NATO ASI Series

Advanced Science Institutes Series

A series presenting the results of activities sponsored by the NATO Science Committee, which aims at the dissemination of advanced scientific and technological knowledge, with a view to strengthening links between scientific communities.

The Series is published by an international board of publishers in conjunction with the NATO Scientific Affairs Division

A Life Sciences	Plenum Publishing Corporation
B Physics	London and New York
C Mathematical and Physical Sciences	Kluwer Academic Publishers Dordrecht, Boston and London
D Behavioural and Social Sciences	
E Applied Sciences	
F Computer and Systems Sciences	Springer-Verlag Berlin Heidelberg New York
G Ecological Sciences	London Paris Tokyo Hong Kong
H Cell Biology	Barcelona Budapest
I Global Environmental Change	

NATO-PCO DATABASE

The electronic index to the NATO ASI Series provides full bibliographical references (with keywords and/or abstracts) to more than 30 000 contributions from international scientists published in all sections of the NATO ASI Series. Access to the NATO-PCO DATABASE compiled by the NATO Publication Coordination Office is possible in two ways:

- via online FILE 128 (NATO-PCO DATABASE) hosted by ESRIN, Via Galileo Galilei, I-00044 Frascati, Italy.

- via CD-ROM "NATO-PCO DATABASE" with user-friendly retrieval software in English, French and German (© WTV GmbH and DATAWARE Technologies Inc. 1989).

The CD-ROM can be ordered through any member of the Board of Publishers or through NATO-PCO, Overijse, Belgium.

Series F: Computer and Systems Sciences Vol. 90

The ASI Series Books Published as a Result of
Activities of the Special Programme on
ADVANCED EDUCATIONAL TECHNOLOGY

This book contains the proceedings of a NATO Advanced Research Workshop held within the activities of the NATO Special Programme on Advanced Educational Technology, running from 1988 to 1993 under the auspices of the NATO Science Committee.

The books published so far as a result of the activities of the Special Programme are:

Vol. F 67: Designing Hypermedia for Learning. Edited by D. H. Jonassen and H. Mandl. 1990.

Vol. F 76: Multimedia Interface Design in Education. Edited by A. D. N. Edwards and S. Holland. 1992.

Vol. F 78: Integrating Advanced Technology into Technology Education. Edited by M. Hacker, A. Gordon, and M. de Vries. 1991.

Vol. F 80: Intelligent Tutoring Systems for Foreign Language Learning. The Bridge to International Communication. Edited by M. L Swartz and M. Yazdani. 1992.

Vol. F 81: Cognitive Tools for Learning. Edited by P.A.M. Kommers, D.H. Jonassen, and J.T. Mayes. 1992.

Vol. F 84: Computer-Based Learning Environments and Problem Solving. Edited by E. De Corte, M. C. Linn, H. Mandl, and L. Verschaffel. 1992.

Vol. F 85: Adaptive Learning Environments. Foundations and Frontiers. Edited by M. Jones and P. H. Winne. 1992.

Vol. F 86: Intelligent Learning Environments and Knowledge Acquisition in Physics. Edited by A. Tiberghien and H. Mandl. 1992.

Vol. F 87: Cognitive Modelling and Interactive Environments in Language Learning. Edited by F. L. Engel, D. G. Bouwhuis, T. Bösser, and G. d'Ydewalle. 1992.

Vol. F 89: Mathematical Problem Solving and New Information Technologies. Edited by J. P. Ponte, J. F. Matos, J. M. Matos, and D. Fernandes. 1992.

Vol. F 90: Collaborative Learning Through Computer Conferencing. Edited by A. R. Kaye. 1992.

Collaborative Learning
Through Computer Conferencing

The Najaden Papers

Edited by

Anthony R. Kaye

Institute of Educational Technology
Open University
Walton Hall
Milton Keynes, MK7 6AA, U.K.

Springer-Verlag
Berlin Heidelberg NewYork London Paris Tokyo
Hong Kong Barcelona Budapest
Published in cooperation with NATO Scientific Affairs Division

Proceedings of the NATO Advanced Research Workshop on Collaborative Learning
and Computer Conferencing, held in Copenhagen, Denmark, July 29–August 3, 1991

CR Subject Classification (1991): K.3.0, K.4.3, C.2.0

ISBN 3-540-55755-5 Springer-Verlag Berlin Heidelberg New York
ISBN 0-387-55755-5 Springer-Verlag New York Berlin Heidelberg

© Springer-Verlag Berlin Heidelberg 1992
Printed in Germany

Typesetting: Camera ready by authors
45/3140 - 5 4 3 2 1 0 - Printed on acid-free paper

Preface

The idea for the Workshop on which this book is based arose from discussions which we had when we both attended an earlier – and more broadly based – NATO Advanced Research Workshop on *Computer Supported Collaborative Learning*, directed by Claire O'Malley in Maratea, Italy, in 1989. We both felt that it would be interesting to organise a second Workshop in this area, but specifically concerned with the use of computers and networking (telematics) as communication tools for collaborative learning outside the formal school setting.

We were particularly interested in examining the ways in which computer conferencing can be used for collaboration and group learning in the contexts of distance education, adult learning, professional training, and organisational networking. And we wanted to ensure that we included, in the scope of the Workshop, situations in which learning is a primary, explicit goal (e.g. an online training programme) as well as situations where learning occurs as a secondary, even incidental, outcome of a collaborative activity whose explicit purpose might be different (e.g. the activities of networked product teams or task groups).

Another goal was to try to bring together for a few days people with three different perspectives on the use of computer conferencing: users, researchers, and software designers. We hoped that, if we could assemble a group of people from these three different constituencies, we might, collectively, be able to make a small contribution to real progress in the field.

We had already decided that we wanted to be able to include demonstrations of new conferencing software products, and we would like to acknowledge the help of Mette Ringsted and Jens Ambrosius, of the Danish Technological Institute, and of Jacob Palme, of the University of Stockholm, in organising such demonstrations at the beginning and the end of the Workshop.

We also wanted to find a unique venue for the Workshop, which we hoped would itself create a special environment for promoting discussion and collaboration amongst the participants. We found this unique venue in the three-masted schooner *Najaden,* in which we travelled the 800 or so kilometres from outside the Royal Palace in Copenhagen, to the *Najaden*'s home mooring in front of the Royal Palace in Stockholm. We would particularly like to acknowledge the support of the members of the NATO Panel of the Special Programme on Advanced Educational Technology, and of its Director, Dr. Luis da Cunha, in agreeing to our proposal to run a Workshop on a ship sailing through the Baltic Sea.

In the event, the *Najaden* provided an ideal setting for intensive group discussion: we were able to work in small groups within sight of each other, without being shut away in meeting rooms; and without any time-tabling constraints we were able to hold both formal and informal discussions continuously throughout each day and evening. Sharing a moving space 40 metres long and 7 metres wide with a crew of eight also meant that we had before our eyes, every day and night, a living example of collaborative work in practice, and of the shared goals, mutual trust, flexibility, and team work on which all successful collaboration is based. We particularly want to acknowledge the way in which Arne Welin and his crew provided exactly the atmosphere we needed for our Workshop discussions, and for their tolerance in agreeing to have the *Najaden*'s mess cabin turned into a floating library, and its decks into 'seminar spaces'.

Drafts of most of the chapters in this book were prepared before the Workshop, and, these, together with a collection of books, reports, and research papers brought by participants, and a simulated paper-and-pencil 'computer conference' moderated by Sara Kiesler, were used as a basis for our discussions and presentations. We worked much of the time in three small groups – on Implementation Issues, Research and Evaluation, and Software Design, discussing and commenting on each other's chapter drafts, and this is reflected in the three-part structure of the book. We would like to thank all the participants for agreeing to work in this way (i.e. to produce drafts which would subsequently be worked up into book chapters on the basis of the Workshop discussions), and also for being prepared to accept the challenge – and potential risks – of the Workshop's venue.

Finally, we would like to express our gratitude to the two people who did not take part in the actual Workshop (Madge Brochet, and Alain Derycke) but who were happy to accept our invitation to contribute their experiences to this book.

Tony Kaye and France Henri
May 1992

FOREWORD

During the summer of 1991, I had the pleasure of hosting the NATO Workshop on *Collaborative Learning and Computer Conferencing* on board our sailing ship *Najaden*, during a four-day voyage between Copenhagen and Stockholm – with stays in port in each city at the beginning and end of the journey.

The atmosphere during the Workshop was very positive, and, according to the reports I have seen, the event was considered a success. Clearly, the participants had high expectations and were open to new situations; they also knew each other through their scientific work, and shared common professional interests. However, I think that the decision to run the Workshop on a ship – rather than in a more traditional venue – also had an influence on the results.

The milieu onboard differs a lot from a normal conference site – on a ship you get to know each other in a much deeper way. You are isolated from the rest of the world, and have only your shipmates for company. After working sessions and meetings, you share your spare time with the same people. You get closer to each other and can therefore meet, socially and professionally, in a more relaxed way. On board a ship, there is also plenty of time to finish discussions without being constrained by rigid timetables, or being interrupted by telephones and visitors.

I believe it is good for people to change their daily patterns and to encounter new situations. To be considered as an expert, especially within a scientific community, may give a feeling of security, but it can also be demanding. One is expected to live up to unspecified and often unconscious roles. However, in an unfamiliar milieu, established roles become less obvious, and implicit hierarchies loosen up. Prestige becomes less important, and cooperation is stimulated.

Being close to nature makes us human beings more humble. On a sailing ship, we are exposed to the vagaries of nature, and gain a new perspective on our own insignificance. After a storm or a beautiful sunset, trifling matters lose their interest, and difficulties are put into proportion.

Everybody who sails with *Najaden* is welcome to participate in the work of the ship, and sailing and manoeuvering a large ship like this is a very special and powerful feeling; it also requires total cooperation amongst those involved. Although the conference participants did not have much time to take an active role – other than providing occasional help in raising and lowering the sails – the proximity to the necessary working activities of the ship helped to underline, in a novel way, the collaborative theme of the Workshop.

The informal environment of the ship, and the autonomy it provided to the participants, combined with a friendly atmosphere and pleasant summer weather, all helped contribute to a cooperative and creative climate, which I believe was a necessary condition for the achievement of good results.

Arne Welin

Captain of the Sailing Ship *Najaden*
Skepsholmen, Stockholm

Contents

1
Learning Together Apart [1]

Anthony Kaye

Institute of Educational Technology, The Open University, United Kingdom

Abstract: This paper defines collaborative learning as "individual learning occurring as a result of group process", and examines some of the issues and problems in using computer-mediated communication (CMC) for collaborative learning. A number of typical applications of computer conferencing, in both the educational context (where learning is the explicit primary goal, as in a course or training programme) and the organisational context (where learning might be a desirable, but secondary, outcome of a task-oriented activity), are reviewed. The influences of social climate, a text-based asynchronous communication environment, and software design features, on the success or failure of CMC for collaborative learning are examined.

Keywords: peer learning, cooperative learning, collaborative learning, process loss, organisational learning, computer-mediated communication (CMC), shared space, virtual seminar, online classroom, online games, computer-supported writing, distance education adjunct, lecture-room adjunct, education utility, project group, computer conferencing, message, organisational networking, social climate, software environment, interface design, groupware, lexical density

---

[1] I am indebted to the authors of *Enterprise Networking: Working Together Apart* [16] for the inspiration for this title.

A Definition of Collaborative Learning

> The thing that distinguishes collaborative communities from most other communities is [this] desire to construct new meanings about the world through interaction with others. The collaborative community becomes a medium for both self-knowledge and self-expression. [43, p. 48]

It is easier to describe what does not count as collaborative learning, than it is to produce a universally acceptable definition. Learning based on a transmissive or information-processing model of education, where the main learning activity is the individual reception and organisation of information from books, lectures, videos or computer-based training materials, is not collaborative. On the other hand, learners constituted into groups (e.g. a school class or a training group) are not necessarily learning collaboratively when they sit around talking before, after, or during a class. [2]

It is important to distinguish collaboration from communication. Clear communication, and effective communication tools and channels, may be necessary pre-requisites for effective collaboration, but they are not sufficient. A good teacher, or an effective meeting chair or manager, equipped with flip charts, slides, and transparencies, may well be an excellent communicator, but will not necessarily know how to create and promote an effective collaborative environment (which, in any case, may not be a requirement of the situation). A lecture or a meeting may be an effective way of transmitting and sharing information, but it would be a mistake for the participants to believe that they are – in any real sense – 'collaborating' with each other in the process.

> Most people kid themselves into thinking that they're collaborating when, in reality, they're just saying words. Traditional modes of discourse in no way capture the subtleties, the bandwidth, the power, and the degrees of interaction necessary for effective collaboration. Presentations and the usual modes of organizational communication are to collaboration what smoke signals are to movie epics; puffs of smoke in the wind just aren't as colorful or compelling as *Gone With the Wind*. The practical reality of collaboration is that it requires a higher order of involvement, as well as a different approach to sharing and creating information. [43, p. 29]

Etymologically, to collaborate (*co-labore*) means to work together, which implies a concept of shared goals, and an explicit intention to 'add value' – to create something new or different through the collaboration, as opposed to simply exchanging information or passing on instructions.

For the purposes of this book, we consider collaborative learning as any learning that takes place as a result of people working together, regardless of whether learning is the primary explicit goal of the collaboration (e.g. a training seminar or workshop) or is a secondary, incidental, outcome (e.g. a work team in which the individual members acquire new knowledge or skills from each other). Successful collaboration assumes some agreement on common goals and values, and the pooling of individual competencies for the benefit of the group or community as a whole – and the teamwork which this implies is more often a feature of work in organisations than it is of learning in schools or universities.

---

[2] Setting aside the part played by informal chat amongst children in school, which clearly serves important roles in language acquisition and in the development of shared understandings. [7]

One reason why collaborative learning appears to be more commonplace in the work environment than in many parts of the formal education system may be because, in our culture, the latter is mainly based on recognition of individual achievement within an essentially competitive environment (collaboration between schoolchildren, in certain circumstances, is still sometimes labelled as 'cheating'). Another reason might be that the formal education system assigns relatively hermetic roles to participants (one is either a student, or a teacher), and these roles imply an unequal relationship based on differential levels of authority and power.

Current interest in collaborative learning, and in computer support for collaborative learning, seems to be associated with a number of positively loaded assumptions, which can be linked to a variety of theoretical perspectives concerning the learning process. Some of the strongest of these assumptions include the following:

– Much significant learning and deep-level understanding arises from conversation, argument, debate, and discussion (often unplanned, sometimes structured) amongst and between learners, peers, colleagues, experts, and teachers; learning is essentially a communal activity [5] involving the social construction of knowledge [30].

– Peer collaboration in learning can directly help to develop general problem-solving skills and strategies through the internalisation of the cognitive processes implicit in interaction and communication [6,11,52].

– The strengths of collaborative learning through discussion and conversation include the sharing of different perspectives, the obligation to make explicit and communicate one's own knowledge and understandings to others through verbalisation or writing [51], and the motivational value of being a member of a healthy group [41].

– A significant proportion of many peoples' jobs involves working in teams and groups, and job achievements often rely heavily on successful collaboration with colleagues; formal education should prepare people to work together healthily in groups.

– Groups of adults following education or training programmes, especially in-service training programmes, often have a valuable repertoire of personal knowledge and experience to contribute to the educational process [29].

– Outside formal educational settings (e.g. within society at large, within organisations), much of the individual learning that occurs results from informal group interactions and the help and support provided by peers and colleagues, through what Illich [24], many years ago, called 'learning webs'. [3]

Valid and inspiring as these assumptions might be (especially when contrasted with a transmissive or behaviourist perspective on learning), there are often major difficulties to overcome in making them operational, particularly in a formal educational context. It is necessary perhaps to make explicit at this point, as a counterbalance, some relevant 'negatively loaded' assumptions:

– Much educational practice is based on a transmissive model, with all authority and knowledge assumed to be invested in the teacher; as a result, it is notoriously

---

[3] The concept has re-surfaced in recent organisational literature in terms of 'networked' or 'competence-based' environments [16].

difficult to initiate and maintain constructive group discussion as a learning medium in a traditional educational context [3].

– Even in situations where teamwork and collaboration are accepted as major elements of the social environment, the experience of working or learning in groups can be associated with 'process loss' [49], and at times be frustrating, time-consuming, and conflict-ridden [28].

– The research findings on the relationship between educational achievement and the use of cooperative learning methods are inconsistent, some reviews suggesting that individual competition produces better results than group conditions, others show no significant difference, others show an opposite trend. [53]; it would appear that, in the classroom situation, cooperative learning methods can only result in improved achievement levels if they incorporate both group goals and individual accountability [46].

– The introduction of possibilities for enhanced group collaboration (computer-based, architectural, or whatever) into an existing organisational structure or educational system can lead to rejection because the new opportunities run counter to traditional working practices, assessment methods, or hierarchies of command.

During the Workshop, in our discussions concerning both the positive and negative assumptions above, we considered the following six elements as being the most important in trying to define the field of collaborative learning:

(1) Learning is inherently an individual, not a collective, process, which is influenced by a variety of external factors, including group and inter-personal interactions.

(2) Group and inter-personal interactions involve the use of language (a social process) in the re-organisation and modification of one's personal understandings and knowledge structures, so learning is simultaneously a private and a social phenomenon.

(3) Learning collaboratively implies peer exchange, interaction amongst equals, and interchangeability of roles, such that different members of a group or community might take on different roles (learner, teacher, information seeker, resource person, facilitator) at different times, depending on needs.

(4) Collaboration involves synergy, and assumes that, in some way, the "whole is greater than the individual parts", so that learning collaboratively has the potential to produce learning gains superior to learning alone.

(5) Not all attempts at collaborative learning will be successful, as, under some circumstances, collaboration can lead to conformity, process loss, lack of initiative, misunderstandings, conflict, and compromise: the potential benefits are not always realised.

(6) Collaborative learning does not necessarily imply learning in a group, but rather the possibility of being able to rely on other people to support one's own learning and to give feedback, as and when necessary, within the context of a non-competitive environment.

In the rest of this book, then, we use the term collaborative learning to mean *the acquisition by individuals of knowledge, skills, or attitudes occurring as the result of group interaction*, or put more tersely, *individual learning as a result of group process*.

We distinguish collaborative learning from group learning, or group productivity, by assuming that only individuals can learn, and that what is called group learning can only reflect the summed learnings of the individual members of the group. We draw a distinction between learning (the acquisition of knowledge, skills, and attitudes by individuals) and group performance (the demonstration of knowledge, skills and attitudes by a group). A football team or a jazz quartet may improve as a group from one performance to another, because the individual members have not only improved their individual skills, but have also learned to be a better group.

We also distinguish collaborative learning from organisational learning [44], seeing the latter concept as referring to the process by which an organisation changes and adapts over time, in response to environmental factors and to development of the organisation's own culture, traditions, and knowledge base, even though individual membership of the organisation might change.

The factors identified by Schrage [43, ch. 11] which determine the likely success of any form of collaboration are undoubtedly relevant to collaborative learning activities. They include: competence amongst group members; a shared and understood goal; mutual respect and trust; the creation and manipulation of shared spaces; multiple forms of representation; continuous – but not continual – communication; formal and informal environments; clear lines of responsibility, but no restrictive boundaries; the acceptance that decisions do not have to be based on consensus, and that physical presence is not necessary; the selective use of outsiders; and the realisation that the collaboration ends when its goal has been achieved.

Computer-Mediated Communication for Collaborative Learning

Computers can clearly be used to support learning in a variety of different ways. Traditionally, most educational applications of computers have involved simulations (e.g. in science teaching) and computer-assisted learning (CAL) applications, where pre-programmed software provides anything from drill-and-practice exercises to 'intelligent tutoring' and access to multi-media resources. Such educational software programmes are available for use in either stand-alone mode, or over networks. Although in some cases, the term 'computer-supported collaborative learning' is applied to these situations (either because two or more learners use the software simultaneously, or because the learner is 'collaborating' with the computer) this is not the sense we give to the term in this book.

In this context, we interpret computer support as meaning the use of computers and computer networks as communication tools by people who are collaborating with each other to achieve a shared goal, which do not require the physical presence or co-location of participants, and which can provide a forum for continuous communication free of time constraints. Specifically, our focus is on the use of computer-mediated communication (CMC) – computer conferencing and electronic mail – for asynchronous, text-based communication. We focus particularly on computer conferencing (as opposed to electronic mail) because conferencing systems can provide shared working and learning spaces, can be used to create both formal and informal environments, and.have a number of properties particularly well-adapted for support of collaborative activity. [4]

---

[4] See Chapter 16 by Jacob Palme for a comprehensive listing of conferencing software functions.

Conferencing supports many-to-many communication (whereas electronic mail is designed essentially for one-to-one or one-to-many messaging), and conferencing software includes features specifically designed to help in the organisation, structuring, and retrieval of messages. Messages can be linked to each other (e.g. as 'comments'), organised in different 'branches' or 'topics' of a conference, and search commands can rapidly identify messages with particular key words in their titles, or in the body of the text. Support is also provided for tracking the activity of individual group members: for example, it is generally possible to see which messages in a conference a given member has read, or which messages have been written by a given member. Special commands are available to the person responsible for a conference (the 'moderator' or 'organiser') which can help in defining the membership of the conference, in keeping the discussion on track, and in scheduling the opening and closing of discussion topics.

Finally, in conferencing systems with large numbers of users (e.g. the in-house systems at IBM and at Digital Equipment Corporation mentioned in Chapters 6 and 11 respectively, or the Open University's CoSy system, or the EuroKOM system), open conferences can be used to promote networking and serendipitous exchanges – and thus enable the selective participation of outsiders – in a way which is impossible in any other medium. For example, a user of the system requiring help on a problem can signal this in an appropriate open conference, and may rapidly receive advice and suggestions from other users whom he has never met and did not even know existed. From such contacts, collaborations of a more substantial nature might then develop – ranging from online self-help groups set up by students taking the same course, to teams being formed to prepare a research proposal or develop a new product.

Applications in education and training programmes

Computer-mediated communication, it has been claimed, is creating a new environment of online education, providing "... unprecedented opportunities for educational interactivity" [18, p. 42] and which "... can be used a powerful tool for group communication and cooperative learning" [26, p. 10]. A wide range of different applications of conferencing has developed within the education and training fields over the last few years, although not all of these are necessarily based on a deliberate strategy of collaborative learning or active group work. Different typical applications are briefly reviewed below.

The virtual seminar

One of the earliest examples of the use of computer conferencing for peer learning and exchange is the International Executive Forum run annually by the Western Behavioral Sciences Institute (WBSI) in La Jolla, California, from 1982 to 1991 [42]. This programme is paradigmatic of the virtual seminar model, in which a small group of articulate peers exchange ideas and information over a period of several months, in a text-based mode entirely free of any time or place constraints. The high quality and value of the resultant online discussions is evident even from a retrospective analysis of the printed conference transcripts [33], which can only represent a pale trace of the intellectual experiences and commitment of the participants during the online discussion period.

The online classroom

Since the first WBSI courses, there have been many applications of the online classroom model, often inspired by the pioneering research into the 'virtual classroom' carried out at New Jersey Institute of Technology, using the EIES system [21]. The common features of most of these applications is that the group size is comparable to that in a normal class (say 10 to 20 people in a group), that there is at least one person responsible in some way for guiding the group's activities, and that computer conferencing represents the principal (and sometimes the only) mode of teaching, learning, and communication.

Different varieties of the online classroom depend on the age groups involved (e.g. college-level or adults) and the educational level (e.g. undergraduate or in-service). They also depend to a large extent on the role taken by the person or people responsible for the group – just as in a normal class situation. Where this person is a teacher, and the evaluator of the participant's work and inputs, a different style of interaction is likely to develop from a seminar or syndicate situation, in which each member of the group has knowledge and skills to share with the others, and the leader's role is more that of facilitator and resource person, as well as being a peer. There are many instances of successful use of conferencing in professional education, postgraduate education, and updating amongst peer groups. Examples include:
– teacher updating, province-wide, by the Ontario Institute for Studies in Education, using the Participate system;
– in-service training for health care professionals in Denmark, by the Danish Technological Institute and Arhus Technical College, using PortaCOM;
– MA courses in Media Studies at the New School for Social Research in New York, organised through Connected Education, and attracting participants from many countries.

The many-to-many and asynchronous nature of computer conferencing suggests that the online environment is more conducive to seminar and syndicate interactions than to the more conventional teacher-directed class. Clearly, in the online situation, the group leader cannot control exchanges and turn-taking in the same way that is commonly seen in many face-to-face class situations – for example, through the classic Initiation-Response-Feedback (IRF) sequence described by Sinclair and Coulthard [45]. However, Hiltz [22] has reported that in undergraduate courses (in sociology, management, statistics, mathematics, and computer science), where the grades of matched groups of traditional classroom (TC) and virtual classroom (VC) students were compared, there were no significant differences in achievement levels – except on the computer science course, where the VC students performed better.

Online games and simulations

A variety of the online classroom which merits further development, as it can build extensively on computer processing power as well as on computer-supported group communication, is the online game or simulation, particularly in the context of management training courses. Hsu [23] describes such an application, using EIES, at New Jersey Institute of Technology – the 'virtual management practices laboratory'. Initial evaluation results (comparing CMC-supported groups with groups using face-to-face meetings for group processes) suggest that levels of group cohesion are higher in CMC groups, and that performance scores are better. Such positive findings are not necessarily found in all cases of group task achievements in management training courses, however. Research by Galegher and Kraut [12] into matched groups of students on an MBA course using computer conferencing, or face-to-face meetings, with and without phone contact, for collaborative drafting of a consultancy report, showed no significant differences in achievement across groups with different treatments, and the CMC groups reported greater difficulty in achieving effective group coordination and in reaching agreement.

Another example of an online game and simulation is the University of Michigan's ICS (Interactive Communications Simulation) programme, that, initially a face-to-face game played during residential weekends, has been running since 1984 on the University's Confer system [14]. Participants in the most widely-used game, which involves active role-playing in the context of a simulation of the Arab-Israeli conflict, were estimated as being in the thousands by the summer of 1990, and are drawn from schools and colleges in the USA as well as in a number of other countries. Since 1987, the game has also been run on Confer for Michigan University students, using terminals on-campus, and it has been noticed that both the quantity and the quality of messages exchanged are quite different from when the game was played in a face-to-face setting. There is now a range of different games available via Confer, including one based on the US Constitutional Convention, a Community Land Use Game (CLUG), and a mathematics game involving teams competing to find solutions to maths problems.

Computer-supported writing and language learning
The essentially textual nature of computer conferencing and electronic mail, combined with the use of word-processing software for drafting, has obviously attracted interest within the field of the teaching of writing and language skills. Examples include creative writing courses offered by Connected Education, courses in creative writing, technical writing, and English composition offered on CoSy to home-based students in Arizona by the Rio Salado Community College, and the 'writer in electronic residence' project for high school English pupils in several different schools, with electronically distant poets and writers, at Riverdale Collegiate Institute in Toronto. Owen [36] in analysing the 'writer in electronic residence' project, notes that the online forum provides greater equity of use than the traditional classroom setting, and gives students more control over what they write, when and 'where' to send it, and how to respond. Karen Smith at the University of Arizona [47], on the basis of research conducted into traditional and computer-supported classes for teaching Spanish as a second language, reports that computers encourage students to write more and to be more creative than their traditional counterparts.

Multi-media distance education adjunct
Many existing distance education programmes try to achieve economies of scale by registering large numbers of home-based students on courses in which the main learning mode is independent study of mediated course materials (print, broadcast, CAL software etc), backed up with varying levels of tutorial support through correspondence tuition, telephone contact, and occasional face-to-face tutorials in local centres. High quality distance teaching materials require considerable investment in time and resources for their production, hence the

need to amortise their cost by large student populations and/or successive presentations of the same courses over periods of several years.

There appear to be strong arguments for introducing computer networking facilities into such systems [19,26,30]. For example, electronic mail can be used for promoting more regular and faster communication between students and tutors; computer conferencing can provide a channel for group discussion and interactive learning, for promoting communication amongst tutors, students, and course development and support staff, and for providing opportunities for socialising and cooperation amongst students who feel isolated; online databases can give access to library and reference resources. A number of multi-media distance education programmes have now started using computer networking on some courses, with varying degrees of success. Two well-known examples are the British Open University, and EuroPACE.

Mason [32], in reviewing the first year's experience of the use of CoSy on an undergraduate course on Information Technology, points out that the relatively marginal role of conferencing on the course (around 10 hours' connect time in a 400 hour course, spread over 6 months) militates against an effective use of conferencing for collaborative learning and group work. The basic problem is one of trying to integrate a new, group-based technology within an existing (and very effective) distance teaching system which is essentially designed around the needs of the individual, home-based, learner. A more central use of conferencing in the OU system would require a re-think of the basic course model, and would imply a need for a higher proportion of time from course tutors to act as effective conference moderators and online teachers [50].

EuroPACE, which provides satellite transmitted video programmes backed up with printed reference and self-study material to over 150 reception sites in companies and universities throughout Europe, makes use of the PortaCOM conferencing system (PaceCOM) [34]. Initially, it was thought that it would provide a useful method of giving participants access to each other and to the academic and industry specialists responsible for the course materials – in fact it is a contractual requirement for these consultants to log on to the system to deal with queries and requests for help. However, in reality, the PaceCOM system is used essentially for administrative communication amongst the 100 or more site coordinators and the EuroPACE headquarters staff, rather than for collaboration amongst participants.

There are similarities in the ways in which conferencing is used (and not used) at the Open University and at EuroPACE, which may to some extent reflect the fact that both programmes are dealing with relatively large numbers of students for whom the primary mode of learning is independent study of multi-media materials. On the whole, participants have not been enthusiastic about taking part in online classes and formal group activities – but they have developed many other valid uses of conferencing, such as administrative communications, practical help with problems, information dissemination, socialising, and inter-personal networking.

Lecture-room adjunct

Just as conferencing has been used to provide possibilities for inter-student collaboration and closer contact with tutors in distance education, so it has been used as an adjunct to large campus-based lectures, for similar reasons. In large lecture classes, there is generally not time for every student to ask questions on areas of difficulty, and the communicative context is usually unsuitable for discussion. In universities where there is easy access to a campus-wide conferencing system from terminals in libraries and elsewhere, some lecturers will set up conferences related to their course, where students can, very conveniently, get help from the teacher, and from other students.

One of the best-documented cases of the use of conferencing as a support for large college lecture classes is the use of VAX Notes to create ancillary 'electronic classrooms' at the University of Indiana, as reported by Hansen *et al* [17]. Three models were tried, as ways of promoting collaboration amongst students and staff outside the largely transmissive lecture classes: ongoing discussion topics, extending the classroom activities; sharing of case studies and class projects written by individual students, or groups of students, prior to classroom discussion of them; and collaborative revision and preparation for examinations. The first of these three models – the most generic – was the easiest for faculty staff to implement. The evaluators conclude that all three models have the potential to increase student participation through online discussion. However, the instructors involved need to actively support the technology, and to re-structure their courses to give sufficient weight to online activities, if this potential is to be realised (many students were not prepared to invest the necessary time in learning to use the technology if it was perceived as marginal, or resulted in a participation grade comprising only 5% or so of the overall course grade).

The education utility

This is a set of networked resources which any education or training programme can plug into and use [15]. An example in Britain is the CAMPUS 2000 system, which provides access to information databases, to CAL and CBT material, to the national and international Dialcom electronic mail system, and to the Caucus computer conferencing system. It also has gateways into other systems in Britain and in other countries. CAMPUS 2000 is jointly run by British Telecom and Times Newspapers, and the majority of its users are schools and further education colleges. For example, it hosts many inter-cultural networking projects, linking children and pupils in different schools in Britain and abroad (e.g. in Japan, the USA, France, Germany, etc) cooperating in language learning and social and cultural studies programmes. CAMPUS 2000 also hosts some distance education programmes. One example is a computer awareness project for nurses, based on a 'cascade system' [38] which trains trainers in local and regional centres using online CAL and database material, together with inter-personal support (including return and marking of assignments) through electronic mail and computer conferencing. These trainers then use the knowledge and expertise they have gained through the networked programme to provide training within their own establishments, using courseware and other resources which they have selected themselves from the network.

An American example is the Montana Big Sky Telegraph, originally set up in 1988 to link the 114 one-room rural schools in the state through a multi-line microcomputer network, for peer information sharing and distribution of resources [35]. Currently, Big Sky – described as an "online co-op", offers electronic mail, computer conferencing, educational databases, library access, information-menus maintained by users, online classes, and an educational software preview loan library. Since the project started, other groups (than rural teachers) have asked to use the system, including a Job Corps, Womens' groups, agricultural groups, disabled groups, and Western Montana College has started running drug education and literacy classes online. The Telegraph is a truly cooperative venture, and is in fact run by only two 'quarter-time' staff, drawing on technical consultant expertise as needed.

Comment

Participation rates in use of electronic mail and computer conferencing in education and training programmes and courses of the types reviewed in the various categories above vary widely: for example, read/write ratios (number of messages read: number posted) typically are of the order of 100:1 in many programmes, and a relatively few percent of active users often account for up to 80% of message traffic [39, p.33]. Differences in participation rates within groups taking part in courses with an online component depend on a variety of factors, including the level of the programme (e.g. undergraduate, in-service training, professional development); the disciplinary focus of the programme; the role of the teachers and conference moderators; the extent of the emphasis on group work and collaboration; and the relative weight of the online component in the course as a whole (totally online courses on the 'virtual seminar' model tend to attract much higher participation than courses where CMC is an adjunct).

The three cases of the use of CMC in formal education programmes analysed in Part 1 of this book (the papers by Simón on in-service teacher training; by Søby on conferencing as a distance education adjunct; and by McConnell on peer learning in a management education programme) well illustrate a number of the major issues which need to be considered in judging the success of such initiatives.

Applications in organisations

Collaborative learning – indeed, learning of any sort – is obviously not a prerogative of formal education or training. It could be argued that formal education and training programmes, for most people, are associated with only a small proportion of their total lifelong learning experiences. Much significant learning occurs in the family and social environment, and, in adulthood, in the work environment, as a by-product of activities whose primary explicit goal is not necessarily 'educational'. To this extent, such learning could be called incidental, in contrast to formal educational programmes where learning is an explicit primary goal. Computer support for activities which give rise to such 'incidental' collaborative learning could have a more significant impact in the social and work environment than in the school setting [2]. Motivation levels for participating in networking activities in the organisational and work setting may often be higher than those encountered in many formal education or training programmes: the 'need to know' factor is probably more urgent, and the penalties for failure may well be higher. In this, the last decade of the twentieth century, we are constantly being reminded of the collapse of hierarchical organisational structures, of the increased prevalence of lateral communication and flexible, team-based working environments, and of the importance of information as a major economic resource. From this perspective, computer networking can play a critical role in helping people to learn from each other, and in facilitating the evolution of new organisational forms and working methods [13,16,48].

Project teams and work groups

Team work is becoming increasingly common throughout many organisations – *ad hoc* task groups, new product development groups, committees, quality circles, all involve group work. It can be argued that healthy, well functioning, work groups are ones where, as well as completing the group task successfully, each member feels they have learnt something as a result of their collaboration with other members. Such learning can be considered as having two dimensions: learning to develop and improve group process skills (developing consensus, coordination, negotiation, management of the transition from one phase of group work to the next etc), and the acquisition of new information and understandings necessary for completion of the specific group task, from other team members and from outside the group. Taking the case of new product teams in high technology industries, for example [1], it has been possible to identify three main phases in the life cycle of a team: an initial exploration phase ending with design decisions, an exploitation phase (during which the product is developed), and an exportation phase (when a prototype is passed on to another part of the organisation for eventual production). A similar phasing can be observed in teams developing distance education course materials [27], with an initial stage of overall course design, a second stage of drafting of course materials, and a third stage of hand-over of materials for print and media production. In both instances, the initial exploration and design phase can be said to imply the need for collaborative learning processes, as it requires team members to collect information and resources from outside the group, to learn about the competences and limitations of team colleagues, and to collectively and creatively develop new ideas.

Computer-mediated communication can potentially play an important role in helping collaborative learning during the initial exploration/design phase of a group's work, whether the group members are co-located, or distributed across different sites. However, access to computer conferencing or to a bulletin board is not a sufficient condition for successful electronic collaboration. A study of one of the few successful uses of CMC for group discussion during the design phase of a software product at Hewlett-Packard suggests that the role and active presence of the team leader in the electronic environment is crucial to a successful outcome [8]. In this case, the team leader was responsible for half of the total messages submitted, and played a key role in the development of 'message webs' containing evaluative comments from other members of the team. These results confirm other research at Hewlett-Packard which suggests that the role of conference organiser in the CMC environment is the major critical factor in determining the quality of online collaboration in work groups [9]. However, it would be naive to assume that all, or even the majority, of inter-personal collaboration in work groups can take place successfully over CMC networks: conferencing is maybe best suited to relatively unambiguous information and learning exchanges, but is often inappropriate as a communication medium for exchanges requiring subtlety, nuance, or tactful negotiation [1,48].

Organisational networking

An increasing number of large organisations run their own electronic mail and conferencing systems, linking the majority of staff throughout the organisation, regardless of their geographical location. Many of the early examples were companies working in the information technology and computing sectors (e.g. IBM, Digital, Tandy, Hewlett-Packard), but cases now exist in many other areas (e.g. insurance, banking, petrochemicals, pharmaceuticals etc), especially in organisations with an international base. These systems not only support formal work groups, but also provide an organisation-wide capacity for the networking of human resources which was simply not feasible with earlier communication technologies [48]. Staff with difficult problems to solve, or requiring information not available in their local environment, are able to put up "Does anybody know....?" type messages in appropriate conferences or distribution lists on the network, and very often obtain useful responses from (maybe unknown) colleagues, within a few days or hours. The human networking and peer learning which is enabled by corporate computer communications facilities has been dubbed a capability-based environment in which "...electronic networks and networking techniques are used to access, communicate, and share the information that fuels the development of modern products and services in a complex and rapidly changing world" [16].

Inter-institutional and intra-organisational networking

It has become common in many universities for academics to use international electronic mail networks such as BITNET, or EARN, for collaboration over research and authoring projects, or simply for staying in touch or for making new professional contacts. News groups on USENET, and list servers and bulletin boards on BITNET and other networks, have large numbers of subscribers, from many academic disciplines, all over the world. The immediacy and convenience of this mode of communication for faculty who have a networked micro-computer on their desk are major factors in helping to develop and maintain inter-institutional links and collaborative projects that might not have survived the delays of postal communication, nor the expense of voice telephone contact. The automatic notification of new mail, list, and bulletin board items whenever users log onto their own local, institutional, network, has undoubtedly been a major influence in encouraging the enormous growth in use of these services over the last few years. Such facilities do not have the functionality of computer conferencing systems for group work, of the type described by Hiltz in her classic study of online communities [20], but they do avoid the need to log on to a remote centralised service, and costs to the individual user are minimal or non-existent. Specialist conferencing services, however, with tailored environments for collaboration between people working in different institutions and organisations, do exist. A successful example is the EuroKOM system, used by several thousand scientists, engineers, and academics from companies, research institutes, and universities working collaboratively on the European Commission's ESPRIT, DELTA, and COMETT programmes.

Comment

There are a number of reasons why we chose, in the *Najaden* workshop and in this book, to put as much emphasis on collaborative learning in the work environment as in the education and training environment (this emphasis is well reflected in Chapters 5, 6, 10, and 11). Firstly, it can be argued that inter-personal collaboration in learning is more prevalent in the work setting than in the formal schooling or training situation. Secondly, the general principles of adult learning [29,4] often seem more consistent with the sort of peer learning and exchange that takes place outside the formal education and training situation than within it; the paper by Rueda (Chapter 6), analysing message types in IBM's computer conferencing system, illustrates this very well. Thirdly, the very availability of computer communications networks is blurring the distinctions between learning in the two contexts – educational and organisational – precisely because they permit and facilitate exchanges and contacts between resource people and 'teachers' from both environments. Shared computer communications networks make it as easy for an expert from a high tech company to contribute to an online course in electronics run by a university, as it is for a university lecturer to share her expertise with a team developing a new product in some other company. In this respect, computer networking is responding to, and evolving in parallel with, the increasing demands for professional up-dating, in-service training, and continuing adult education which are apparent in so many sectors of employment.

Issues and Questions

The *Najaden* Workshop brought together people with at least three different perspectives and backgrounds to the uses of computer conferencing for collaborative learning:
– the implementation of projects (e.g. courses, networked collaborations etc) involving computer conferencing;
– the research approaches and methods appropriate for analysing what happens in such projects;
– the design of appropriate conferencing software and networks for collaborative learning.

These perspectives are, to a large extent, reflected in the three Workshop sub-groups, and in the related Parts of this book. The workshop provided an occasion for implementors of networked collaborative programmes, researchers, and software developers, to exchange ideas and experiences, and to compare their different perspectives. From these discussions – and the papers in this book – it is possible to identify a number of general issues which seem important in determining the quality and outcomes of attempts to use online facilities for collaborative learning. These are briefly developed below, in such a way as to provide an introduction to the rest of this book.

The social climate

The experiences of the use of CMC for collaborative learning described and analysed in this book (particularly the cases presented in Part 1) clearly reinforce a view that is becoming more and more widely accepted, namely that social, more than technical, factors, are the main determinants of the success or failure of a CMC application. In discussing the organisation of computer conferences, and the need for a new profession of 'social network designers', Feenberg points out that:

> It would be a mistake to treat this as essentially a technical issue. Although technology is important for any mediated activity, it cannot 'automate' what is in reality a social encounter based on specific social practices. These social practices are unusually complex because of the difficulty of mediating organised group activity in a written environment. Failures and breakdowns occur at the social level far more often than at the strictly technical level. [10, p. 28]

More recently, Riel and Levin, in analysing cases of success and failure in the use of computer networking via electronic mail by teachers, conclude that:

> The most important factor leading to successful networks is the presence of an important function that the network serves for the participants. The nature of this function determines the particular form that the network should have. [....] As communication technology advances, "user friendly" interfaces will become the norm and the technical barriers to networks will disappear. At that point, the social design of networks will become the dominant issue: what should be the nature of the interactions, how should leadership be provided, and how should activity be organised in this new communication medium? [40, p. 168]

I would argue that the social design of CMC applications, broadly interpreted, has been the most important issue ever since the earliest attempts at using conferencing as the primary vehicle for collaborative learning (e.g. the WBSI programme, which started in 1982). For any meaningful and useful collaboration to occur within a (technically functioning) CMC system, it is essential that the users are motivated to participate, that there are shared goals and aims, and that there is some sort of structure to the collaboration environment. The structure may be fairly open (for example, the use of organisational networking to obtain advice on a specific problem, and the social expectation that such advice will be forthcoming, illustrated by the example from IBM quoted in Chapter 6), or more tightly defined (such as the different conferences set up for specific functions within the distance education programmes described by Søby in Chapter 3 and McConnell in Chapter 4).

The role of the conference manager (or moderator) is often seen as crucial in determining the success or failure of the use of CMC for collaboration and education. The literature on computer conferencing abounds with advice and prescriptions for effective moderation of CMC discussions, and with guidelines for teachers on how to develop appropriate techniques for tutoring in the online environment, which, it is sometimes argued, is so different from the face-to-face classroom environment that it requires special skills.

Certainly, there are particular techniques that need to be mastered by a conference moderator (e.g. the system commands needed for setting up conferences, adding members to a conference, moving or deleting messages, changing conference status from read-only to read-write, setting up voting procedures etc), but many of the key social skills needed for nurturing online collaboration are not specific to the CMC environment. They are the skills needed by any tutor, facilitator, or chairperson involved in a peer learning situation – as pointed out by Simón in Chapter 2, these include the ability to make group members aware of the fact that their own experiences are important and worth contributing, and that other peers can be as valuable a source of knowledge as the course materials. Clearly, educators whose professional experience before using CMC is that of the traditional classroom teacher who tightly controls turn-taking, and who is perceived by students as the main source of expertise and knowledge, may have difficulty in adapting to the far more open and less controllable environment of computer conferencing. On the other hand, learners and tutors who are comfortable with the basic premises of peer learning and small group work (in the face-to-face situation) will – as McConnell's case study shows – adapt well to the CMC environment, and take collective responsibility for progressing the online discussions.

An examination of the guidelines on 'moderating' of computer conferences confirms the view that the skills involved are those appropriate to group work and peer learning in the face-to-face environment as well as the online setting. It is often stressed that the conference moderator needs to work hard at the role of 'social host' and 'meeting chairperson', and Feenberg lists contextualising functions (opening a discussion, setting norms and agendas), monitoring functions (recognition of participants' contributions, prompting) and meta functions (meta-commenting and weaving) as being very important [10]. We would argue that people who can deploy such skills successfully in small groups in the seminar room or workplace will also be able to apply them to the online environment with little difficulty.

It is probably important to make a distinction between the social structure of formally constituted CMC groups (e.g. participants in an online course or a task group) and that of people who are regular users of a network and who may 'come together' without even knowing each other, in solving a problem or providing help and information to colleagues. Such spontaneous, voluntary, and self-organising group processes (such as those in the company-wide networks described by Rueda in Chapter 6 and by Gundry in Chapter 11) seem to occur without any formal 'moderation', because they arise within organisational cultures which value information-sharing and participation.

"The message is the medium"
Computer conferencing is a unique form of group communication – based as it is on a manipulable database of text messages on a common theme, contributed at different times by the different members of a group. The para-linguistic cues of face-to-face or telephone communication are absent, and yet the medium offers greater communicative richness than more familiar forms of textual communication used by groups and communities (such as the Readers' Letters pages of a daily newspaper, an office or parish notice-board, or the minutes of a meeting). The open nature of conferencing, where members can contribute messages directly themselves without submitting them to prior editing or control by others, differentiates this medium from other forms of public or semi-public written communication. The public, recorded, and textual nature of the medium sometimes leads to expectations concerning the content and style of messages which may not be shared by every member of the group or wider community. Cases have been recorded where the 'textualisation of sociality' which occurs in conferencing systems can lead to rejection of the system by an organisation's managers [55, Ch. 10].

The novelty of conferencing, and its ambiguous position in the spectrum of public to private communication media, is reflected, for example, in the agonising over the drafting of 'codes of conduct' for university or corporate conferencing networks, or in the uncertainties over whether the *messageries roses* on the French videotex system should be subject to legislation covering the press, the telephone system, or the broadcast media [31].

Although computer conferencing discourse shares some of the features of speech (interactivity, spontaneity, etc.) and of writing (permanency, re-use, etc.), it is probably not fruitful to attempt to consider whether it is 'more like' one or the other of these forms of communication. Recent work on calculation of the lexical density[5] of a range of conferencing discussions clearly shows that computer conferencing can support a "... continuum of linguistic styles from highly interactive spoken forms through to academic writing" [54]. Conferencing interactions can range from rapid-fire exchanges of short messages typed online on the spur of the moment, to carefully edited and relatively lengthy texts, prepared off-line over a period of several days before being uploaded into the system. Conferencing exchanges take place in front of an invisible 'audience' – the members of the conference – that may be a small, closed, group (as in the student groups described by McConnell in Chapter 4 below), or a totally open community of unknown people (as in the company-wide conferences at IBM described in Chapter 6). As a vehicle for group communication, computer conferencing possesses unique features which make it qualitatively different from either spoken or written communication, and which raise new opportunities – and problems – as a result.

As a medium for collaborative learning, the cumulative record of message contributions in a conference, and the tools provided by the conferencing system for retrieving and organising messages, provide perhaps a greater potential for reflective and thoughtful analysis and review of earlier contributions, and hence for mutual elaboration and development, than would, say, participation in a face-to-face seminar. In the conventional seminar situation, if the right opportunity for a contribution is missed, it may be gone forever; subsequent review has to rely on partial recollections or selective note-taking, and continuation of the discussion and the re-investment of the results of analysis and reflection have to be postponed until the time of the next group meeting. Potentially, conferencing provides more opportunities for participation in group discussion and collaboration than face-to-face meetings, because it is not possible for turn-taking to be controlled in the same way, nor for dominant personalities to forcefully take over the discussion.

On the other hand, the lack of control over turn-taking, the difficulties in providing contextual cues for framing different discussion genres, and the frequent development of multiple threads of discussion within the same message space, can provide serious obstacles to effective collaboration in the conferencing situation. Attempts to use metaphors drawn from familiar educational or work situations to define different message spaces and functional areas in the conferencing environment (e.g. online 'cafés', 'libraries', and 'seminar rooms') are not always successful. In a face-to-face setting, the framing of, for example, informal chat opportunities by coffee and meal breaks is an accepted and familiar convention. In the conferencing environment, messages which reflect social support and informal discourse, or off-topic discussion threads, are often intercalated with messages reflecting the substantive purpose and content of the conference. Different members of a group may react in different ways to this phenomenon; those who perceive it as a source of frustration and annoyance are likely to either withdraw from the conference, or enter messages which reflect their annoyance which, in turn, can rapidly sour the social environment of the conference. The lack of social context cues – as compared to the face-to-face situation – may thus lead to more extreme forms of behaviour in the

---

[5] A measure of the ratio of lexical items or 'content' words to grammatical items or 'function' words.

conferencing situation, which may outweigh some of the advantages of conferencing for collaboration and group learning.

When we look at transcripts of conference discussions, it would be naive in the extreme to equate the number or frequency of messages in a conference, or the recognisable links between messages, as an indicator than any form of useful 'collaborative learning' is occurring. Terms like 'communication', 'interactivity' and 'collaboration' need to be used with care and precision in this context. The fact that a group of people may be communicating within a shared conference space (even if they are 'lurkers' only reading messages contributed by others), and that some messages – such as a comment on an earlier message – might indicate some form of interactivity, does not necessarily imply that there is any real form of collaboration occurring amongst the members of the conference. In many cases, when one looks at the actual messages exchanged, the interactivity is limited to brief exchanges of information, rather than to any collaborative analysis and development of earlier contributions.

To establish whether any meaningful form of collaborative learning is occurring, it is necessary to undertake an analysis of the messages in a conference, and to situate the analysis within the social and organisational context of that particular conference. Examples of such analyses in this volume are included in Chapters 4 and 6 below: they each demonstrate the existence of collaborative learning in the sense we have tried to define the term, in that – in each case – the participants in the conferences in question were able, through the messages being exchanged, to create 'added value' and new understandings amongst the members of each group.

However, if there is to be real progress in the development of conferencing applications for collaborative learning, then it is necessary to provide educators and conference organisers with tools for content and message analysis which will help them to understand what is happening in the conferences in which they are involved, and which they can use as a basis for facilitating collaborative processes amongst group members. The framework proposed by France Henri in Chapter 8 of this book is an attempt to develop such tools, enabling us to identify messages in a conference which demonstrate the application of higher level cognitive skills (such as inference, judgement, problem-solving strategies), of in-depth processing of information, and of meta-cognitive knowledge and skills (evaluation, planning, regulation, self-awareness etc). The incorporation of tools based on such an approach to content analysis into the repertoire of conference moderator skills could be an important step in the direction of amplifying the potential of conferencing for intellectual collaboration.

The software environment

How important are specific software and interface features in determining the success or failure of a conferencing application? At one level – following the argument concerning social factors above – one could say that, as long as some sort of readily available facility for group messaging exists, people will use it successfully if they are motivated to do so, regardless of its functionality. In recent years, there has been an extraordinary growth in the use of e-mail lists and bulletin boards on academic research networks worldwide (even though they contain few specific tools for enhancing and managing group activity) simply because they are available. The IBM TOOLS system described by Rueda in Chapter 6 of this book does not possess the full set of features found in dedicated conferencing systems such as SuperKOM or Caucus, yet is successfully used on a large scale for collaboration and organisational networking, because it is a readily available feature of the users' normal work environment, and because it links together a large and globally dispersed community of users.

In a contribution to our discussions during and after the Workshop, Palme [37] answered this question from a different viewpoint by pointing to specific software features which have been shown to influence user behaviour:

One way to answer this question is to look at the experience with existing systems, and see if the actual behaviour of the user differs with different system design. There do not exist very many studies to investigate the user behaviour in different systems. Some information is however available from a number of cases:

Writing personally addressed mail versus conference contributions: Studies on use of the Forum-Planet computer conferencing system have shown that new users of these systems tend to write mainly conference contributions, while experienced users write more personally addressed mail. This is peculiar, since experience with most other conference systems is the opposite: beginners tend to write mostly interpersonal mail. The explanation is however easy if one looks at the user interface of Forum-Planet. This user interface makes it much easier to write a conference contribution than to write a personally addressed message.

Multi-conference messages: Many group communication environments have ethical rules which strongly discourage the sending of the same contribution to more than one group. This is peculiar, since it might seem natural in many cases to send a contribution to more than one group, if the topic of the contribution overlaps the areas of both groups. The explanation for this rule is however obvious. The systems which have these ethical rules are designed in such a way, that if a contribution is sent to more than one group, and a recipient is a member of both groups, then that recipient will see the contribution twice. Interesting to note is that no requests for such ethical rules have appeared in the KOM family of conference systems (KOM, PortaCOM, SuperKOM) where the software is designed so that a user is not shown the same contribution as new more than once, even if it is sent to more than one conference.

Allowing the sender to check if his/her message has been read: Some message systems allow the sender to find out if and when his/her messages have been read by their recipients. The existence of such a facility is controversial, some people claim that it is an infringement of privacy. However, such critical views are often heard for mail systems with distribution lists, but very seldom for conference systems. The probable explanation is that because the conference systems allow the recipient more control of what to read or not to read than pure mail systems with distribution lists, the users do not feel the same need for protection of privacy in the conference systems as in the mail systems.

Controlling who may start conferences: In a conference system at the Royal Institute of Technology in Stockholm many years ago, the administrators of the system decided that ordinary students (who were the main users of the system) should not be allowed to start conferences. The effect of this was that the students instead discussed the topics they wanted in the conferences available, which meant that the discussion in the conferences often did not agree very well with the intended topic of the conference. This however, led to rather violent clashes between those who wanted to discuss the intended topic of the conference and nothing else, and those who wanted to discuss other issues.

... The conclusion from this is that system design does influence user behaviour, often in peculiar and unintended ways. To some extent, however, users will try to circumvent bad systems design by finding ways of getting around the limitations.

In this book, we are interested in features which can promote collaborative learning. If conferencing is to develop as a widely used tool for collaboration, outside the normal work environment of a university or of large corporations such as IBM and Digital, then – as a first step – improvements are required in current system and interface designs to ease rapid and enjoyable initial learning by novice users. As Vallée stresses in Chapter 12, CMC systems must provide an environment which people find personally motivating and enjoyable to enter, which allows the 'magic' of CMC to occur. Once the initial familiarisation phase is over, it is important that the design of the system encourages feelings of 'groupness' and 'telepresence', encouraging users to identify with the the the other members of their group, despite constraints of time and space. Features which allow users to see which messages other members of the group have read and contributed within a conference, which facilitate consensus (e.g. through polling or voting tools), which make it easy to branch into sub-groups or sub-topics, and which can assign special functions to conference organisers or moderators, are all important in this respect.

The dominant metaphor in the interface design – as proposed by Sorensen in Chapter 13 – needs to be that of a tool for group communication and collaboration, which allows the users to maintain their focus on the group task, rather than on the medium through which the group task is accomplished. Alexander (see Chapter 14) proposes a number of specific graphic style interface features which make it easy for the user to navigate within the conferencing system, to maintain a sense of group identity, and to keep a focus on the collaborative learning task being undertaken. He proposes four different 'views' into a conferencing system to achieve these goals:
– a view of the system as a whole, using the metaphor of an 'electronic campus' to help users find their way around;
– a view of each conference, with information on each member's status, and information on new comments in each of the main discussion topics;
– a view onto each individual message, with ready access to reply and comment facilities;
– a personal view, giving access to information on each group member, and their roles and contributions within the group task.

Such features can provide an appropriate context within which groups can use the explicit forms and procedures of the conferencing tools (e.g. for moderating, for commenting, for reviewing etc). However, collaborative groups exist over time, evolve, and change. Their activities follow natural rhythms. Between the software environment and interface which defines the context of a group's activity, and the toolbox of procedures and functions provided by a conferencing system, there is, effectively, a gap in the current generation of software primitives. Peter and Trudy Johnson-Lenz, the original developers of the concept of 'groupware' argue that the next generation of conferencing software needs to provide more support for processes over the life of a group project. They propose the inclusion of four new categories of primitives (fundamental and orthogonal constructs) to " bridge the gap between groupware as context and groupware as mechanism":

– **timing**: appropriate tools for current stage of group evolution; to punctuate transitions, beginnings, endings
– **rhythms**: patterns for periodic contact and participation
– **boundaries**: to define group membership, delineate group identity; mark rhythms, beginnings, endings
– **containers**: to hold group energy, life, identity, "presence"; give meaning and purpose to group life. [25, p. 405]

It is true that not enough attention has been paid in design of current systems to the natural processes and rhythms of group work. The asynchronous nature of computer conferencing (a great advantage in many respects) tends to lead to a neglect of the need for some sort of punctuation, or scheduling, which sets temporal limits to discussion, indicating deadlines by which specific stages of a collaborative activity should be completed. Most other forms of social and group work are paced by specific events (e.g. classroom schedules, due dates for assignments, meeting dates etc). The fact that computer conferencing allows collaboration to progress without the need for set places and times for meetings and other highly visible decision-points does not mean that there should be no rhythm or pacing to conferencing discussions. Tools which provide help in organising the life cycle of a group (including the natural processes of group formation, of inter-personal negotiation, and of constructive collaborative work leading to satisfactory task completion by an agreed date), are essential if computer conferencing is to develop its full potential for collaborative learning.

Conclusions

During the *Najaden* Workshop, and in this book, we have tried to establish whether computer mediated communication can provide an appropriate medium for collaborative learning, and if so, under what social and technical conditions. Certainly, computer conferencing fits a number of the (technical) requirements which Schrage [43] lists as pre-requisites for effective collaboration: it provides a shared communication space, and allows for continuous communication; one can construct formal and informal environments within a CMC system; the physical presence of the participants is not necessary; and computer networking allows for the selective use of outsiders. Clearly, there are examples of successful use of computer conferencing and networking for collaborative learning, some of which are analysed in this book. But provision of a CMC system as part of an education or training programme does not, of course, of itself, in any way imply or guarantee that collaborative learning will occur. There are also successful examples of the use of classrooms for collaborative learning – yet the overall trend of educational activity in the classroom environment is generally far from collaborative, and many other types of activity occur there.

Just as the classroom can provide an environment suitable for a whole range of learning models and activities, so can the CMC environment provide for other functions than collaboration. Only some of the applications of CMC reviewed briefly in this chapter – in particular the virtual seminar application – use computer conferencing discussion groups as the main learning vehicle, and the groups involved are usually fairly small (10-15 people), are often composed of professional peers, and are generally run by very experienced conference moderators

In most other applications, conferencing is one of several communication media (and may even be an optional add-on) within the CMC system, and constructive collaborative learning in groups is only one amongst several elements. Other activities supported by computer-mediated communication include one-to-one mail, socialising, information-exchange, trouble-shooting, posting announcements, trading insults, swapping jokes, playing games, submitting homework assignments, conducting opinion polls, developing written communication skills, co-authoring documents, social networking, organising events and meetings, and so on. Such online activities, combined with the groupware features of a conferencing system, provide the necessary – but not sufficient – social and technological conditions and facilities for the development and support of collaborative learning activities. But just as in the face-to-face classroom or organisational context, the successful inclusion of collaborative learning activities within the CMC environment depends also on the value attached to inter-personal collaboration, on the way such collaboration is planned and organised, and on the extent to which it meets the needs, interests, and goals of the participants. Networked communities capable of supporting and nurturing successful learning collaborations do not just arise spontaneously within the electronic webs and circuits linking their members. Like other communities, they require active and planned involvement within a context of shared goals, interests, and commitments.

References

1. Ancona, D.G., and Caldwell, D.F.: Information technology and work groups: the case of new product teams. In: Intellectual teamwork: social and technological foundations of cooperative work (J.Galegher, R.E. Kraut, C. Egido, eds.). Hillsdale, N.J.: Lawrence Erlbaum 1990

2. Bannon, L.: Issues in computer-supported collaborative learning. In: Computer supported collaborative learning. (C. O'Malley, ed.). Heidelberg: Springer Verlag (in press)

3. Beard, R. and Hartley, J.: Teaching and learning in higher education. London: Harper and Row 1984

4. Boyd,R.D., and Apps, J.W.: Redefining the discipline of adult education. San Francisco: Jossey-Bass 1980

5. Bruner, J. S.: Actual minds, possible worlds. London: Harvard University Press, 1984

6. Damon, W.: Peer education: the untapped potential. Journal of Applied Developmental Psychology, 5, pp. 331-343 (1984)

7. Edwards, D., and Mercer, N.: Common knowledge: the development of understanding in the classroom. London: Routledge, 1987

8. Fafchamps, D., Reynolds, D., and Kuchinsky, D.: The dynamics of small group decision-making over the e-mail channel. Proceedings of the First European Conference on Computer-Supported Cooperative Work. Gatwick, Sept 13-15, 1989

9. Fanning, T. and Raphael, B.: Computer tele-conferencing: experience at Hewlett-Packard. Proceedings of the Conference on Computer-Supported Cooperative Work, Austin, Texas, 1986

10. Feenberg, A.: The written world. In: Mindweave: communication, computers and distance education. (R.D. Mason, A.R. Kaye, eds.), pp. 22–39 Oxford: Pergamon 1989

11. Forman, E.A, and Cazden, C.B.: Exploring Vygotskian perspectives in education: the cognitive value of peer interaction. In: Culture, communication, and cognition. (J.V. Wertsch, ed.). Cambridge: Cambridge University Press 1985

12. Galegher, J. and Kraut, R.E.: Computer-mediated communication for intellectual teamwork: a field experiment in group writing. Mimeo. Arizona: University of Arizona 1989

13. Galegher, J., Kraut, R.E., and Egido, C. (eds.): Intellectual teamwork: social and technological foundations of cooperative work. Hillsdale, N.J.: Lawrence Erlbaum 1990

14. Goodman, F.L.: Instructional gaming through computer conferencing. In: Empowering networks: computer conferencing in education. (M. Waggoner, ed.). Englewood Cliffs, N.J.: Educational Technology Publications 1992

15. Gooler, D. D.: The education utility: the power to revitalize education and society. Englewood Cliffs, N.J.: Educational Technology Publications 1986

16. Grenier, R. and Metes, G.: Enterprise networking: working together apart. Bedford MA.: Digital Press 1992

17. Hansen E. et al.: Computer conferencing for collaborative learning in large college classes: final report of a grant project. Division of Development and Special Projects. Indiana: Indiana University 1991

18. Harasim, L. (ed.): Online education: perspectives on a new environment. New York: Praeger 1990

19. Henri, F.: Distance education and computer-assisted communication. Prospects, 18, 1, pp. 85-90 Paris: Unesco 1988

20. Hiltz, S.R.: Online communities: a case study of the office of the future. New Jersey: Ablex Publishing 1984

21. Hiltz, S.R.: Evaluating the virtual classroom. In: Online education: perspectives on a new environment. (L. Harasim, ed.), pp 133–184. New York: Praeger 1990

22. Hiltz, S.R.: Collaborative teaching in a virtual classroom. Proceedings of the Third Symposium on Computer-Mediated Communication, May 15-17, pp. 37–55. Guelph, Ontario: University of Guelph 1990

23. Hsu, E.: Running a management game in a computer-mediated conferencing system. Proceedings of the Third Symposium on Computer-Mediated Communication, May 15-17, pp. 201-208. Guelph, Ontario: University of Guelph 1990

24. Illich, I. D.: Deschooling society. London: Calder and Boyars 1971

25. Johnson-Lenz, P. and Johnson-Lenz T.: Post-mechanistic groupware primitives: rhythms, boundaries, and containers. Int. J. Man–Machine Studies. 34, pp. 395–417 (1991)

26. Kaye, A. R.: Computer-mediated communication and distance education. In: Mindweave: communication, computers and distance education. (R.D. Mason, A.R. Kaye, eds.), pp. 3–21. Oxford: Pergamon 1989

27. Kaye, A.R.: Computer networking for development of distance education courses. In: Computer Supported Collaborative Writing (M. Sharples, ed.) London: Springer Verlag (in press)

28. Kling, R.: Multivalent social relationships in computer-supported workplaces. Mimeo, 1991

29. Knowles, M.S.: The modern practice of adult education: from pedagogy to andragogy. New York: Association Press 1970

30. Lamy, T.: La télématique: un outil convivial? In: Le savoir à domicile: pédagogie et problématique de la formation à distance (F. Henri, A. Kaye, eds.), pp. 303–328. Québec: Presses de l'Université du Québec 1985

31. Marchand, M. et al.: Les paradis informationnels. Paris: Masson et CNET/ENST 1987

32. Mason, R.D. : An evaluation of CoSy on an Open University course. In: Mindweave: communication, computers and distance education. (R.D. Mason, A.R. Kaye, eds.), pp. 115–145. Oxford: Pergamon 1989

33. Mason, R.D.: Moderating educational computer conferences. In: DEOSNEWS 1 (1), Pennsylania State University 1991 (also to appear in Electronic Networking: Research, Applications, and Policy, 1992)

34. Nipper, S.: Developing acceptance: how can integrated systems be used for industry-oriented distance education and training? Workshop on Telematic Networks for Distance Education and Training – 'Electronic Universities'. Brussels: Commission of the European Communities, October 3, 1990

35. Odasz, F.: Grassroots networking on Big Sky Telegraph: empowering Montana's one-room rural schools. In: Empowering networks: computer conferencing in education. (M. Waggoner, ed.). Englewood Cliffs, N.J.: Educational Technology Publications 1992

36. Owen, T.: Computer-mediated writing: the writer in electronic residence. In: Mindweave: communication, computers and distance education. (R.D. Mason, A.R. Kaye, eds.), pp. 208–210. Oxford: Pergamon 1989

37. Palme, J.: Does software design matter? Written contribution to the *Najaden* ARW 1991

38. Proctor, P.: M. ENB Computer-assisted learning project. Campus World 1989/90, pp 79–80 Cambridge: Hobson's 1989

39. Rapaport, M.: Computer mediated communications. New York: John Wiley 1991

40. Riel, M.M. and Levin, J.A.: Building electronic communities: success and failures in computer networking. Instructional Science, 19, pp. 145–169 (1990)

41. Rogers, C.: Encounter groups. London: Allen Lane, The Penguin Press, 1970

42. Rowan, R.: The intuitive manager. New York: Little 1986

43. Schrage, M.: Shared minds: the new technologies of collaboration. New York: Random House 1990

44. Senge, P.M.: The fifth discipline, the art and practice of the learning organisation. New York: Doubleday / Currency 1990

45. Sinclair, J.M. and and Coulthard, R.M.: Towards an analysis of discourse: the English used by teachers and pupils. London: Oxford University Press 1975

46. Slavin, R.E.: Co-operative learning: theory, research, and practice. Englewood Cliffs, N.J.: Prentice Hall 1990

47. Smith, K.L.: Collaborative and interactive writing for increasing communication skills. Hispania, 73, pp. 51–61 (1990)

48. Sproull, L. and Kiesler, S.: Connections: new ways of working in the networked organization. Cambridge, MA.: MIT Press 1991

49. Steiner, I.D.: Group process and productivity. New York: Academic Press 1972

50. Thomas, R.: The implications of electronic communication for the Open University. In: Mindweave: communication, computers and distance education. (R.D. Mason, A.R. Kaye, eds.), pp. 166–177. Oxford: Pergamon 1989

51. Vygotsky, L.S.: Thought and language. Cambridge, MA.: MIT Press 1962

52. Vygotsky, L.S.: Mind in society. Cambridge, MA: Harvard University Press 1978

53. Webb, N.M.: Student interaction and learning in small groups, Review of Educational Research, 52, 3, pp. 421-445 (1982)

54. Yates, S.: Speech, writing, and computer conferencing: an analysis. In: Computer conferencing: the last word. (R.D. Mason, ed.). Victoria, B.C.: Beach Holme Publications (in press)

55. Zuboff, S.: In the age of the smart machine. New York: Basic Books 1988

PART I

Computer Conferencing in Practice

The cases analysed in these five chapters represent only a sample of the variety and number of applications of computer conferencing relevant to collaborative learning that have appeared over the last few years. Nevertheless, they give a fair picture of the issues involved in trying to create appropriate conditions for group learning, and each case illustrates particular features which represent recurring themes throughout the book.

In the selection of cases, a number of criteria were taken into consideration:
– the nature of learning collaborations, to include examples where learning is the primary goal (e.g. education and training courses), and examples where learning is a secondary, highly desirable, outcome of action-oriented teamwork or of organisational networking for creativity and brainstorming;
– the level of incorporation of networking within the course, project, or organisation, ranging from the use of conferencing as an add-on to an existing structure or course design, or as a novel feature, to its acceptance as a mundane communication tool within the work environment;
– scale, to include examples of relatively small and structured groups (e.g. the management students at Lancaster University) to extremely large and open groups (e.g. those using IBM's extensive and well-established in-house network);
– geographical spread, ranging from the province-wide programme for in-service teacher training in Catalonia, to development programmes involving teams using inter-continental networking;
– coverage of a range of technology related factors, including access locations (the home, the workplace, and local centres), conferencing systems (Caucus, CoSy, AGORA, PortaCOM, and TOOLS) and access devices ('dumb' terminals, personal computers and modems etc);
– inclusion of cases which had not so far been widely published in the literature on educational applications of networking, and which we hope will be new to the readership of this book.

The first three chapters are illustrations of the use of conferencing within education or training programmes. The chapter by Cristina Simón concerns the first application in Spain of networking for a public education project, and focuses on the use of a variety of telematic tools – videotex electronic mail and data-base access, file transfer, and conferencing – as components of an in-service teacher training programme in information technology. These supports were associated with printed teaching texts and articles for each course module. There was a highly differential use of media within this programme, with videotex being the most used, followed by the file transfer facility. Conferencing proved to be of relatively minor interest, possibly because the course design did not incorporate the role of tutors as animators and moderators of online debates and conferences.

Two of the cases analysed in the next chapter, by Morten Søby, represent approaches to adding computer conferencing and electronic mail to a standard distance education or correspondence course model, and also include an example of a totally online course. Of particular interest in the context of this book is the use of closed conferences on PortaCOM for small groups of learners to organise their group activities and to prepare group reports as part of their assessed coursework.

The chapter by David McConnell on use of CMC for management learning by the University of Lancaster (UK) is an excellent example of the implementation, de novo, of a pedagogical approach based on peer collaboration – in design of the programme, in management of individual and group learning, and in assessment of participants' contributions. It is also a good example of the use of CMC in conjunction with residential workshops, with each environment (the electronic and the face-to-face) being used in alternation.

The next two chapters present examples of the use of conferencing in cases where education or training is not the primary explicit goal, but where collaborative learning occurs as an important secondary or incidental outcome. Elaine McCreary and Madge Brochet summarise the findings from several years' experience of work groups using computer conferencing to manage development programmes involving institutions and groups spread across several continents. Jesus Rueda analyses the use of computer conferencing within IBM's world-wide network, with particular emphasis on the issues raised by the large numbers of members of many conferences, and the use of networking internationally within IBM.

In the discussions within this group (The Implementation Group) on Najaden, one of the main issues raised was the importance of recognising the variety of different scenarios within which collaborative networked learning can occur, and that these are not restricted to situations where education or training of some kind is the primary goal. Collaborative learning undoubtedly takes place in the project teams described by McCreary and Brochet, and through IBM's company network. What these cases hold in common with specifically education-oriented examples such as Lancaster's management programme, and some of the NKS courses, is the recognition of the importance of learning through exchanges between peers, where individuals feel able and willing to help each other, and learn from each other, over the network. The likelihood of such free exchanges occurring was seen as being related to the 'social climate' on the network, which in turn is dependent upon factors such as the feeling of being part of a non-threatening community of equals, and the recognition of appropriate norms for the various roles (information-seeker, collaborator, organiser, animator, moderator, resource person etc) which members of the network might take on at different times. The building of such a social climate takes time, and – particularly in new educational applications – requires considerable initial input in personal time and moderating skills from online tutors and animators before members of online groups begin to realise, and then take for granted (as in the case of IBM), the potential of the network for peer exchange and learning. A key role for the setting up of new projects was seen as being that of the 'diffusion manager' – the person who takes on responsibility for ensuring that the innovation of computer conferencing is introduced effectively, and through the appropriate formal and informal channels within the organisation.

The framing of the networking environment was also seen as being of great importance. By this we mean the elements which form the framework within which the different actors will operate, such as:
– the explicit purposes and goals of conferencing within the programme or organisation, including both task-oriented goals and social maintenance processes;
– the appropriate places within the conferencing environment for messages and discussions related to particular tasks, goals, and processes;
– the timing and phasing of conference discussions, particularly where deadlines are crucial for the completion of a given task, or of a specific phase of a programme (e.g. a particular module of a course);
– the role of conferencing *vis-à-vis* other communication modes (personal electronic mail, telephone, fax, face-to-face meetings) and information sources (texts, data-bases etc), and the integration of conferencing with these other facilities.

Problems experienced with the use of conferencing, including its failure to live up to expectations as a medium for group learning and effective collaboration, can often be attributed to lack of attention to these and other framework factors – especially in contexts where peer learning and support is not seen as being the main paradigm for participation in the activity (whether it be a course or a group task). Paradoxically, views on the importance of specific software design features in determining the success or failure of conferencing applications were contradictory. On the one hand, it seemed clear that instances of perceived success or failure could not be attributed to the attributes of a specific conferencing system. On the other hand, the importance of software design features which promote feelings of 'groupness' was constantly stressed as being of utmost importance, and this is one of the key issues to which we return in the third Part of the book.

2
Telematic Support for In-Service Teacher Training

Cristina Simón[1]
Educational Technology Office, Technical University of Madrid, Spain

Abstract: This paper describes a pilot experiment carried out in Spain involving the use of various telematic media (file transfer, a videotex electronic mail application, and computer conferencing) in support of in-service teacher training courses. The experience is analysed with respect to the balance to be achieved between technological facilities and design features in order to promote collaborative learning processes, and thus maximise instructional effectiveness. Results show that learners made a highly differential use of media, with individual support being much more accepted than support for collaborative processes. Some design factors are studied in the light of these results: minimum estimated conditions for users' participation, tutors' changing roles, and the bridge to be built towards new instructional models by both learners and teachers.

Keywords: telematic media, electronic mail, videotex, computer conferencing, file transfer, in-service teacher training, tutor role, dropout rate.

---

[1]I feel deeply indebted to the other members of the evaluation team (Carmen Viorreta, Pablo Martín and Daniel Cabrero) for their invaluable help and discussions both during the evaluation itself and the elaboration of this work. I also want to thank the PIE experts (in particular Jordi Vivancos and Ferrán Ruiz) for their useful inputs throughout the whole process.

Introduction

The setting up of effective group dynamics in a computer-mediated educational situation poses a set of problems which are not easily solved by designers and implementors. First of all, there is a range of possible technological solutions [3] from which the most adequate one needs to be chosen. And here we face the first question: is technology in itself so important in the promotion of a collaborative distance learning environment? Current European R&D programmes underline the point that pilot experiments with training technologies should aim at applying educational features and not at testing the latest developments in computer science and telecommunications [6]. On the other hand, any practitioner in this field knows that some technical requirements are essential to guarantee participation and success. Even more, when technology fans (and I admit to being one myself) are placed in front of the latest version of a software package, they frequently wonder how they managed before, without this new facility that the previous version didn't offer! Where is, then, the balance between technological features and pedagogical designs?

Many of the discussions in the Implementation group during the *Najaden* workshop centred on which software features would be desirable to promote collaborative learning. The experience described in this chapter has two very important conditioning factors. Firstly, the technological infrastructure used is a mixture of media, with two access points for the different media, as well as diverse kinds of software; and secondly, as the results show, collaborative learning processes have been reduced to a minimum (though this has not reduced learners' perception of success and effectiveness of the courses).

This work consists in the evaluation of the first experience carried out in a public institution in Spain using telematic media as a support for distance training. It was undertaken by the *Programa d'Informática Educativa de Catalunya* (Catalonia is one of the autonomous regions of Spain). It is hoped that this analysis will raise some issues that should be taken into consideration in the implementation of electronic collaborative learning environments.

Telematic Supported Courses for In-Service Teacher Training

The problem

The Department of Education of the *Generalitat de Catalunya* (Catalonia Autonomous Government) has 2165 centres widely spread over the various provinces. These centres cover the range of primary and secondary education as well as vocational training. As a support to the teachers at all the centres (mainly through the running of courses and pilot experiments) there are about 77 Pedagogical Resource Centres (CRP's) in the region.

In 1986 the Programme of Information Technology in Education (PIE) was created, to promote the use of these technologies within different aspects of the primary and secondary education curriculum. In-service teacher training has become an important part of this programme. Teachers are given instruction in the application of technological media to various areas of their teaching activities. During the 1989-90 academic year, 244 courses were organised and attended by 4000 teachers [5].

Up to this year, courses were arranged within a face-to-face scheme. This meant considerable effort from the learners, who had to move from their homes and working centres to Barcelona and pay for their travel and subsistence expenses. This problem led the PIE experts to consider using information technology not only as a topic to teach, but as a training communication channel as well.

The design of the solution

In 1988, PIE had set up a telematic educational network called XTEC (*Xarxa Telemàtica Educativa de Catalunya*). This mainly provided access to a videotex database of educational resources which could be consulted by teachers in order to incorporate a wider range of materials into their classes. The network also offered a computer conferencing service (AGORA), used by students in different schools for getting to know each other and for communicating with experts to discuss different topics. It was decided to use the facilities offered by the XTEC as the medium to reach teachers for their in-service training.

Thus, for the academic year 1990-91, a set of two telematic-supported pilot courses was organized. The initial design was for two groups of 25 participants each, and with this idea in mind a brochure was sent to the centres asking for applications. The demand was so high (more than 200) that an initial selection of candidates had to be made, with a requirement that they should have some previous experience with computers. It was also decided to duplicate the number of groups per course.

The final group of learners consisted of 111 teachers in both primary (42) and secondary (69) education, aged between 25 and 45 years. They were all graduates in different disciplines, with their roles changed from teaching to coordinating the Pedagogical Resource Centres referred to above. The fact that they were experts in teaching at different levels was considered an advantage, since it would probably elicit lots of thinking on the comparison of instructional processes, and lead to conclusions concerning the best way to implement them through telematic media.

Courses were then composed of two different groups with 26 to 31 members, and each one with a different tutor. The courses were about the use of spreadsheets in education, and the use of online information retrieval services (in particular, the SINERA documentary database). The duration of the courses was estimated at six months, running from late November to May. Each course consisted of 7 modules, requiring 2 weeks to study each module. Materials were adapted from already existing courses on both subjects for self-study and distant interaction with a tutor. Learners received the following materials:
– text for each module, consisting of an explanation of the module structure, the main set of materials, and a description of the related practical work;
– a CBT (Computer Based Training) tutorial on how to log into the system;
– additional materials depending on the contents of the module, either text (complementary readings) or diskettes (examples of applications);
– a user handbook.

Learners were then supposed to work through the materials, practice navigation through the software, carry out exercises on the application of software to hypotheses or pre-defined situations and send the solutions to the tutor, and answer theoretical questions posed by the tutor. A final assignment had to be prepared by the end of the course, which was proposed as the course progressed. Participants were given extra time to complete this.

Telematic support

The XTEC network is managed by a central host, a DPS8 BULL computer running GCOS8 operating system with 4.4 Gb of disk storage. It works with the DATANET front-end, allowing 44 simultaneous users. This configuration offers the learners the following services:

– A videotex system with e-mail facilities that provide personal contact with the tutor (since, as we will see later, the computer conferencing system did not permit one-to-one messages); videotex was also used for consulting databases using the MISTRAL software (especially a documentary database, whose enquiry techniques formed the basis of one of the courses).

– A file transfer system called HERMES, through which learners were supposed to send all their exercises. They had to state a code for each item sent reflecting their user ID and the exercise number. Files were stored in a common space equally accessible by learners and tutor.

– A computer conferencing service (AGORA) in which students entered comments and reflections on a series of so-called 'proposals'. These proposals were given in the text corresponding to each module, and were mainly general topics for discussion proposed by the coordinator. With these topics, conferences (or 'teledebates', as they were commonly referred to by learners and tutors) were created. Some of them were permanent throughout the course, while others were deleted when the module finished.

Access to the network was only available at fixed hours (Mon-Fri, from 09.00h to 20.00h). Time restrictions were not expected to be a problem, since learners connected from their schools and not from their homes. Learners' workstations were hard disk MS-DOS computers with internal V22/V23 modem boards.

Leading learners on their way to technology

Given the low levels of prior use of technological media by the learners and tutors at the beginning of the course, various steps were taken in order to foster as comfortable a working environment as possible.

First of all, both the user handbook and all written material (except for additional readings) made continuous reference to the different activities learners should do through the course by means of special icons, so that they knew at each moment which media to use to perform the exercises.

Face-to-face meetings were also arranged, in order to help learners with the use of the services and counsel them about their problems with working at a distance. The first was held as a starting point to the course, the second one after two modules were over, and the last one at the end of the whole course.

At the first meeting learners were given basic guidance on how the various activities should be carried out using the different technological media. Personal questions to the tutor or to peers, and notifications (e.g. of meetings or deadlines) were to be directed through videotex e-mail, using one-to-one or one-to-many letters, as appropriate. General and public issues or questions were to be dealt with through computer conferencing, whilst the file transfer facility was to be used for sending material to the tutors, and receiving their corrections. Finally, there was a telephone hotline for technical problems, but due to the scarcity of technical staff, learners were recommended to use it as little as possible.

Evaluation Methodology

The team of evaluators designed and carried out several analyses. They were supposed to work as 'external eyes' to the process, making a set of recommendations at the end of the course in order to plan and design the next courses. It could then be considered a formative evaluation within a pure positivist paradigm (see Chapter 7 in this volume, by Mason). Both quantitative and qualitative analyses were carried out.

Quantitative analysis

A first questionnaire on initial expectations concerning the general use of telematic support was drawn up, which covered the following variables:
– estimated effectiveness and comfort of distance learning
– the adequacy of the contents themselves
– ease and friendliness of use of the telematic services
– user skills regarding written expression and typing
– estimated frequency of connection
– availability of equipment
– estimated contribution of computer conferencing to decreasing learning time and increasing quality of learning and interaction with tutor and peers.

A post-use, final evaluation questionnaire was also designed, to provide a comparison with the above expectations, and also covering the following variables:
– estimated reliability of the system
– factors that were identified as preventing effective use of the network
– perceived global usefulness of the system
– selection and justification of aspects of the course to be improved.

Finally, there was a withdrawal questionnaire, which was sent to learners who decided to drop out of the programme. The quantitative analysis was complemented by usage statistics provided by the host computer.

Qualitative analysis

Evaluators were provided with hard copies of all the messages entered on the computer conferencing system by the four groups. In addition, one of the tutors released the contents of his mailbox on the videotex e-mail system. Messages from the computer conferencing system were classified according to the kind of activity underlying the communication situation.

Learners' messages covered the following categories:
– greetings
– responses to a proposed activity
– descriptions of personal experience with computer conferencing
– reactions to a peer's comment or interaction
– proposals for debate (which were mainly to discuss applications to the classroom of ideas drawn from the course itself)
– questions and requests for further information on a topic.

Tutors' messages, on the other hand, were classified into:
- presentation of modules
- proposals for activities
- proposals for debate
- posing of examples
- 'weaving' activities
- references to other comments
- explanation of questions
- public correction of exercises
- expression of personal opinions on a topic.

There was also a monitoring questionnaire that learners filled out six weeks after the start of the courses. The intention of this instrument was to gather the first reactions to the use of the system and the methodology of the course, in order to introduce corrective actions if necessary (for example, by increasing technical help with connection problems). These responses were also analysed qualitatively. Finally, at the end of the course the evaluators held two meetings with the tutors and a group of students, respectively, in order to collect final reactions and conclusions regarding the use of these services as a support to their distance learning processes.

Results and Findings

Expectations and first reactions

It seemed clear from the very outset of the experience that the learners had built up great expectations of the new training scheme. The chance to experiment with the new media appeared as the most important reason for their applying for the courses. The main advantage expected was increased communication with the tutor; contact with other peers was also considered important, but not so much (these priorities are clearly reflected in the dynamics of communication throughout the course, as will be shown later).

Learners expected to connect to the telematic services at least once a week (80.5 %). Only 7 % had a workstation available at home; some of the rest had to share their computer with other colleagues at the schools, which could limit their connection chances.

Final results reflect a very high withdrawal rate (only 57 out of the initial 111 completed the course). It is noticeable that 19 of them had not even finished the first module of the courses. The main causes for giving up as reported by the dropouts, in order of importance, were: lack of time, as the course required much more additional effort than estimated; technical problems over connection, which caused a great delay in the follow-up of the modules; and lack of knowledge of the software (especially for e-mail and computer conferencing, rather than for file transfer).

A delay in the start of courses (from early to late November) caused an overlap of the first modules of the course with a peak in teaching activities (final examinations for the term, Christmas holidays). Difficulties in completing this first phase of the course were an important factor in the final withdrawal rate; only 3 learners had finished 3 modules or more before giving up.

The initial monitoring questionnaire filled out after two months revealed problems with connections to the services. This constrained very much the range of activities open to the participants, because they could not send the exercises or communicate with anybody. The resultant feeling of loneliness was very difficult to overcome in many cases. Learners asked for an extension of technical support. Other problems were also detected, such as those derived from sharing the computer, which restricted the available connection time. Finally, learners also complained about deadlines for the modules, considered too tight and strict.

The use of telematic services

There was a highly differential use of telematic media: 87.8% of participants used videotex e-mail at least once a week or more, whilst 73.1% did the same with file transfer. However, only 26.8 % logged in as frequently to the computer conferencing system. The reasons for this restricted use of group communication facilities could be found in the design and dynamics of the courses themselves. The file transfer facility was used to send the exercises, which were an essential part of the course. And videotex, being the communication channel with the tutor, was also considered relevant. However, learners did not grasp the relative importance of AGORA as a component of the course. This factor was combined with the connection difficulties, turning AGORA into an unreliable medium. This had important consequences such as the decision (conscious?) to use e-mail for leaving notifications or important messages to the whole group by using a distribution list instead of using the conferencing system. In fact, learners estimated that e-mail was a better medium for increasing interaction with their peers than computer conferencing!

Results from the analysis of messages reflect this scarce use of the medium. One of the course conferences on spreadsheets only had 41 messages during the whole period, with just 3 interventions from the tutor. When analysing these messages, the largest percentage in each course corresponded to 'responses to activities' and 'questions' posed by learners, but there were few messages on peer interaction or expression of personal opinions that could elicit collaborative learning processes.

We tried to explore at the group meetings and interviews why learners seemed so reluctant to participate in computer conferencing, while being so active in other aspects of the course that also required their effort. Most of them considered the medium as "very cold", and pointed out the fact that they did not know each other very well, despite the face-to-face sessions arranged at the beginning of the course. They also found it difficult to express their ideas in writing, because it was hard to imagine "... who you are addressing".

The interviews and group meetings corroborate the above results. Learners reported that their lack of time determined their allocation of priorities, and that participation in the computer conferencing did not seem important for the progress of the course. Some learners even considered logging on as a waste of time (e.g., because they left a message that no-one answered), and one of them reported: "I don't think I've learned more from getting into AGORA".

When asked for their personal experience with telematic media as a whole, learners considered its potential for individualisation as the most important feature. They also perceived the technology as being comfortable, easy and exciting to use. Videotex e-mail, as the channel of communication with the tutor, was of course chosen as the most useful service contributing to this individualisation.

Computer-mediated communication in a broad sense was considered worthwhile incorporating as a tool for the later courses. It was estimated as "good" to "excellent" in comparison with both face-to-face courses and traditional distance education media. Among the factors to be improved in future projects, the large majority of respondents to the questionnaire chose the need to include animation activities on the AGORA system, and to give it a thematic orientation in order to increase participation, together with more realistic time planning for each course.

Some Issues Arising from the Experience

Minimum conditions for participation

We conclude from our results that sophisticated software features are not necessary to enable learners to log in to the services. Some of the factors that our experience did prove to be essential were:
– Straightforward access, which can frequently be split up into two aspects: an easy procedure (solved with an automatic logon script installed on the communications software) and lack of problems with the telephone lines (this was in fact one of the problems that created a high degree of reluctance over use of the computer conferencing service).
– A planned structure of tasks that gives learners a clear objective, with the subsequent motivation to connect to and use the service; as we have seen, learners reported that file transfer and videotex e-mail were worthwhile to use because they mediated specific and relevant tasks for course progress.
– A shared perception of the medium as reliable, that is, the trust that one's communication objectives and requirements will be met by the system (e.g. the successful use of e-mail by tutors for public notifications to the whole group); a feeling of insecurity within the communication situation created by AGORA led to withdrawing from the use of this medium.
– Realistic planning and allocation of time for the different modules of the course; it seems likely that time pressures and an overlapping of activities caused the high mortality rate at the beginning of the course.

Changing tutors' roles

Tutor presence and use of media has been considered essential to foster learners' participation. In this sense, a change in the tutor's role would have been desirable for the initiation and continuity of collaborative learning processes. Results show that tutors acted as subject-matter experts, answering questions and correcting exercises and practices, and that this role has been successfully played, with a corresponding satisfaction and approval from the participants.

Nevertheless, inputs from tutors to promote collaborative learning in itself have barely been detected. Successful experiences of peer collaboration [2] tell us that the tutor has to make group members aware of the fact that their own experiences are relevant and worth telling to the group, and that other peers are as valuable a source of knowledge as the rest of the components in the course. As expressed by McIhenny:

> The tutors have to face a change in role from 'teacher as authority' to 'tutor as supporter'. No longer are they to be the providers of information; they have to become fellow searchers for knowledge with their students. [4]

Tutors were well aware of the importance of this factor for the effective use of AGORA. But again, time pressures imposed their priorities, and preference was given to dealing with individual problems rather than to stimulating group processes.

A changing instructional model

A very interesting parallel can be observed between traditional face-to-face instructional models and the use which participants made of telematic media. Especially in the courses on spreadsheets, videotex e-mail acted as a substitute for the telephone, and file transfer played the role of ordinary mail. Following this scheme, the teaching-learning process remained the same as that of traditional distance study methods. Users considered these media as an improvement, but just because they were "faster" and "more comfortable". In this sense, media were satisfactorily used but in our opinion their wider potential was not fully exploited. How could we optimise the use of these services? Again, the role of the tutor is essential in making learners aware of the functionalities of technology, not only to speed up information exchange with the tutor, but also as a way to enrich their learning processes through peer interaction, joint practice and generation of ideas [1].

Conclusions

The implementation of computer supported instructional environments, as stated in the first part of this chapter, has to strike a balance between technological features and capabilities. Our experience shows that advances in computer science or telecommunications, though desirable, are not essential to increase participation. Some minimum requirements have appeared as a result of learners' reports. The importance of tutors' interventions in creating a collaborative learning environment has also been pointed out, as well as the need to introduce learners to teaching-learning models different from traditional face-to-face classroom situations. The combination of acceptable technical conditions with a careful group design seems, in conclusion, the key to achievement of effective instructional results.

References

1. Davie, L.: Facilitation techniques for the on-line tutor. In: Mindweave: communication, computers and distance education. (R.D. Mason, A.R. Kaye, eds.), pp. 74–85. Oxford: Pergamon 1989

2. Goodlad, S. and Hirst, B.: Peer tutoring. A guide to learning by teaching. London: Kogan Page 1989

3. Johansen, R.: Groupware: computer support for business teams. New York: The Free Press 1988

4. McIhenny, A.: Case study: tutor and student role change in supported self-study. Educational Training Technology International, 28, 3 (1991)

5. Ruiz, F.; Vivancos, J. and Baldrich, J.: XTEC Online in-service teacher training project. In: Proceedings of the Conference DELTA and Beyond – Telecommunications for Distance Learning, October 1990

6. Telematic services in flexible and distance learning: Workplan 91. Brussels: Commission of the European Communities, Directorate General XIII 1991

3
Waiting for Electropolis

Morten Søby
Institute for Educational Research, Faculty of Social Sciences, University of Oslo, Norway

Abstract: Computer mediated communication constitutes a method for overcoming time and space gaps in distance education, and the media can enhance collaborative environments electronically. Three cases: the NKS Electronic College, Competence Networks in the Public Sector, and the Pedagogical Online Seminar, illustrate various practical implementations of computer conferencing and collaborative learning in Norway. From an optimistic 'global village' perspective, new events like computer conferencing can deconstruct computing, education and training. At least, computer conferencing could be a fragment of a new developing groupware and a part of multimedia for the 'Telematic Man'.

Keywords: computer mediated communication, distance education, NKS Electronic College, competence networks, collaborative learning, computer conferencing, education and training, groupware, telematic man.

Dimensions of a New Didactic Model

Since the early 1970's in particular, collaboration and cooperation have been focal points for Nordic social science inquiry. Educators have stressed the importance of group processes in learning. Organisational theorists have emphasized team work as a means of achieving greater productivity and as a socialisation mechanism in the organisational culture. In psychology, a wide range of group therapies are practised.

Collaborative learning may be conceptualised in various ways. It is fundamental, however, that learning is a social activity. And yet, distance education has been based upon instructional design and an industrialised approach where the social perspective has been peripheral. The merging of distance education and the features of computer conferencing is about to change this [9].

Until the 1980's, distance education systems relied on a large scale model involving traditional correspondence courses. The institution-centred correspondence systems supported primarily individual learning, and the distance student could normally follow an independently tailored learning pace. The term 'distance education' covers various forms of study at all levels which are not under the continuous or immediate supervision of tutors present with their students, but nevertheless benefits from the planning, guidance and tuition of a central tutorial organisation [3]. Distance education has a large component of autonomous learning and is heavily dependent on the didactic design of materials which must substitute for the communication between student and teacher in face to face instruction. Distance learning includes elements of flexibility that make it more accessible to students than courses provided in place based centres of education and training. This flexibility arises variously from the content of the course and the way in which it is structured, the place of provision, the mode, medium or timing of delivery, the pace at which the students proceed, the forms of special support available and the types of assessments offered. However, the communication possibilities in traditional distance education were limited, and the learner was relatively isolated. The use of computer mediated communication in distance education and training offers new facilities and opportunities to improve the collaborative aspects of learning, without reducing individual flexibility.

Computer mediated communication constitutes a method for overcoming time and space gaps in distance education, and the media can enhance collaborative environments electronically. The use of computer mediated communication can move distance education from an institution-centred model involving pre-planned structuring, towards a person-centred model involving interactive learning processes in a collaborative environment. Flexible learning programs with computer conferencing can become a substitute for the classroom and the face to face seminar. In the 80's a variety of experiments showed promising dimensions of a new flexible learning model with elements from both traditional distance education and traditional methods of instruction. [5]

The following case material from the NKS projects in Norway can be used to illustrate various practical implementations of computer conferencing and collaborative learning.

The NKS Ernst G. Mortensen Foundation

The aim of NKS Ernst G. Mortensen Foundation is to contribute to the distribution of knowledge and competence in Norwegian society. This is accomplished through the development and implementation of flexible networks of distance teaching accessible to students from where they live or work. NKS covers all educational levels, from secondary school to university degree programmes.

NKS has built up competence as a traditional correspondence school, but has recently developed in the direction of a modern distance education institution relying on a variety of media. The school receives 80,000 course enrolments per year and a small but increasing number of NKS's courses are offered as computer conferences. The aim of the computer mediated communication projects at NKS is to develop improved forms of flexible learning generally, and to contribute to the development of new electronic distance education models based on the PC as a tool in the learning process. [10]

The NKS Electronic College

NKS College offers degree courses in Business Administration, Marketing and Public Management. All the programmes are organised as part time courses, implying a study load of 50% of full time study per semester. The scheduled time for the study programmes is two years. NKS courses can be combined with full time jobs and/or family obligations. All courses are offered as distance teaching. In 1991, the total number of students was about 500. Nearly 45% of the total number of admissions in 1989 was a result of in-service training contracts with private and public institutions. The average student is a male, about 35 years old and in a full time job. He is married and lives either in our largest cities or in a rather rural area.

The distance education model

The five main 'pillars' of the NKS distance education model are:
- a pre-produced course package based on instructional design
- a delivery system based on the correspondence element
- a large scale administrative system
- a distributed faculty, drawn from higher education institutions country-wide
- face-to-face tuition once a semester
- regular computer conferencing.

The college's computer conferencing activities were initiated in 1989 and are part of an ongoing effort to develop an advanced distance education model based on electronic networking and computer conferencing. The conferencing system PortaCOM provides the technical platform for the development of the College's activities. Clearly, one of the major shortcomings of distance education has been the general lack of communication and collaborative environments. Electronic distance education deals with this problem in a new fashion by allowing two-way, asynchronous communication between students, tutors and administration.

The Electronic College offers a number of features which parallel those of a traditional college:
- electronic mail for students, staff and administration
- electronic bulletin boards with information from staff and administration

– an online 'Café' and other social arenas for all students
– substantial course-related conferences
– student seminars
– a Student Council to represent students' interests
– a general meeting arena for staff and administration ('staff room')
– an online library
– an area for general assistance/help-desk.

In the presentation of the various courses, the metaphor 'NKS Electronic College' is illustrated visually as a traditional college building. For beginners, this improves understanding of the features of the conference system. Our experience is that this is just as essential as technical instruction in how to use the system.

In the Spring Term of 1991, there were four courses running in the Electronic College: Business Administration (with 180 students), Statistics (55 students), Computer Applications (110 students) and a Business and Management course for post office employees (with 40 students). The courses supported by computer conferences in NKS Electronic College are included in the formal national credit-giving education system. Additionally, the students automatically receive practical knowledge in the use of computer mediated communication and participation in the electronic micro-societies.

NKS Electronic College assumes responsibility for course contents, administration and social functions by means of computer mediated communication. The challenge is to adapt and integrate computer conferencing so as to satisfy the requirements of distance education programmes based on pre-produced written course material.

Tutors serve as coordinators/moderators in all course-related conferences. Their duties include responding to questions and moderating all discussions. Moderators are either lecturers from other educational institutions or NKS teaching staff members. They are required to log in and check the conferences for which they are responsible at least every other day.

Technical questions about personal computers, computer mediated communication and PortaCOM are addressed in specific conferences and instruction is the responsibility of teaching assistants. The telephone can also be used to solve acute technical problems.

Learning and electronic sociability

Course-related conferences contribute to the students' learning process in three ways, which may be labelled the guidance form, the seminar form and the electronic socialising form.

The guidance form is the most frequent communication form, involving questions from the students regarding substantial matters and assignments, to which the teacher responds by referring to cases, examples, theories, etc. The general perspective of the course is in focus continually, in order to provide answers which will be useful to other students. Fellow students may contribute, and in some cases, such guidance discussions may develop into a seminar form.

The seminar form evolves from the guidance form and may be scheduled during certain periods of the course semester. It is primarily driven by eager students and engaged staff members. The seminar may depart from questions regarding interpretations of assignments. However, a further institutionalised development of the seminar form in the Electronic College does not seem as a realistic goal at the present stage. The main reason for this is the large size of the conferences. As they may include between 50 and 100 students, the forum is too large for an in-depth seminar. The concept is based upon computer conferencing as a voluntary add-on. Though the conferences are mainly dominated by the guidance form, the subject-oriented conferences clearly stimulate the students to complete their courses.

The popularity of the electronic socialising form leaves no doubt that participation in conferences has a beneficial effect on motivation. There is evidence indicating a positive relationship between participation in conferences and course completion or success in the final examination. The importance of the social dimension of computer mediated communication should not be overlooked. Students get a sense of belonging as a result of participation. The 'Online Café' conference – a forum for unbridled self-expression and discussions of just about anything – is extremely popular. It also serves as a more or less synchronous chat-line around midnight.

As positive side-effects, students also gain proficiency in practical computer mediated communication as well as online peer counselling and cooperation. Furthermore, participation in such electronic communities promotes a more democratic atmosphere in distance education institutions – students have the opportunity to 'talk back', and to participate in the planning process. Students are also encouraged to evaluate the teaching and administrative staff.

The majority of the computer conferencing projects initiated by NKS (e.g. the courses in business administration, statistics, and organisation and leadership) have been based on a 'minimal' model. This model rests on the assumption that computer conferences should supplement printed course material and that student participation is voluntary. Assignments are returned to tutors by regular mail. Though course related conferences and seminars are not mandatory, the majority of business administration students choose to participate in them.

The course on Computer Applications illustrates an approach where the computer conference is to a large extent an integral part of the learning experience. Tasks typically assigned in this 'maximal' model include assignments uploaded from students to tutors as text files, and notices about specified topics entered in the course conference. In 1989 and 1990, the maximal model was extended to include group tasks carried out by groups of three to five members. This combination was not very successful, since computer conferencing is not yet sufficiently user-friendly. Secondly, it was complicated to co-work on large documents. And lastly, it also proved difficult to carry out small group co-working when also following the minimal model in other courses.

Competence Networks in the Public Sector

This project is in its initial phase at the present time. Participants include employees in several government organisations and agencies who are offered learning opportunities in three major areas: access to several government databases; use of PortaCOM conferences for sharing ideas and experiences (SIGs); and on-the-job-training based on pre-produced material, PortaCOM interaction, and face-to-face meetings.

Participants are recruited from local, state and national authorities, all with access to a nationwide electronic network. Norwegian Information Technology (NIT), one of Norway's leading IT companies, is responsible for project administration, cooperating with NKS on the design and implementation of on-the-job training programmes. This cooperative effort also illustrates the potential of computer conferencing as a tool for project administration.

The first course, Leadership, was completed early in 1991, and lasted for five months. Twenty five females, all inexperienced computer users, participated actively in the substantial conferences as well as in the social conferences. The lessons were based on an existing correspondence course, modified to fit the computer conferencing format. PortaCOM participation was mandatory.

While adult students typically value the flexibility of distance training, they often appreciate the imposition of structure and a fixed time schedule in order to facilitate their progress. Computer conferencing is one of the few media technologies which allow for collaborative learning at a distance. Group assignments serve to pace the progress of the students, because, to make contributions to their group, the participants must follow the same schedule.

Some assignments were sent directly to the tutor's electronic mailbox and subsequently returned to the students with comments, while others were posted as notices in the appropriate conference. Groups consisting of five members organised their activities and coordinated their writing of reports in closed conferences, receiving occasional input from tutors. Discussions of drafts and proposals were carried out in the groups. The final version was mailed to the tutor for evaluation and comments. The users worked with terminals – not microcomputers – which were connected to an IBM mainframe running PortaCOM. File transfers and the use of a personal text editor were therefore difficult or impossible, adding to the technical difficulties encountered in this form of group activity.

Another course, called Administrative Procedures, was initiated in the Spring of 1991. The course lasted for six months. Computer conferencing was not emphasized in this revised approach. Alternatively, local groups were organised which met regularly. Discussions of drafts and proposals on individual assignments were carried out in small face-to-face groups, of five or six members, before the final version was mailed to the tutor for evaluation and comments. While some of the students experienced technical problems, several groups still cooperate through the conferencing system. As an indication of the success of the course, the participants organised electronic conferences for informal exchange of experiences and knowledge after the course was completed. Such an informal development of competence is one of the primary goals of Competence Networks in the Public Sector. In the Spring of 1992, more than 400 people were participating in various conferences of the Network, without taking part in explicit training.

Technical difficulties and practical solutions related to group work may vary, but networks of the type described above, connecting government agencies and organisations, promote cooperation at several levels. They act as communication tools connecting local, state and national government, as a forum for Special Interest Groups which unite various professional communities, and as a medium for coordinating the activities of LAN and database dealers and course administrators.

The Pedagogic Online Seminar

Computer networking technologies introduce unprecedented opportunities for international communication and cooperation. While this chapter was being completed (February 1992), the Pedagogic Online Seminar(POS) started. POS is a seminar under the direction of COSTEL (Course Systems for Telecommunicated Training of Trainees and Innovation Management) which is a pilot project under the European COMETT II program. The seminar is arranged by USIT (University Centre of Information Technology Services, University of Oslo) and NKS College and 27 students from the Nordic countries participate. POS uses the approach of a virtual seminar and operates in a small scale mode. Activities in POS will also be the framework in the development of a new Nordic network offering a Nordic infrastructure for research, education, business and social interaction.

POS is a part time course and lasts 12 weeks. POS started with a face to face seminar in Oslo and will be taught at a distance through computer conferencing. The intention with POS is to offer future teachers, consultants, and educational administrators an introduction to online teaching in a computer conference. The participants will learn how to use the computer conferencing system PortaCOM, and acquire practical experience and theoretical knowledge in the field of online teaching. Theoretical knowledge is gained by reading and discussing articles written by well-known authorities in the field. All the discussions will take part in computer conferences, where people with pedagogical and technological experience will serve as moderators. One moderator is situated in Pennsylvania (USA) and the other in Oslo. Practical experience is gained through actual use of the computer conferencing system. The participants will also act as 'lurkers' in computer conferences used by students and teachers at NKS College and USIT. All the participants are required to deliver a short essay at the end of the seminar and 'publish' it in the conference.

Beyond Distance Education

Traditionally, computer mediated communication has been limited to 'computer freaks' and researchers in computer science related fields. However, computer conferencing has recently been adopted by various distance education institutions and organisations. From a distance education perspective, expectations have been high, because such media are particularly well-suited to overcome the restrictions of time and space in distance education and can create a collaborative learning environment.

The objectives of the various NKS projects have varied, as have our objectives when using computer conferencing in distance education. Although computer conferencing has been used in different ways, collaborative learning is an essential element in all projects. Prior to 1988 the NKS distance education system was heavily dependent on a large scale model and relatively few technologies: print, radio and video/television. Communication and student support depended on correspondence. Learning and working in a tele-communicated environment implies new roles for tutors, learners, administrators and project managers. Implementing computer conferencing and collaboration through networks implies a challenge to the organisation.

Large front end investments in pre-produced material for a large target group combined with low current tuition expenses, fit the NKS distance education format relying on correspondence and television. From an economic and management perspective a large scale model is not the optimal platform for small scale courses based on intensive support from tutors through computer conferencing. Additionally, a large scale platform is not a good starting point for advanced formal or informal learning through advanced telecommunication networks. Computer conferencing applications and networking implies another cost/benefit structure. In the long run, institutions like NKS or, for example, the Open University in the UK, must develop their models and organisations further if they wish to offer small scale courses with computer conferencing.

Distance education methods have been equated with various practical implementations of instructional design. These methods focus on an individual learning approach. Alternative lines of research and methods with a focus on learning as a social process are desperately needed. A mixture of educational theory based on social practice, phenomenology and communication theory can become a new starting point for flexible learning. The essence of computer conferencing means communication, feedback and more immediacy – we can traverse the distance.

The moderator in computer conferencing combines "... elements of teacher, chairman, host, facilitator and community organiser" [6]. In *Moderating Educational Conferencing* Robin Mason categories the role into three levels – organisational, social and intellectual.

I have tried to summarize our experiences in Table 3.1. Many of the issues mentioned serve as guidelines for the training procedures used with tutors and staff.

The Limitations and Potential of Computer Conferencing

Today's user-unfriendly computer conferencing systems limit the range of collaborative learning applications, qualitatively as well as quantitatively. Areas which must be further explored include:
– more thorough analyses of problems in one or more areas
– advanced decision making and clarification
– social psychological group processes / group therapy
– quality in personal communication
– use of pictures, graphics, sound and special characters
– long and complex documents (even in ASCII).

Computer conferencing is clearly distinguishable from human networks characterised by close physical proximity. For this reason, a clarification of the limitations and potential of computer conferencing is crucial. The basis of a potential alliance of computer conferencing and collaborative learning may be found in work and educational tasks related to the following categories:
– brainstorming and generating new ideas
– counselling and exchange of experiences and views, offering suggestions
– counselling services related to specific professions
– production/service, e.g., maintenance crews at a computer centre, user or customer support, etc.
– project development, e.g., research and development groups in the DELTA and COMETT Programmes
– communication channels for political groups, trade unions, etc.
– 'Electronic College' projects, with conferences devoted to teaching as well as administrative and social functions

– on-the-job-training with conferences devoted to teaching, administration and socialising in addition to groups sharing personal and job-related experiences.

Table 3.1 Factors to consider in planning courses using computer conferencing

Introductory Phase

Main Points	Adequate user instruction
	Manuals
	Telephone help-line
Typical student problems	Technical
Moderator /support role	Provide solutions to practical and technical problems
	Accommodating profile

Start of Course

Main points	Introduce the course and methodology
	Getting to know one another
Typical student problems	Insecure social climate
	Uncertainty about framework, norms and written communication
Moderator's role	Structuring and providing a framework for further discussion
	Reducing tension and making students feel comfortable

Conferencing

Main points	Planning/time frame
	Forming groups
	Decisions regarding conference format
Typical student problems	Formulating precise questions and comments
	Structuring and adhering to perspectives and plans
Moderator's role	Maintaining an overall view of the situation
	Being aware of each individual's contribution to the discussions
	Problem oriented, providing inspiration and provocation as needed
	Serving as a catalyst
	Directing attention to the inner dynamics of the group
	Pointing out mistakes and correcting them
	Distinguishing between problem solving with correct answers and decision making with no correct answers
	Providing references to literature

The idea of using computer conferencing for collaborative learning is normally met with enthusiasm and optimism. However, in spite of considerable media attention, a recent survey in the Nordic countries indicates that computer conferencing/collaborative learning applications have only a small share of the market. The total number of participants is probably no higher than 2000. [8]

Thus, the market in Norway is clearly not ready for electronic teaching media. In another recent survey, Bø and associates conclude that the market for electronic distance education has not yet begun to realise its potential [2]. The majority of respondents in the survey, representing influential educational organisations and institutions, lack information about how computer mediated communication can be effectively utilised in education and training programs. Thus, regular application of computer mediated communication in education, training, and project-oriented cooperative activities is still a marginal phenomenon. Only a small minority of PC and computer terminal owners use their equipment for communication purposes.

In Western Europe and in the United States, rapid growth of electronic education is predicted, and the Commission of the European Communities is investing heavily in this area. Current economic, technological and social trends require flexible and continuous learning. Mounting competition and increased specialisation and innovation compel companies to continually monitor and update the knowledge and skills of their employees. The development of user-friendly systems, ISDN, and multimedia applications will have a great impact on the market share of electronic flexible learning in the future. [3]

To Be is to Connect

Whenever new media technologies emerge, predictions arise about the creation of 'mediated communities'. The melting pot of computer networks – 'Electropolis' – is no exception [7]. The communication and information channels in 'Electropolis' are instantly available all over the globe and may be stored and retrieved as long as electricity and telephone lines are available. We are waiting for 'Electropolis', but what happens to us when we get online? What kind of system do we tap into?

From an optimistic 'global village' perspective, new events like computer conferencing can change education and training and recast our schedules and concept of time. Individuals in 'Electropolis' will multiply their number of connections so that their points of intersection become a rich and juicy locus of choice. Already today networking and computer conferencing interweaves thousands of organisations and personalized complex schedules. At least, computer conferencing could be a fragment of a new developing groupware and a part of multimedia for the 'Telematic Man'.

'Electropolis' is a metaphor of a general process of change in society at large. There is no off switch to information technology. From a pessimistic perspective the following questions emerge: Will 'Electropolis' be a post-industrial nightmare of total administration for the future generations? Will networking and advanced computer mediated communication penetrate every aspect of work, consumption, social relations, leisure and play? Will the 'telematic man' cross over life as if it were airspace, fastened to his seat and immobile in front of the computer? Will the computers be 'integrated' into the body as transparent genetic prostheses after the year 2000? "Am I a man, am I a machine?" [1].

References

1. Baudrillard, J.: Xerox to infinity. London: Touchepass 1988
2. Bø,I., Carlsen, T., Rekkedal, T. & Søby, M., Elektronisk fjernopplæring - om undervisning og kompetanseutvikling gjennom datakommunikasjon og nettverk. Oslo: SEFU 1990
3. Commission of the European Communities: Open and distance higher education in the European Community. SEC(91) 897. Brussels: Commission of the European Communities 1991
4. Feenberg, A.: From information to communication: the French experience with videotext. In: The social contexts of computer-mediated communication. (M. Lea, ed.). Brighton: Harvester-Wheatsheaf 1992
5. Kaye, A.R.: Computer networking in distance education – multiple uses, many models. In: Proceedings NEK 91. Oslo 1991
6. Mason, R. D.: Moderating educational conferencing. In: DEOSNEWS 1 (1), Pennsylania State University 1991 (also to appear in Electronic Networking: Research, Applications, and Policy, 1992)
7. Reid, E.M.: Electropolis: communication and community on Internet relay chat. (unpublished, downloaded from the CuD archives, Internet). University of Melbourne 1991
8. Rekkedal, T. & Søby, M.: Fjernundervisningsmodeller, datakonferanser og nordiske utviklingstrekk. In: Proceedings NEK 91. Oslo: University of Oslo: 1991
9. Søby, M.: The postmodern condition and distance education. In: Distance education: development and access. (M. Croft, I. Mugridge, J.S. Daniel, A. Hershfield, eds.). Caracas: ICDE 1990
10. Søby, M.: Traversing distances in education – The PortaCOM experiment. In: Media and Technology in European Distance Education. (A. Bates, ed.), pp. 241–248. Milton Keynes: The Open University 1990

4
Computer Mediated Communication for Management Learning

David McConnell
Centre for the Study of Management Learning, The Management School,
Lancaster University, United Kingdom

Abstract: The paper addresses some issues to do with the running of a self-managed, collaboratively designed MA in Management Learning, using a mixture of computer conferencing, electronic mail, and periodic face-to-face seminars. The nature of professional practice in the online environment is discussed and analysed.

Keywords: management learning, open learning, knowledge, educational design, computer-mediated communication, cooperative learning, tutor, online environments

Introduction

In this paper, I want to address some issues to do with running a self-managed, collaboratively designed MA programme mediated by computer conferencing and electronic mail. In addition, I want to present some thoughts on the nature of professional practice in online environments. First though, some background information about the programme and the nature of the educational enterprise.

The computer mediated MA in Management Learning (CM MAML) is a two year part-time programme for professionals in Management Education and Development. Participants range in age from mid-twenties to early sixties. We try to get a balance of genders on each cohort, and a spread of public, private and voluntary organisations as well as those who are self employed.

The design of the MA (which is modelled on a well established part-time course) is based on educational principles broadly shared by staff, who neverthe - less bring influences from different academic backgrounds (including Organisational Behaviour, Educational Research, Educational Technology and Linguistics). These principles are :
– participants should have as much choice as possible over the direction and content of their learning;
– they are responsible for managing their own learning and for helping others in theirs (the notion of a 'learning community' is generally used to denote this);
– the work of the programme integrates the idea of critical perspective to the academic tradition, with participants' day to day professional experience;
– the opportunity presented to the students by the MA should be equally for learning about and developing themselves in their professional roles, as for engaging with relevant ideas and concepts in the public domain;
– the marked degree of participation inherent in the design assumes a commitment to taking collective responsibility for attending to the 'process' of the community i.e. reviewing and modifying the design, procedures and ways of working.

In practice, this means for instance that the staff often, but not always, design in some detail only the first day or so of each workshop. Thereafter, activities are planned collectively. Reviewing progress and subsequent planning is also a collective activity. Topics which arise emerge from the interests of staff and participants, as do the choice of methods and online tutorial groups. The topics for course assignments are the choice of each student and assessment is collaborative i.e. peer, self and tutors [10].

The programme is structured round two learning environments – a residential one and an electronic one. The residential learning environment is made up of six intensive residential workshops spread fairly evenly throughout the two years, at which participants examine relevant research and theory, and experiment with and plan alternative strategies for their continuing learning in their normal working contexts.

In the electronic learning environment there is continuation of some of the issues raised in the workshops, and the 'meeting' of tutorial sets. The sets usually consist of three or four participants and a tutor. Their main purpose is to provide support for each individual in choosing, planning and writing course assignments. Participants also discuss matters arising out of the programme and out of their work experience. These activities are supported by computer conferencing and electronic mail (using Caucus). The whole year group also has the opportunity to 'meet' via the medium. Participants on the programme link into the system from various parts of England and Wales, with one even connecting from Hong Kong. Tutors (usually three or four per programme) use the local area network on campus, or link in from their homes.

The Nature of the Educational Enterprise

Although the staff on the programme work as a team and broadly share those principles mentioned above, we do 'act' from various views of education. In order to understand some of the issues I will be considering in this paper, some explanation of my own views on education is necessary.

The concept of liberation education [6] is at the root of my professional practice: " liberation is a praxis: the action and reflection of men (sic) upon their world in order to transform it." This educational philosophy is underpinned by the challenge of uniting action and reflection [7]. This leads to informed action [1]. In our case, with students and staff who are management trainers and developers, action is based on reflection on one's professional practice, as well as on one's role as a learner.

We espouse a theory of knowledge which has much in common with Habermas' knowledge constitutive interests [9]. Knowledge is not a commodity made up of a series of 'truths' (scientism); it is not propositional, but rather a process of knowing in which we engage with our reality, and through dialogue with others and with ourselves we give meaning to the world. This process acknowledges that there are different forms of knowledge such as tacit or personal knowledge [17] and experiential knowledge [15], besides others.

One of our principles is the integration of a critical perspective to participants' academic and professional work. Talking of a critical social science, Carr and Kemmis[1] state that :

> ...its epistemology is constructivist, seeing knowledge as developing by a process of active construction and reconstruction of theory and practice by those involved; that it involves a theory of symmetrical communication (a process of rational discussion which actively seeks to overcome coercion on the one hand and self-deception on the other), and that it involves a democratic theory of political action based on free commitment to social action and consensus about what needs to be and should be done. In short, it is not only a theory about knowledge, but also about how knowledge relates to practice. [1]

The dialectical nature of our educational enterprise is supported by the medium of CMC. Here we can engage in praxis in a way that may not always be possible face-to-face. If we see this medium as an empty space to be moulded or designed in whatever way supports our purpose, then it is not difficult to imagine it supporting a form of education which is based on a resolution of the contradiction of the teacher-student relationship (without this resolution "dialogical relations...are otherwise impossible" [6]). This is a fundamental aspect of our approach to academic professionalism on the MA.

---

1 Some of these ideas are not particularly new, of course. John Dewey talked of reconstruction as part of the educational process : "I believe finally, that education must be conceived as a continuing reconstruction of experience; that the process and the goal of education are one and the same thing." (J. Dewey, 1897, *My Pedagogic Creed*)

Our programme is a form of open learning, not of the conventional packaged learning or distance learning variety, but one which is based on a philosophy of openness [11] rather than one of expediency [2]. For some of us, the work of Rogers is central to our thinking about these issues :

> In persons who are moving towards greater openness in their experiencing, there is an organismic commonality of value directions. These common value directions are of such kinds as to enhance the development of the individual himself (sic), of others in his community, and to contribute to the survival and evolution of the species. [18]

The contradiction posed by Roger's inevitably individualistic theory of education and our concern to establish a community of learners who support each other and work cooperatively provides a useful dilemma for us all to address as part of the educational process in the programme. I share Freire's viewpoint :

> It is not always easy, even for those who identify with the people, to overcome a petit-bourgeois education that is individualistic and intellectual.... [7]

Some Characteristics of the Programme

In order to show something of the way in which we use CMC, I will focus on three aspects of the programme, namely: the process of feedback and assessment of participant's course work; decision making on the programme; and the role of the tutor. In doing this, I hope to show how the medium offers a unique environment for putting into practice those principles outlined above.

The process of feedback and assessment of participants' work

Our aim of providing an environment where participants choose what to work on for the course assignments (there are five assignments over the two years) requires a context and process whereby each person can talk about their interests knowing they are supported by other participants and tutors. We manage this by forming electronic learning sets – small groups of three or four participants and a tutor. Each group opens its own set-conference and contracts to support each other in their assignments, amongst other things. In the preparation of the assignment, and in giving feedback and assessment, each participant and tutor is involved in the following process :

(1) Each participant offers suggestions on what they would like to do for their assignment. This is done in an item opened by them for that purpose. Other participants and the tutor offer comment, and a dialogue evolves. Peoples' approaches to the assignment often change as we sound each other out and offer references and other resources.

(2) Each person plans their assignment and writes it, at the same time.

(3) Criteria for assessment are mutually agreed, and we think through what's involved in assessing each others' work.

(4) Copies of papers are sent from one member to another so that we all have copies to work from.

(5) We start the process of giving and receiving feedback.

(6) We assess/mark each assignment (self/peer/tutor assessment).

This may appear rather idealised, but in reality it is not far from the truth. Other events sometimes get in the way of the process, so prolonging the exercise; but eventually all six stages are covered in one way or another.

In order to illuminate some of the processes and issues that arise during feedback and assessment, I will discuss two items from one of the early set-conferences on the programme. The first item was a platform for the exploration of issues around peoples' criteria for being assessed, and for discussion about the assessment process itself (item 11). The second one was set up by one of the participants to plan and discuss her current assignment (here referred to as her Project Essay – PE) (item 17). Each conference is of course also concerned with other issues which are 'happening' at the same time (in this particular set-conference there were about 24 items in all).

Dialogues about assessment

Item 11 was set up by the tutor involved after a general discussion at the first residential workshop about assessment (the programme starts in January each year). At the workshop, staff had introduced three criteria that they use when assessing participants' work. This was the starting point for the item: [2]

```
===================================================================
Item 11   30-JAN-91   23:05   Daniel

CRITERIA AND ASSESSMENT - THOUGHTS ON

Thought it might be useful at this point to start an item to look at criteria that you all want to
think about using for assessing your assignment, and also maybe give our thoughts on the
nature of peer/self/tutor assessment ?

124 Discussion responses
===================================================================
11:1) Daniel                                                    30-JAN-91  23:18

Some of my criteria that I implicitly use when 'assessing' someone's essay :

 * does the essay look at issues critically i.e. is there critical thinking or are things merely seen
as 'unproblematic' or taken for granted

 * is there a combination of personal thoughts and ideas as well as some use made of theory,
concepts and ideas from what you have been reading

 * is the essay about some aspect of Management Learning/Development ( you can make
your own case for saying it is !!)

Needless to say I also use the criteria that you want to apply to your essay too.

What are your thoughts.........?
Daniel
===================================================================
```

What followed (124 entries, 20084 words) was an exploration of the nature of learning and assessment. Participation in the item, in terms of the number of entries made and the total number of words entered, is fairly evenly spread, apart from Greg's contributions which were relatively low (Table 4.1).

---

[2] Throughout these extracts I have used pseudonyms to maintain the anonymity of persons and organisations.

Table 4.1 Entries Made to Items 11 and 17

	Daniel	Malcolm	Mary	Greg	Sandra
Item 11 (criteria and assessment)					
Entries (N=124)	27 (22%)	21 (21%)	36 (29%)	10 (8%)	30 (24%)
Words (N=20084)	5388 (27%)	2872 (14%)	4984 (25%)	1908 (9%)	4932 (25%)
Item 17 (Mary's project essay)					
Entries (N=49)	12 (25%)	9 (18%)	20 (41%)	3 (6%)	5 (10%)
Words (N=10660)	3492 (33%)	1236 (12%)	5040 (47%)	636 (6%)	256 (2%)

A content analysis of the item shows the main activities engaged in. The diversity of activities gives some indication of the issues discussed in the item and the quality of the experience:
– participants explaining the criteria they would like applied to their paper
– people voicing concern about their 'ability' to meet some of the Lancs criteria
– people organising the set's 'work' against timescales
– self-disclosure
– statements about the focus of their assignments
– some direction (from tutor and participants)
– discussion about theory
– checking out understandings
– posing questions about each other's work
– planning
– making (collective) decisions, about contracts for working as a set, about timescales, and about how we would assess each others work
– summarising discussions so far
– asking for support and help
– giving support and help
– dealing with technical problems/issues
– giving feedback on peoples' papers
– some self-analysis/critical reflection
– reviewing.

Are participants engaging in a self-managed, open learning enterprise? I think there is evidence to suggest they are. On analysing the transcripts of this and other items, two sorts of activity which are particularly important indicators of this can be seen to be happening: participants taking control of the learning process; and participants reflecting on the nature of what they are doing in the assessment process.

The following extract from the item shows something of the way in which the participants were beginning to assume responsibility for managing the learning process and making decisions about how to proceed with assessment. By this point, we had already given feedback in other items on each other's assignments.

```
===================================================================
```
11:88) Sandra   14-APR-91 20:26

Daniel, Mary, Thanks for all that, how do you think we should go about this, any ideas? If we
are going to asses each others work and our own with the lanc givens, and our own criteria to
give a % has anybody got any "plan" as to how we should do it? I feel that this is dragging on a
bit as we are now in April and we have not started to "talk" about our next piece of of work.

 Can we have a timescale when we agree to have it done by. I know we all agreed to have the
feedback and assessment completed by a certain date but that does not seem to have
worked, I might be wrong, what do you all think? Sandra...(edit)
```
===================================================================
```
11:93) Malcolm   16-APR-91 15:56

 I agree with Sandra about this issue dragging on and feel we need to take the plunge, getting
into the marking. I thought Greg's suggestion of grades at 13.8 (why there Greg ?)rather
duplicated the suggestion Daniel made at 11.33. Like Mary (11.80) I think we should use
Daniel's marking scheme. If I haven't said so clearly elsewhere I would prefer to use the %age
mark and Daniel's "b)" suggestion.

We appear to have personal criteria for everyone except Greg, unless Greg you have tucked it
away somewhere, could you say what yours is? My "plan" for getting over this impasse, is that
we all need to record our % marks for all the papers including our own. If there are any
significant differences (and by significant I mean the mark being outside the bands Daniel's
item 11.33 suggests) we discuss that difference and agree a mark collectively. Otherwise for
the sake of convenience agree an average mark which will be within the bands anyway. Does
this make sence (sense) ?

......(edit) I am ready to put in my marks if evryone else agree the format for doing so. I will
check each day to see if we have agreement. Malcolm

```
===================================================================
```
11:94) Mary   16-APR-91 20:27

 Malcolm - Your suggestions above all look fine to me and I'm happy to go with what you
suggest. Like you, I'll therefore check daily. I'm very conscious of being a beginner at this and
so I like your idea of agreeing a mark collectively if poss. Thanks.
```
===================================================================
```

Although the tutor had offered some suggestions about the assessment
process (mentioned by Malcolm), he held back from initiating the process itself,
waiting for the participants to address the issue. Within the dynamics of the
programme, this is not as contrived as it may appear. There is no expectation that
the tutor should necessarily 'lead' discussion, nor initiate the assessment process.
By holding back, the tutor was 'allowing' the participants to take control
themselves. This action is part of the trust building that is needed for participants
to believe that they are indeed being allowed to manage their own learning.

The next extract shows a participant reflecting on the nature of what she is
doing in the assessment process. She is struggling to understand the educational
process she is engaged in, and reflects on similar experiences in other settings and
acknowledges that our relationships online are an important aspect of the
process.

```
========================================================================
11:102) Mary                                                    21-APR-91
21:41
```

This is my 1st attempt at uploading solo, so here goes.................

Here's my assessment of our seminar papers.
I'm finding this quite difficult and was trying to work out why. I've had a couple of goes at
assessing work our managers at (Organisation) have done on the management development
progs. we run and so it's still quite a new thing for me to do. However, I haven't found it too
difficult. I think the difference between assessing them and assessing you all and me, is that
we're needing to work fairly closely together and we've been through (and no doubt are
continuing to go through), some pretty fraught times together. I'm feeling very aware I
suppose of potential "halo" effects on how I do this and the differences in our relationships
with each other. I'm struggling therefore, to put all this aside, (I shan't succeed of course!), and
look with clear eyes on what we've tried to do and how well we've done it.

Having now experienced this process, I really have felt that the feedback has been the most
valuable part of it all - apart from writing the actual thing of course!! I've also found seeing what
we've all chosen to do and how we've approached it a useful experience.

...(edit - she proceeds to give her assessments)
```
========================================================================
```

The next extract (from a different set-conference) again shows the participant
struggling to make sense of the whole assessment process. She points out some
of the difficulties and contradictions we are often faced with in the programme
(and on reading it I'm reminded of something Freire says "Existence is not
despair, but risk. If I don't exist dangerously, I cannot be." [7]).

```
========================================================================
21:2) Anna
                                                      25-APR-91   17:11
```

...(edit) Some reflections on assessments - and subsequent discomforts
For me the first seminar paper was undertaken in three broad phases :

THE PRODUCTION OF THE PAPER
this involved reading;writing and rewriting;dialogue;struggling;testing out ideas;being
confused and becoming clear and then confused again;excitement;application of learning to
improve my professional practice;challenging myself;making things explicit,or trying
to;gaining confidence;identifying learning needs;discovering;using my work to know both
myself and others better.

FEEDBACK
this involved.....struggling with defensiveness;pro-activity;risking being first; self
disclosure;...touching;enjoyment of what had been created.

ASSESSMENT
involved receiving;being judged;wanting to move on;being involved in a game I didn't
understand;being focussed on what hadn't been achieved;feeling afraid and little.

When I reflect on the phases described above it occurs to me that in phases 1 and 2, I felt as if
I was managing the process and was engaged, whereas in the third phase I was submitting
myself to an introject. Painful. And running away. Painful...(edit)

My current position regarding academic assessment is that I don't know the rules of the game. It would be relatively easy to pretend. I have done much pretending in my life and have some well developed skills which I could use. However, I don't want to waste my time or abuse the work of others. Nor do I want to create processes which are introjects.

I have still to learn how to engage in academic aassessment, in a way which is congruent with my concept of self managed learning. I am also struggling with the notion of numeric assessment as an integral part of the MAML programme. Perhaps colleagues have perceptions of the process which might facilitate my understanding. I would be grateful for dialogue to enable me to move on...........(edit)
===

As time passed, and we proceeded with giving feedback and finally assessing each others' work, the dialogue became reflexive as we began to use our experience of the process to talk about the nature of the enterprise. This element of experiential learning [15] was not unique to the assessment process (the whole programme is in a very real sense experience based), but it brought here an urgency to what we were doing and made a bridge between theory and practice [3] which we all actively lived through. The process is not problem free; it not only involves intellectual engagement, but just as importantly it involves legitimate emotional engagement [19]. Working with emotions in an online environment is a new experience to us all. We don't shirk from it, but we tread softly because we are unfamiliar with some of the consequences of doing so in this new medium.

Support in doing one's assignments

Item 17 was a place for Mary to make explicit issues relating to her assignment. Its dynamic (Table 1) is different to that of item 11, as might be expected from the purpose of the item. She started off by talking at some length about what she wanted to do for the PE (how to get managers in her organisation more involved in the development of their staff), carefully outlining her own position in relation to the managers (she is a management developer), defining her terms, offering justifications for tackling this issue and presenting her initial thoughts on the way she might go about doing the research. This opening statement was a very detailed and well constructed statement of some 684 words. She concluded this opening entry by inviting us to join her in working through this.

===
17:1) Mary   04-MAY-91   12:01

...........(edit) To progress on this, I'd really like comments on my ideas from you. I am wondering whether it's too big an area to tackle for the PE, but I'd really like to do something towards it if poss. To help me along the way, I've been dipping into "Management Development - Strategies for Action", Alan Mumford and "A Manager's Guide to Self Development", Mike Pedler, John Burgoyne and Tom Boydell. I've also come across a very helpful article in "Personnel Manager" on the manager's role in staff dev, but I don't have it at home with me , so forget who wrote it!
What do you think?
===

Here is a place for Mary to be 'heard' by the others; for her to use for her own purposes. The level of dialogue and engagement between Mary and the others in the set was reasonably high. There is evidence that participants are listening to what she is saying and engaging in a meaningful exploration with her about her work:

```
=========================================================================
17:2) Malcolm                                              06-MAY-91 15:15
```

Mary - getting the involvement of the line manager in the development of their staff is a big issue with the (his Organisation) and my dept. One of the problems I can see is that there are many people all too keen to come up with instant solutions without looking at the issues first. I think your Project will/would help address this problem for (his Organisation).

I am tempted to start to discuss the problems with you but I will hold back for now and concentrate on the methods you are proposing to use. In establishing what development means to the policy makers I wonder if you should go a step further and establish what it means to them in terms of practical outcomes. There seems to be a gap between what is "policy" and practical "application". Would it be useful for you to discover what methods policy use to evaluate their policies......(edit). The communication process between policy and managers might also be an area for work...(edit)

Malcolm
```
=========================================================================
```

and later :

```
=========================================================================
17:33) Malcolm                                            24-JUL-91 10:40
```

Mary - I find it really exciting to see how you are progressing with your PE and to read your thoughts on conducting research...(edit)

I was interested to see you had taped an interview. Do you think it affected the quality or depth of the information you obtained ? I have not attempted this as I believe that using it with the senior managers I have interviewed will inhibit them from being fully open. One or two have noticeably altered the body posture when they have seen I was taking notes ! This is an assumption I plan to explore in my PE......(edit)

Malcolm
```
=========================================================================
```

Also, Mary's thoughts on her PE are having an influence on other participants' ideas for their own work :

```
=========================================================================
17:10) Greg                                               16-MAY-91  0:50
```

Hi Mary
I have just downloaded your item 17 to view tomorrow and will join in the discussion. I would like to contribute now only its 12:45 and I'm getting a little tired. There are questions in my mind from reading your initial proposals from the PE in looking at managers and their staff which may also help me to focus my thoughts from the FE (further education) point of view but I will come back when my head is clearer.
Cheers
Greg

```
=========================================================================
```

and he came back the following night :

```
=======================================================================
17:11) Greg                                              16-MAY-91   23:45
```

Hi Mary
I have been reading the issues in your item and two thoughts came immediately to mind and
I'm sure a few more will follow. The first question is around comments of Daniel and Malcolm
that of involving both parties in identifying and understanding 'development'. For example is
this just a manager developing staff or do you see this as a team development process. I have
two models in my mind from my own experience which may have no bearing on your thoughts
what so ever but here goes....(edit)

```
=======================================================================
```

and proceeds to explain the two models and how they apply to developing
managers.

What I think we can see happening here, and in similar items set up by
participants in this and other set-conferences, is a supportive group dynamic; one
which has indicators of self-management, openness and a willingness to share
and take some risks.

How We Make Decisions About the Online Environment

Decision making and the ongoing design of the programme are collective
activities. Much of this occurs in the residential workshops as well as online. The
collective involvement of us all in these processes means that ownership of
decisions and programme design lies with us all, and not just the tutors.

The negotiation of decisions about the nature of our online work and the
design of the conferences is a major aspect of this. Each time we do this it is
inevitably different because we are always building on past experience and
reviewing past plans and decisions in the light of experience. Even for those
tutors who are now experienced in the use of the medium, the procedure of
reviewing is appropriate and necessary in order to engage them in thinking
about *recent* experience with the *present* group of participants. We do not believe
that the experience of one group cannot inform that of another, but we do
believe in the uniqueness of each group and that each has its own dynamic,
purpose and life.

How do we go about doing this in practice ? The following extracts from notes
taken at a workshop give some indication :

> Tuesday evening - met in the large group (all participants and all tutors) to discuss the
> assumptions and "taken for granteds" about the programme and around the concept of
> learning sets. Question and answer session, with tutors being put on the spot about their
> "taken for granteds". Decided that we needed to meet in our present sets to establish how
> we are working together and to review business that requires completion, before deciding on
> design for the next online period.

> Wednesday afternoon - met in our present sets to review past experience and think ahead to
> what we need to do online in order to finish the business of the set. Some frank discussion
> about online relationships......

> Wednesday pm - reviewed in large group such things as "purposes" of online environment;
> possibility for forming new sets online rather than face-to-face at the workshop. Discussed
> how to have fun online!! Reviewed how we make decisions, how they work out in practice
> and peoples' subsequent engagement with them. Posed the question: how can we
> accommodate everyone's needs within different designs of the online environment?

Thursday am - met in the large group to deal with where we are "ourselves" in relation to the programme, and where we are in relation to sets and the next period online. Discussed various ideas for new ways of working online. Eventually decided to try working as one "large" online set, rather than three smaller ones. Thought through the implications of this (eg possibility of over thirty items in the conference and consequently considerable information to deal with). Decided it was worth trying. Thought through the design of the conference and how to manage it.

These reviews and decision making sessions have allowed us to collectively design our online environment and put a social as well as educational focus on the use of technology in the programme. By doing this we are taking into account "the boundaries around the computer" [14], peoples' social worlds. This I see as being similar to what Kling describes as the "infrastructure of computer support" [14]: dealing with the computer system, the people who use it, their own computer equipment at home, and the ways in which we all take part in this online experience, in order to make sense of what is happening. Some innovations that we have tried as a consequence are described below.

'Snapshot' conferences

These are conferences where each of us has our own item to use for personal review of the programme. We called the conference 'snapshots' since essentially each item would become a series of snapshots about our experiences of the programme. The conference will run for the duration of the course (two years), and will afford us all a series of personal evaluations of being on it. Procedurally, we can read each others' items but not contribute to them. The intention is for each of us to have a 'space' of our own in which to talk in any way we want about issues to do with the programme. The conference is grounded in personal ownership (the idea came from one participant, and was discussed by us all before being agreed). No one has to 'hear' other people's thoughts *now*; it allows us to decide when we want to listen to each other by going into *others'* snapshots when we are ready to. The experience is similar to talking to yourself in a personal journal or log – but you are also being *heard* by others and getting some *full* attention. In practice, people are commenting on others' contributions in their own item. The items are also being used to 'talk' about personal professional practice in the work place.

Large learning set conferences

In these, we all work as one large group, instead of the usual three smaller set-conferences. This design emerged from discussion about peoples' experience of set-conferences to date. Some felt that the idea of being able to 'look into' but not contribute to other set-conferences wasn't working for them. It took too much time to keep up with the other set-conferences as well as actively contribute to your own. And there was sometimes a sense of frustration at not being able to take part in the dialogue of other sets – a feeling of being barred from them. We discussed the possibility of us each having our *own* open conference which people could join if they were interested as an alternative, but thought that this would be too cumbersome and could lead to some people being forgotten altogether. The preference for one large set-conference, with items for each individual completely open to us all, seemed worth trying, although there was some reservation about how we might deal with the mass of information that would inevitably accumulate (the number of words at the end of most set-conferences is considerable, often in the region of 40-50,000). We would spend some time reading each item and responding in those we chose to. Once we have established who we want to work with, we would make any other items 'invisible' to us, so progressively limiting the number of items we visit and the amount of information we have to deal with. We would then have tailored our environment to suit our present interests and concerns. The items we work in, and therefore the people we work with, would be the focus for discussion about the current assignment, amongst other things. Triads (self/tutor/peer) for assessment would be formed, with people inviting a tutor and another participant into their item for that purpose.

Readings and resources conferences

The purpose of these was for us all to share what we were currently reading – papers, books etc. The conferences had an initial flurry of activity with some very detailed summaries and reviews, and draft papers people were working on, placed in them. However, activity soon waned. The act of preparing a review or summary solely for the purpose of putting it into this rather abstract conference is perhaps inappropriate given that people talk about their readings in their set-conferences as a natural part of dialogue with their colleagues. The potential benefit of sharing those readings formally with everyone else perhaps was not enough to justify the time and effort required to do so.

Tutor conference

This conference was the outcome of a face-to-face staff meeting at which we were aware that we were not involving the participants in our staff reviews of the programme. This seemed somehow inappropriate given the open philosophy of the course. We do still continue to have our 'closed' off-line staff meetings, but try to report back to the course members in this conference. In addition, the conference is a place for tutors to discuss general issues to do with the course, and is a bridge for staff between each new programme. Participants have 'read only' rights in the conference, but those who join it regularly, often raise their views on some of the issues discussed by staff in one of the other conferences.

Joint programme conference

This conference was set up shortly after the start of the second intake of the programme. It is a place for participants on both intakes to come together, share thoughts on their experiences of the course, discuss their professional work lives, plan meetings and so on. One particularly interesting development in this conference is the formation of a small group to discuss the possibility of running an online PhD learning set once they have completed their MA. This might include some of our part-time overseas research students.

Comment

These reviews of our online 'life' have freed us up in our thinking about the programme generally. The comment was made that the programme is not made up of residential workshops and online activity; rather it is complete and organic. I call this 'seamless' activity. "We are finding ways of doing the things we *want* to do " was the comment of one participant. Someone else said that "usually, at the end of other programmes or workshops there is a 'nothingness'; it has ended until the next time people meet." But not on CM MAML. The online environment continues immediately from the face-to-face one, and it's often the case that, on arriving home from the workshop, people immediately go online that night, or the next day.

The Role of the Tutor Online

Conventional CMC wisdom suggests that the tutor should 'moderate' any computer conference [4,5,13]. If not the tutor, then at least it is assumed that someone has to take on the job of moderating. This orientation to the place of the tutor in a CMC environment is problematic in an open learning or self managed context such as ours. It is built on the premise that the tutor takes control of the learning situation; from this premise follow a series of 'leadership' strategies designed to ensure that the conference achieves its stated purposes.

> In most conferences, the moderator's main function is to facilitate discussion by deciding *unilaterally* a great many procedural questions that would otherwise require prolonged and *wasteful* discussion. These questions may include such things as *when to begin discussing a topic*, when to pass to a decision and new topic,.....what are the *boundaries of relevance*, of emotional tone, of length or complexity of comments, and so on. The authority delegated to the facilitative moderator.... [5] (*my emphasis*).

In our context it would be antithetical for me as tutor to unilaterally decide on procedures for our use of the medium or the way we should conduct ourselves. Although discussions about process can be prolonged, we see them as integral to the purpose of the programme: the process is indefinable from the content, and discussions about such things are not only important, they are vital to the proper conduct of the programme and for the relationships between us all, tutors and participants alike.

Tutors and participants share responsibility for ensuring that the conferences are operating to our mutual satisfaction. This again is consistent with our philosophy of self management. It is usually a tutor who sets up a conference, mainly because it is technically too complex for all participants to learn to do, although several have done so. But this is only done after discussion with participants about its purpose, and after a suitable title has been agreed (we choose conference titles that have some association with our work together: for example, when one of the participants was leaving for Hong Kong to take up a new job, we called one of the new conferences *orient*). Once a conference is established, everyone plays a part in its design – setting up items, discussing protocol, setting contracts and so on.

In our setting too, the need for "strong leadership" [13] online would be to view our role as tutor from a particular educational perspective, one which presumably is based on hierarchies and divisions between learner and teacher:

> *Strong leadership* has been shown to be required in this medium if groups are to be successful.....The nature of the medium, including the different kinds of group structures that emerge and the absence of pressure to sign online and participate, create the need for strong and active leadership. The lack of adequate leadership is one of the factors sometimes responsible for conference failure; unless a moderator sets an agenda and keeps the group working to its goal, nothing much will occur. [13]

Our experience to date tells us that leadership of this kind is not necessary. If the group has a real purpose for being online and has established a sense of collective ownership of the conference, and if issues of power and control within the group are part of the group's focus and agenda, then the concept of leadership will not only be unnecessary, but it will be unhelpful. Setting agendas, and keeping work to its goals, are activities which we try to achieve democratically.

Since we are all regular visitors to the conference, issues of information overload [12] are less likely to be a major problem – although sometimes even a week's absence can leave someone with a considerable amount to catch up on if activity in the conference has been high. But the need for the tutor formally to netweave ("summarizing the state of the discussion and finding threads of unity in the comments of other participants" [5]) on behalf of everyone else, on the grounds that participants need to be kept informed of what is happening, is not necessary. Active participation (most people come online at least twice a week, if not more often) means we are all keeping up with what's happening in a conference. When it appears that a summary is needed, netweaving is done spontaneously by us all (see, for example, Malcolm's summary of where we were in the assessment process mentioned above).

Some problematic areas

There are a certain number of areas where our role as tutor could be said to be problematic. Firstly, there is the question of the impact of our interventions; this is not unique to the tutors, but it does have serious implications for our formal role of supportive facilitator. Our position as tutor can carry with it a power and authority which could be abused [7, 8, 21]. We are constantly confronted with the contradiction in playing the dual role of tutor-participant. This is especially so in the assessment process. Any intervention we make has the likelihood of being received differently to interventions made by other participants. Our wish to remove the iniquity of unequal power relationships takes some considerable time and active work – as tutors, we have to establish a sense of trust and partnership online with participants. But in this medium it is not always possible to be as aware of your interventions as you might be in a face-to-face situation. Participants may construe your intervention in an unintended way, perhaps reading more into what you say than you intended. There is no way of checking this out (other than constantly asking how an intervention was received, which would get in the way of discussion if done frequently, although it has to be done from time to time). You can be aware of the ongoing climate of the conference and glean some information about your position in it and how you are being 'received' and perceived. But from time to time it emerges that a tutor intervention has had some unanticipated affect. Sometimes participants confront us about the issue immediately and we are then able to discuss it (for example, issues to do with giving and receiving grades). Sometimes its effects are dormant and it is only in time in discussion over other issues that we become aware of its significance. This may not appear any different to what a tutor has to confront in a face-to-face situation, but online it does have a different impact on all concerned and seems in practice to be more difficult to manage. It requires critical awareness through dialogue with participants.

A second issue is how best to obtain a sense of being effective online. In face-to-face situations we receive information (verbal, body language, etc) which helps tell us something about our effectiveness as a tutor. Online we can only be told, indirectly or directly, about our professional practice. If, however, we are constantly trying to develop honest, trusting and open online learning environments then we can trust our intuition at times to tell us something of our effectiveness (Polanji [17] talks of such commitment saving us from mere subjectivity). Participants will 'say' something about us as tutors in the normal ongoing dialogue, and if the climate is good we will be able to 'see' ourselves in the process and make judgements about our effectiveness. However, I have found it helpful at times to set up an item about my role as tutor (the contradiction here of forcing a focus on me as tutor in an environment that tries to diminish roles is not lost on me, although it might be seen as being no different to the individual items each participant sets up to focus on them?). This has been reasonably useful and when it works well participants have engaged in discussion about 'me as tutor' in a meaningful way.

Thirdly, our role as largely non directive tutors sometimes feels compromised online. This I think has much to do with the asynchronous nature of computer conferencing, and with attaching meaning to silences online and to the nature of our 'voices' online.

The medium can have the effect of making what we say stand out more than we would wish. Interventions which, when made face-to-face and supported by non-verbal cues which help to present intention and other meaning beyond the words we use, can only be 'said' online. This sometimes strips the intervention of its richness, so that a comment intended to be non-directive is sometimes 'heard' as direction.

Interpreting a silence online is difficult. With Caucus everyone can check when anyone else was last online. If someone is frequently online but silent, or if they are online but only silent in particular conferences or items, we can assume that they have actively chosen to be silent, so any intervention on our part to draw attention to their silence may well be seen as directing them in an unhelpful way. This is of course a conundrum for a tutor. But if the conference participants are being supportive of each other, then it is likely that one of them will offer a way back into the discussion for the silent partner before a tutor has to. Being open and 'able to talk' about one's silences doesn't always come easy in this medium. [3]

Prologue

As I reflect back on the voyage of the *Najaden* over the Baltic Sea, I am struck by the apparent familiarity about the use of this medium which the members of the Workshop seemed to share. At the same time though, I am left more aware than ever of the gulf that exists between professionals like ourselves who purport to "have things in common". That gulf is about not knowing how in practice (and in detail, not generalisations) we each use this medium in our everyday work. For myself, until we know something of the micro-politics of our own and each others' online educational process, we might well be unable to claim we

---

[3] One particularly difficult interpersonal experience presented us with the problem of how to manage feelings in an online environment. We spent some time trying to work with the issues; but they were only resolved later when we met face-to-face. Talking of the experience online, one person involved did however say: "I have found that trying to express feelings through this medium one thing, but there are some feelings that one first has to come to terms with before one can express them. By that I mean how can you express feelings online when one does not know what the feelings are about and why one is feeling them. I now feel that it has not anything to do with this medium and I would have had to work through this even in a face-to-face situation."

understand very much about what we are personally achieving, and what we collectively imagine we have to say about the medium.

Making judgements about the conduct of professional practice in online environments presents us with a new arena for discussions about professional practice generally. The issues are complex – whose reality are we talking about, and what social (and research) standards do we apply to the process of making sense of our claims to 'knowing' and to the development of educational knowledge?[4] By approaching issues of professional development from a critical perspective, and working out of a theory of professionalism which is based on such questions as "How do I improve the process of education here?" [20], I believe we have a way forward [15]. Otherwise, how will we know if claims often made about the educational benefit of this medium are not mere rhetoric rather than the outcome of analyses grounded in the realities of those involved?

References

1. Carr, W. and Kemmis, S. : Becoming critical : education, knowledge and action research. Brighton: Falmer Press 1986

2. Boot, R. and Hodgson, V.: Open learning: philosophy or expediency? Programmed Learning and Educational Technology, 25, 3 (1988)

3. Boot, R. and Reynolds, M.: Rethinking experience based events. In: Management development : advances in practice and theory. (C. Cox, J. Beck, eds.). New York: J Wiley & Sons 1984

4. Brochet, M.G. : Effective moderation of computer conferences: notes and suggestions. Guelph: University of Guelph Computing Support Services, 1985

5. Feenberg, A.: Network design: an operational manual for computer conferencing. IEEE Transactions on Professional Communications, Vol. PC-29, 1 (1986)

6. Freire, P. : Pedagogy of the oppressed. Middlesex, England: Penguin Education, 1972

7. Freire, P:. The politics of education: culture, power and liberation. Basingstoke: Macmillan 1985

8. Giroux, H.A.: Theory and resistance in education: a pedagogy for the opposition. London: Heineman 1983

9. Habermas, J.: Knowledge and human interests. London: Heineman 1972

10. Hardy, G., Hodgson, V., McConnell, D., and Reynolds, M.: Computer mediated communication for management training and development: a research report. Lancaster, England: C.S.M.L., Lancaster University 1991

11. Harris, D.: Openness and closure in distance education. Brighton: Falmer Press 1987

12. Hiltz, S.R. and Turoff, M.: Structuring computer-mediated communication systems to avoid information overload. Communications of the ACM, 28,7 (1985)

---

[4] See the following for discussions of such research issues :

– Lincoln, Y. & Guba, E.: Naturalistic inquiry. London: Sage,1985

– Reason, P. & Rowan, J.(eds): Human inquiry: a sourcebook of new paradigm research. Chichester : John Wiley & Sons 1981

– Whitehead, J. How do we improve research-based professionalism in education? A question that includes action research, educational theory and the politics of educational knowledge. British Educational Research Journal, 15, 1 (1989)

13. Kerr, E.B.: Electronic leadership: a guide to moderating online conferences. IEEE Transactions on Professional Communications, Vol. PC-29, 1 (1986)

14. Kling,R.: Computerization and social transformations. Science, Technology and Human Values,16,3 (1991)

15. Kolb, D.A.: Experiential learning: Experience as the source of learning and development. Englewood Cliffs, N.J.: Prentice Hall 1984

16. McConnell, D.: The educational use of computer conferencing. Educational and Training Technology International, 27, 2 (1990)

17. Polanji, M.: Personal knowledge: towards a postcritical philosophy. London: Routledge & Kegan Paul 1958

18. Rogers, C.: Freedom to learn in the 80s. Columbus, Ohio: Charles E. Merrill 1983

19. Snell, R.: Graduating from the school of hard knocks. Journal of Management Development, 8, 5 (1989)

20. Whitehead, J. How do we improve research-based professionalism in education? A question that includes action research, educational theory and the politics of educational knowledge. British Educational Research Journal, 15, 1 (1989)

21. Young, M.F.D.: Knowledge and control: New directions for the sociology of education. London: Macmillan 1971

5
Collaboration in International Online Teams

Elaine McCreary
Baha'i World Centre, Haifa, Israel

Madge Brochet
University of Guelph, Ontario, Canada

Abstract: This paper examines the use of computer-mediated communication (CMC) by four international online teams active in rural and environmental development projects on three continents. These cooperative teams engage in mutually supportive learning, as they utilize electronic mail and computer conferencing facilities, to help overcome challenges to effective communication presented by geographic isolation and time zone complexities. The groups' experiences are examined in terms of their transition to CMC use, the types of communication tasks carried out via CMC, problems encountered and benefits received. CMC is reported to play a key role in developing an electronic or paper database to act as a project's 'collective memory', increasing the feasibility of inter-continental projects, and viewing modern team communication as an orchestration of media. Recommendations are made regarding the effective use of CMC in international project management and the benefits of team learning to advance communication at the frontiers of cross-cultural problem solving.

Keywords: computer-mediated communication, rural development, CMC, collaborative learning and international development projects, CoSy, electronic mail, computer conferencing, CMC and project management, time zone challenges to communication, collective memory, team work across time zones.

Introduction

The present vital need to accelerate human learning has a deeper meaning than the desire to graduate more experts from our centres of higher education. We urgently need to assist open-minded and cooperative teams to engage in mutually-supportive learning, as they endeavour to ameliorate some of the world's increasingly more pressing problems. The four case studies that follow recount the implementation experiences of cross or multi-cultural teams engaged in rural research and development. Each team described herein is learning-as-a-group at the frontiers of cross-cultural problem-solving. They demonstrate how CMC technology is being used to restore the synergistic process of 'learning together' to the forefront of practical human welfare.

The Four International Teams

Rural change in Europe: A research programme spanning 12 countries

The European Community sponsored this five-year research program to examine trends in 24 farming areas dispersed throughout nine EC member states and three non-member states, namely Austria, Switzerland and Sweden. Arkleton Trust (Research) Ltd., the executing agency, coordinated the 24 study teams from its own base in Scotland using a wide area network and computer conferencing software [1]. The research examined current evolution of farm household behaviour, including the phenomenon of multiple income sources (referred to as pluriactivity), in relation to common policies of the Community regarding such agricultural structures as quotas, levies and other planning restrictions. Each of the 24 study areas encompassed baseline and final surveys of 300 farming households, and required in-depth annual interviews with 60 selected families during three years of the project. The 12-country study required integrated planning and collection of both quantitative and qualitative data, and joint analysis at different spatial levels in order to understand better the socio-economic evolution of these regions. Formidable communication challenges resulted both from the distribution of the project staff throughout most of Europe, and from the complexity of qualitative data analysis required, which involved relating farm decision-making patterns and diversification of income sources in response to a variety of socio-economic conditions, agro-rural environments, and trends in structural policies regionally and nationally, in a comparative cross-national framework.

The need for integrated planning and close coordination led those initially involved to seek alternatives in communication technology that would be equal to the scale, speed, and complexity of the project. The diffusion of CMC tools into project work followed a classic sequence: the Project Director adopted conferencing (using the CoSy software) in 1984; some of the project steering group undertook design work with it in 1985; a joint meeting of most research staff participated in discussions, demonstrations, and training in its use in 1986, after which it was formally incorporated as a key communication tool in the work of the project [2]. The actual, daily, informal adoption of CMC by staff also followed a now-classic sequence: confidence in the reliability of the physical links (microcomputer to modem to telephone lines); logging on and off the system; reading messages; sending messages; downloading, working off-line, and uploading messages. All 24 regional research teams were encouraged to establish such linkages early in 1987. By 1988, a staff member had been hired to handle user training and answer questions and to revise the user manual in cooperation with British Telecom, for what was now known as the Rurtel network (the online team of rural researchers).

Over the next three years (1988-91) the pattern of adoption of CMC never became either universal or uniform – three of the participating countries had technical problems such as telephone lines, and individuals varied considerably in the frequency and intensity of usage. The transition to online work did noticeably increase in volume: the original host computer (near Inverness, Scotland), running the UNIX version of CoSy, offered users eight simultaneous lines open 24 hours a day, and had the capacity to handle approximately 60 regular participants; work was later upgraded to a DEC-VAX computer substantially increasing line and storage capacity [7]. Online work also evolved in the kinds of communication tasks undertaken: in the early stages CMC was applied to managerial discussions over contracts, financial arrangements, timing and meetings; as design work progressed more field-staff researchers were involved in development of the research instruments, pilot testing early questionnaires, refining ambiguous items, and re-thinking the coding of data. An expert observer of the process remarked on the strong sense of group purpose which emerged from designing the highly complex data gathering instruments through a consensus-driven process, and further estimated that the design phase had thereby been cut in half, from two years to one year. As data from the project flowed in, to be assembled in a central archive at the University of Essex and forwarded to Scotland, a new set of part-time project researchers, working from remote sites, accessed the CMC host to examine the data and discuss it together online. The final stage of re-writing is being facilitated by ready access to all products of the research in machine readable form.

Members of the Arkleton Trust research staff evaluated CMC as a crucial component of team building in the early phases of the project despite technical and learning difficulties among some of those involved. Its administrative support functions throughout included such elusive details as airline flights, agenda for meetings, hotel reservations, and financial aspects of the 12-nation project. Its broadcast functions included the distribution of such commonly useful items as European Community information and legislation relevant to the rural research community in Europe, as well as extracts of bulletins and newsletters of interest to either the entire group or to subsets of the group. But group consultation was the hallmark of CMC in this project for joint discussion, analysis, interpretation and reporting of project findings. Overall, the level of interaction of this continent-wide network of researchers was estimated to be five to six times greater than their experience led them to believe would have been possible using the telephone and mail services only.

The Sulawesi regional development project in Indonesia

This extensive rural development project covers all four provinces of the island of Sulawesi, the fifth largest Indonesian island group. Indonesia itself is an archipelago of 13,000 islands which stretches a distance equal to that from coast-to-coast in North America, and is home to 160 million people [8]. The Sulawesi regional development project is a bi-lateral undertaking between Canada, through the Canadian International Development Agency (CIDA), and

Indonesia, through its Department of Home Affairs, operating since 1984 through five-year phases. The University of Guelph, through its University School of Rural Planning and Development, is the Canadian Executing Agency for the CIDA portion of the project. The joint staff who provide training, technical assistance and support for district and provincial planners and community groups face considerable challenges to communication. The mountainous terrain of Sulawesi, dispersion of rural sites involved, and hemispheric distance between the team members exacerbate communication problems identified by Keen [6] such as stress caused by working across time zones, the need to reduce the amount of paperwork shipped from point to point, and the need to increase direct, flexible contact between people.

From the beginning of the project, staff used the CoSy conferencing software to send private and group-directed messages between sites in Canada and Indonesia. Senior project staff used CMC during the start-up phase, and established the first linkage of the project itself between the two principal offices in Jakarta (Indonesia) and Guelph (Canada). Transition experiences were described by new staff who joined the project after start-up. One informant with prior experience on development projects and a high level of comfort with microcomputers, noted that it still took approximately two months to become completely familiar with CMC as part of one's day-to-day work habits, and yet even before a comfort level was reached it became obvious that there was a free flow of information possible with CMC that had not been experienced previously. Training was provided informally to new CMC users as part of the regular workload both in Canada and Indonesia.

The Indonesian telecommunications provider, PT IndoSat, established communication routing via a satellite positioned over Indonesia in 1986/87. The link was later expanded so that the project field office staff in Ujung Pandang could also send messages to Jakarta and to Guelph in Canada. Curiously the 12-hour difference in time zones becomes an asset for the intercontinental joint staff, such that a 24-hour cycle of almost uninterrupted work becomes the norm. When staff on one continent end their work-day with messages transmitted almost instantaneously, those reports are picked up shortly thereafter by their counterparts on the other continent who are just starting the day.

A variety of communication media are currently used in concert to carry out the work of the Sulawesi project, including telephone, Fax transmission, surface mail, courier service and CMC. A single criterion can determine the specific mode employed for a particular message or document; for example, courier service is used for sending final reports, as it is necessary to obtain receipts of delivery for these documents. Urgent messages are often handled by CMC, although Fax is also used, or, if the time window is appropriate, a telephone call is placed. When matters are both urgent and confidential, managers use computer conferences set up exclusively for the management group, and may also use private two-point, simple e-mail messages. Early use of any new communications medium can be irregular, perhaps tentative, indicating experimentation rather than whole-hearted adoption. Lack of experience can lead to such *faux pas* as sending a message but omitting some of the significant players in its distribution; accidentally copying to inappropriate readers, or placing confidential information in conferences with a wider readership than appropriate. Over time usage stabilizes and becomes differentiated in systematic ways. Sulawesi project staff have standardized their use of CMC in its many possibilities for private, group, and public consultations, into a model that operates in three-dimensions:

– access: "... who needs to know?"
– urgency: "... how essential is speed?"
– duration: "... for how long will they need this communication channel?"

Variations of the 'access' dimension are observable in the variety of conference groupings that have been established. For example, one conference serves as a bulletin board for all staff. Information about personnel movements, new project developments, and all non-confidential information is placed here. A new conference of this name is established annually, and the old one archived in a read-only form that becomes a searchable database for everyone in the organization. Both homebase offices, in Jakarta and Guelph, have the capacity to circulate information just among their respective staff groups consisting of 5 or 6 people each, to take care of strictly local matters. Other closed conferences exist jointly between Jakarta and Guelph comprised of only senior management from both offices to deal with such issues as hiring, salary negotiations, contract concerns, project directions, project and development philosophy. On the access dimension there can occur a degree of 'underlap' where information is missed, or 'overlap' where it is read in a couple of different locations. At least for the question of repetition, it was reported that it is easier to scan and discard previously read information on a microcomputer screen, than it is to interrupt a colleague who is repeating information you already know.

The Philippines environment and resource management project

This four year project began in the autumn of 1989, with C $4.9 million from the Canadian International Development Agency (CIDA) and in-kind contributions from the University of the Philippines at Los Banos (UPLB) and Dalhousie University. Staff have been contributed from the University of the Philippines at Los Banos (UPLB) and from Dalhousie University, Nova Scotia, both universities operating through their respective environmental teaching and research units.

The Philippines had been experiencing rapid exploitation of natural resources, rapid increase in population and increasing poverty among resource based communities. The overall goal of the project was to strengthen UPLB's capacity to contribute to environment and resource management in the Philippines through Canadian assistance with policy development; development action programs; human resource development with an explicit focus on women in relation to training, rural development, and environment; institution building within the University, and within the Environmental Network of the Philippines; and strengthening of communication linkages within the Philippines, and between the Philippines and Canada [5].

Of the 7,000 islands in the South China Sea which comprise the Philippines, only 1,000 are inhabited, with two-thirds of the population settled on the two largest islands, Luzon and Mindanao, at opposite ends of the archipelago. Arab missionaries in the 1300's gave the Moslem religion to the south, and Spanish missionaries brought Catholicism to the north, in the 1600's. Communication is complicated by the several languages and many dialects, as well as by geographic variability from rice terraced mountainous regions to humid tropical lowlands with heavy rainfall. Distances are hard to cover and roads difficult to install and maintain. Political, economic and religious tensions are exacerbated by both pro-Marcos and pro-Communist groups engaged in opposition to the government, expressing themselves in random bombings, even in the urban areas. Telephone communication is particularly unreliable, being only intermittently available, if at all, outside of Manila and Quezon City.

Amid these communication difficulties the joint project set about intensive human resource development. It provides fellowships for the training of professionals to work with government, non-governmental (NGO) and university agencies in such areas as environmental administration, land use management, water resources development, geographic information services, and environmental economics. The work on environmental management information systems emphasized the transformation of data into easy-to-use formats so that policy makers could easily integrate data from remote sensing and ground surveys, local community information, historical data, ecosystem studies, and policy support studies. Community-based action programs integrated community organizers with government field personnel, members of the Dalhousie University team, and student interns from both Canadian and UPLB graduate programs. All these activities involving exchanges of personnel generated considerable movement of people with a variety of travel arrangements, orientation meetings, review and selection of candidates, requiring an uninterrupted flow of communication with rapid turnaround times between the two countries.

At the time this project began operation in early 1990, the Dalhousie management group already had the benefit of four years of experience with implementing CMC, first in an experimental setting through a CIDA sponsored prototype project and later through their own implementation of CMC in an Indonesian project. For those working in Halifax with such prior experience, a 24-hour cycle of message management had become routine, whereby messages were printed off, distributed to the intended recipients, with copies filed in chronological daybooks, and replies collected and dispatched. But for the project staff in the Philippines, six months still did not produce a dedicated phone link for computer communications, a desperate requirement since the building which houses the entire environmental institute had only one telephone, which was often in use all day and frequently subject to interrupted service – a situation complicated no doubt by the fact that there are 35 non-compatible telephone companies in the Philippines! Fortunately, the International Rice Research Institute (IRRI) is only 15 minutes away by car, and they agreed to send messages for the project through their CGNET[1] connection. The Project has its own CGNET-id and pays a monthly mailbox charge, plus connect charges for this service. The transfer process requires messages for Canada to be typed onto a disk at the project office, driven to the IRRI office where they are copied electronically from the floppy disk and sent via a DataPac call connection to CGNET. Due to time differences, messages sent from Los Banos at the end of the working day are received moments later at the beginning of the working day in Halifax. Frequent complications include the irregular availability of the driver to take the disk

---

[1] CGNET is a conferencing system specializing in agriculture, founded in 1985 by the Consultative Group on International Agricultural Research, Palo Alto, California. [9]

from UPLB to IRRI; IRRI staff accumulating a stack of messages before sending them to Canada and messages being misplaced accidentally, with consequent loss or mis-sequencing of information. To cope, one side may request the other to send a complete hard copy set of a week's messages in the courier bag so that people can get the information into proper sequence again. Courier service has proved a particularly valuable communications tool, positioned where, in another project, one would expect to see Fax machines listed. Due to the low reliability of the Philippine mail service, a four-day courier delivery is preferred for handling floppy disks, newspapers and personal mail to expatriates, copies of official documents, large documents and original documents for signatures.

Despite this now legendary degree of inconvenience, the e-mail link is felt to be vital to communication between the two offices. There are approximately 12-16 people in the bi-lateral staff of the project who need to communicate on a regular basis. The Los Banos staff, having waited so long for their own phone line, regret the imposition on the kindness of IRRI colleagues and are aware that the aid of a third party means loss of confidentiality of project messages between Halifax and Los Banos. In addition, IRRI's phone link is occasionally non-functional, meaning that no CGNET connection is possible at all. When CMC messages are interrupted for more than three days, attempts are made to place a telephone call to the Project Team Leader's home in the Philippines, but given the difference in time zones, there is a very small window in which such a call can be placed. Given the extreme measures required to forward messages in this telecommunications environment, less experienced team members might have abandoned the effort were it not for the senior team members' equally convincing experience of the efficacy of CMC in Canada/Pacific joint projects, and their high level of awareness that quick turn-around of communication is vital in project management on this scale.

CMC has been used to facilitate the collaborative decision making which characterizes the operation of this project. It is used for the joint preparation of terms of reference for consultants hired in Canada to serve in the Philippines, providing a democratic, timely way to process these complex documents. Financial spreadsheets, on the other hand, are always sent on disk in the courier bag due to the characteristics of the financial software being used by the team. With the number of faculty and short and long-term consultants travelling, CMC is used for scheduling and planning meetings, and for making travel arrangements. For exchange students, CMC is used during the selection process, and to keep in contact after their selection, providing them with instructions and information. Although CMC is not used as the formal method of distributing minutes of meetings, project staff are in constant touch, reporting on meetings attended in both countries, and providing informal accounts of external developments connected with the various program areas, through daily CMC messages. The Project Assistant Team Leader in Halifax reports that CMC "sets the agenda for the day" as it often contains questions to which the Los Banos group need answers, or responses that allow the Project Assistant Team Leader to proceed with work to be done. Messages dealing with discussion of goals, longer range planning, and strategies are also sent back and forth via CMC. Theoretical aspects of planning are discussed, as are serious issues such as levels of responsibility. Extremely large files are not sent via CMC due to the cost of transmission, nor are confidential items, due to current logistical circumstances.

Environmental management development in Indonesia

A joint undertaking of the Indonesian Ministry of State for Population and Environment, and the School for Resource and Environmental Studies, Dalhousie University, Halifax, Canada, the project described here is actually Phase 3 of work begun in 1983, that has progressed from early investigation of the need for environmental policy, through development of proposed environmental legislation, to its enactment, and in some cases to its application. Funding from CIDA has increased dramatically from C $2.5 million for Phase 1 (1983-86), to C $7.7 million for Phase 2 (1986-89), to C $31.1 million for Phase 3 (1989-94) [4]. The Canadian commitment has matched that expressed by the Indonesian government in its intention to make "environmental management, including its ecological, social and cultural aspects, an integral component of all development decision-making in Indonesia" [3].

Phase 3 of the project was designed to upgrade environmental management capabilities through institutional strengthening and human resource development, within the Ministry of State for Population and Environment, beyond the Ministry within agencies charged with the work of implementing environmental management and sustainable development, and between Indonesian and Canadian institutions by facilitating stronger professional linkages. A large number of sub-projects have been designed to take place concurrently in Phase 3 providing technical cooperation, linkages and exchanges covering such areas as: spatial planning, environmental standards and impact assessment, pollution control, the means of formulating national level policies, environmental information systems, marine and coastal management, environmental law, publication of a book series on the ecology of Indonesia, and the establishment of professional linkages through all relevant sectors (public, academic, private, and NGO) in Indonesia and jointly with Canadian colleagues through Dalhousie University.

The project dispenses approximately C $17,000 per day, weekends included. A small group of management staff, located in offices on either side of the world, monitor all aspects of project work. By increasing the budget from C $ 7.7 million to C $31.1 million between Phases 2 and 3 of the project, CIDA clearly expressed confidence that the management communication challenges were being met. The Project Director, Dr. Shirley Conover, had been introduced to CMC by colleagues in 1985, and participated in a prototype conference across the Pacific in the winter of 1986-87, sponsored by CIDA and coordinated by Dr Maria Cioni, which allowed participants to evaluate the effectiveness of computer-mediated communication. Then, in 1989 during the first six months of Phase 1, before CMC had been installed as a project tool, staff reported that difficulties were experienced when fast decisions were needed, and that telephone costs were high, both in actual dollar costs and in time spent placing and waiting for calls.

A staff member with expertise in e-mail served as a resource, and messages began to be handled using the mail-mode of CoSy software, identifying each message with distribution lists for readership and topic headings for purposes of filing hard copy – an ingenious re-invention of functions actually available within the software itself. Although 'learning time to comfortable use' varied from a few weeks to a few months, it was obvious that corporate culture influenced new staff to feel curious, to realize CMC's integral place in management as a result of its advantages, and to find the help they needed from co-workers. The project, through all its phases, has been a client of the CoSy Service Bureau of the University of Guelph, rather than buying, installing and running its own copy of the software.

Such customers use a variety of communications software on their local microcomputers and connect to the Guelph CoSy system either via a local phone call, via a Datapac port from elsewhere in Canada, via Tymnet from the USA, or via an international packet-switched network connection from overseas. For project staff in Jakarta, this meant dialing into the IndoSat packet network to place a call to Guelph CoSy. Messages stored at Guelph can be accessed by customers 24 hours a day. Costs are comprised of a flat-rate, monthly user-charge, a per hour connection charge, and a chargeback on connection costs, where applicable.

Far beyond merely coping with separation by vast distances and many time zones, CMC has proven itself to the project staff as a superior and preferred way of doing business. All aspects of the project have been handled to advantage when CMC was added to previous communication media. The aspects include:
– *day-to-day operational management* such as travel arrangements and scheduling of itinerary for faculty and student exchanges, project review teams, and diplomatic officials; timing, budget, and purchase details of the relocation of Jakarta offices; joint drafting and revision of terms of reference for consultants to the project; personal conversations between isolated team-mates to develop familiarity, maintain rapport, vent frustrations harmlessly through humour, and diffuse tensions during periods of high stress and intense activity;
– *crisis management*, where speed was the critical factor, and cost-effectiveness coincidental, as in the real-life drama in which an Indonesian student selected for participation in the project, suddenly needed a lifesaving operation, and Canadian sponsorship was obtained within 12 hours, making the surgery possible;
– *financial management* in which the Project Comptroller, who happened to be located in Canada and responsible for the financial accountability of hundreds of activities both there and in Indonesia, was able to maintain close tracking of expenditures and fine tuning of allocations over the fiscal year, in particular because budget irregularities could be discussed and resolved in an average of five CMC messages;
– *collaborative research and writing* in which a team from the University of British Columbia, Canada, is co-authoring a book with project staff for a series on the ecology of Indonesia, and the project librarian who manages the Halifax-based South East Asian collection provides information to staff and consultants 14,000 miles away.

Once again, as in the Philippine project described earlier, drivers for the project were used as a courier service to deliver messages by paper or disk from one Jakarta office to the other which contained the CMC connection for transmission to Canada. Thus the automobile joined Fax, phone, and computer in the chain of communication technologies. Similarly admirable adaptations were required for the style and content of messages between staff members of different cultures. For managers experienced with CMC the incidence of miscommunication was low, clarifications were requested when necessary, offense was not taken quickly, or answers given sharply. But senior staff who joined the project without prior CMC experience were at first given to both take offense and give angry responses. Several conventions were adopted to overcome this: messages became longer, composed with the ear of the listener in mind, edited with greater care, and always reviewed by a colleague for cultural sensitivity. Nevertheless, CMC was considered a comfortable medium because of the relatively low cost and leisurely pace of message preparation and transmission. In comparison, telephone was 'formalized by cost', with repeated efforts to make contact increasing frustration to the point where one sometimes forgot some of the reasons for placing the call, with the result that its communication value was diminished by the tensions caused. Fax transmission was also considered to be a relatively formal medium, constrained by cost and the tendency to restrict a message to the lowest number of pages. Yet, the final choice was always to use these media in concert as appropriate.

Comparison of the Four Teams' Experiences with CMC

Strategies for adoption and implementation

All four of the cases reported here were designed from the beginning to incorporate CMC as an essential management communication tool because their leadership had previously evaluated CMC in another beta test site, as with the European Community group, or participated in a prototype conference across the Pacific, as with the two Dalhousie projects in Asia, or had been exposed to CMC as a management tool within a university, as was the case with the Guelph leadership of the Sulawesi project in Indonesia. For the key decision-makers the essential question was not whether to use it, but how best to initiate inexperienced staff members into this mode of working.

Whereas the Sulawesi Project Director was able to express his enthusiasm through direct influence, orientation and training of staff on both sides of the Pacific, the European Project Director promoted interest in the adoption of CMC through informal demonstrations and discussion of precedent setting CMC applications with senior management. This gradual creation of a base of acceptance was accelerated in 1986 when Arkleton Trust sponsored a five day seminar for all European staff entitled New Technology and Rural Development. As it happened, the Dalhousie project in the Philippines followed the successful implementation of two phases of its Indonesian project, and furthermore shared some of the same staff, so assumptions about relative advantage of computer communication had developed into convictions by the time the second project was launched.

Transition period

All groups interviewed experienced difficulties in the transition period including technical frustrations (particularly with the installation of modems), and frustrations with the learning curve for staff when senior staff were only available intermittently for training, printed materials were insufficient for problem-solving, and support was not always available even by phone – and when it was, the single phone line could not be used for CMC connection, thus excluding the possibility of long-distance advice during an actual online session.

The Rural Change in Europe project experienced additional complications due to the twenty or so sites involved, whereas the others had two to three primary sites and a maximum of six. This dispersion of sites, rather than the actual distances between, necessitated several months of travel and staff training by the Project Director, followed by the hiring of a staff member exclusively for CMC user support, and finally the preparation of project-specific training materials and a user manual.

CMC message management

Three of the four projects have undertaken to transform the stream of day-to-day information into systematic project archives (a 'collective memory'). Standardized routines have been established by each of the joint projects in the Pacific to provide centralized tracking and control of messages. In the two projects with which Dalhousie University has been involved, this is accomplished with extensive paper copies, distributed according to lists indicated by the message sender, posted to a daily logbook, and cross-posted to topic books according to project activities. Although labour-intensive, this ingenious re-invention of the software's ability to store messages by the topic they address, corroborates the critical need in complex, collaborative work to upgrade simple e-mail exchanges to a systematic storage of messages by topic.

The University of Guelph Sulawesi project in the Pacific also keeps a hardcopy, daily logbook as central backup, but stores its messages-by-topic in 'softcopy' databases that are then electronically searchable by date, speaker, or any specific word in the full text of the messages. This dynamic archive can then be used to extract the historical development of any issue or activity over the lifetime of the project.

In contrast, the Rurtel project of the European Community has no standardized system for recording electronic project management. A large number of messages are exchanged between individuals, among sub-groups, and broadcast to all participating staff from project management, but these are typically not archived systematically. While some discussions are in a searchable form because they take place among managers who appreciate the conferencing mode's advantages over e-mail, the principal example of systematic message management by this team are the central data collection files used to assemble and manipulate the 12-country, comparative research.

Communication tasks

Because the four teams all had mandates related to international collaboration on rural development, it was to be expected that they would have similar management tasks, but not necessarily that they would orchestrate their communications media in similar ways. In fact, with emphases varying between groups and over time, they nevertheless all reported using CMC for i) informal messaging within a group, ii) formal correspondence, iii) information gathering, iv) collaborative planning and report writing, v) staff support services, vi) travel and meeting coordination, and vii) research related work.

The principal variation among cases was their use of CMC for handling of financial information. In the Sulawesi project this is transmitted directly to Guelph from Indonesia and uploaded into spreadsheet software. Other groups are unable to do this, but mention it as a desirable technique. Re-typing of financial data is tedious and error-prone. Attention to new developments in file transfer software may provide solutions for the other three groups so they can take advantage of this method of speeding up financial reporting.

Implementation problems

Online teams universally reported problems in establishing their tele-communication linkages, with resultant costs in the form of slow adoption of CMC, delays in project decision-making by using slower technologies, attenuated training periods, and depleted enthusiasm for an innovation constantly pending. A second common problem was the tendency for granting agencies to sanction one-time outlays for equipment and software and to ignore the on-going equipment costs for maintenance, repair, and telecommunication charges, and human resource costs for staff to introduce, trouble shoot, train and provide higher levels of user support in the emerging networks. A third problem encountered was the variability in new-user openness to CMC adoption, whereby personal attitudes or prior experiences seemed to account for some staff viewing CMC for management as a welcome innovation and others reacting to it as an inconvenience or interruption of their more familiar work patterns. A fourth common problem was the long-familiar range in reading-to-writing ratios, some participants commenting frequently, others being virtually silent partners. Staff felt that reticent writers could be drawn into dialogue by sensitive online leadership.

A curious paradox emerges when CMC is felt to be successful in closing the gap between a team's central office on one continent and its field offices on another. One project reported that the issue of control between offices occasionally detracted from their healthy dialogue, and required a tempering of all extremes: field office isolation and autonomy on one hand which could keep head office underinformed, as well as head office intrusions on the other hand to press for fiscal reporting or interim project schedules when field office staff were preoccupied with implementation or data collection.

Another complaint arose from two teams, who felt that CMC was inappropriately controlling or driving their work day. This was attributed to several factors: the novelty of early morning messages from across the world, the atmosphere of anticipation when information had been requested from counterparts at the end of the previous working day, and the experience (as with Fax), of confusing speed of transmission with urgency of need to respond. In these two teams, staff felt the importance of re-asserting their own work priorities over the agenda inadvertently set by incoming CMC messages.

A third problem, unique this time to the European, Rurtel project was inequality of access among the 24 dispersed sites to their project's wide area network. This situation was partly due to technical infrastructure and partly due to the variety of sponsoring agencies (universities, research institutes, and others) at which project participants were employed or located. Those who were delayed in the funding and installation of micros, modems, and communication lines expressed an intense feeling of disenfranchisement from the early online brainstorming sessions which produced the first benchmark research instrument and the formation of group identity among researchers. This problem led to including provision of CMC access as one of the contractual obligations of any agency wanting one of its staff to be a participant in the European Rurtel research network.

Benefits Reported

Praised in all cases for accelerating the rate at which project goals were achieved and improving overall project well being, staff from the four teams reported specific benefits with: improvement in fiscal control of projects, improvement in the management of wide-ranging project activities, increased ability to meet project deadlines, increased freedom to elaborate on long distance communication, increased freedom from the constraints of the telephone, improvement in dealing with urgent matters, and provision of improved personal communication links in support of staff working at remote sites.

The Rural Change in Europe project enjoyed a unique collaboration in the design of a mass data collection instrument for its 12-country comparative study – a feat that would have been impractical within their timeframe using other means. Another unique advantage was reported by the Indonesian environmental management development project, which attributed its four-fold budget increase to the credibility its staff had acquired as online managers of inter-continental activities.

Conclusions

Team operation

Top-down endorsement was influential in all cases, to stimulate group curiosity, encourage adoption, assist in training, demonstrate commitment, and help others to recognize that CMC was being internalized as part of the communication infrastructure of the organization. When senior managers opted out of online communication, it required extra time to produce a typed memo in addition to the copy for CMC transmission, and led to more junior staff being informed earlier. In these precedent setting cases, it was possible to detect the influence of a 'messiah figure' who was a senior staff person having both considerable technical knowledge and outstanding abilities to encourage innovation.

Perseverance in the face of considerable obstacles was not only universally necessary but forthcoming, especially as staff experienced a significant improvement in their ability to get answers to questions or to broadcast information to all project colleagues. Day-to-day message management differed considerably between groups, demonstrating a variety of operational preferences, despite the fact that all four teams had comparable rural development mandates and objectives and the internal goal of good organizational communication. While CoSy computer conferencing software was a constant in three of the four cases studied, the methods of message creation, transmittal, distribution, storage, searching, and application of the enormous body of project messages varied widely, indicating that far from compelling a uniform pattern of operation, groups could tailor their uses of the software dramatically, finding sufficient flexibility to permit this diversity of implementations.

Transitions to online collaboration

It takes time to advance beyond mere technical skill with the software to a level of personal communication skill online that advances beyond standard transfer of information.

Peer review of messages to new users/readers was adopted independently by three projects to assess messages thought to be complicated or sensitive in nature. Staff informally agreed to freely ask and quickly respond when a message needed review for clarity, completeness, appropriateness of distribution, or the potential to offend, particularly in cross-cultural communication.

The expansion of communication linkages to include additional sites for an existing project re-activated transition phenomena such as the needs for training, technical support, and the re-establishment of work routines and communication norms.

Although only one of the teams studied had a long-term training and user-support person on staff, all four reiterated the importance of taking the human resource needs seriously when planning for success.

Communication tasks

While no communication tasks were excluded from the CMC medium, neither was it ever the only medium in use. Urgent questions were deferred from CMC to telephone communication only during the very small daily window possible between Southeast Asia and North America. Certain long documents not originated in computer form were sent via courier or Fax to avoid the necessity of keying them in. Project staff seemed to gravitate to CMC as their main communications carrier, with other media being orchestrated to complement it where possible.

Problems encountered by online teams

All teams experienced numerous problems, some of which were protracted, and at best ameliorated with compromise solutions. The most at-risk phase was start-up, where problems in establishing basic technical linkages were formidable, but once accomplished the daily contacts quickly became indispensable to team operation.

The most underestimated budgetary allotment, and one essential to project success, was human resource development in the form of initial professional development time, support materials, and staff resources assigned to provide orientation, training, and on-going support to the balance of staff new to online collaborative project management.

The benefits of online collaboration

All four teams praised the quantum advance in close cooperation made possible by working together online despite the thousands of miles separating their work sites.

For the Canadian/Indonesian environmental management project, CMC made possible the expansion of bi-lateral environmental management activities such that the scale of their operating budget quadrupled to C $30 million.

For the Rurtel researchers of the European Community the benefits far exceeded the central collection of comparative data, to include the collaborative, consultative, design process that produced a common research instrument, and later, the daily online conversations that led to the interpretation of results.

For the environmental project in the Philippines, despite unusually difficult circumstances related to telephone lines, staff have identified CMC as essential to their teamwork, especially in drawing all parties into the preparation of terms of reference for consultants, the planning of working missions from Canada, and satisfying the Project Comptroller's need for timely data.

For the Sulawesi regional development project in Indonesia, CMC was not only an essential daily management tool for a large scale undertaking, but its use produced the additional benefit of a collective memory, documenting project activities across the life of the project in an accessible electronic project archive.

Hard-won, obvious truths about implementation

In the briefest possible form, this is what we discovered:

Essential elements for CMC implementation

1. The urgent need to communicate frequently
2. The pressing desire to communicate frequently
3. Commitment from senior management
4. User access to equipment
5. Access to reliable communication connections
6. Staff time to learn
7. Access to basic training
8. Access to technical support
9. Critical mass of users and messages

Desirable elements which promote CMC success

1. Well designed software
2. Planning a communication strategy
3. Access to in-depth training
4. Attention to the communication styles of others
5. Conference leadership (filling the moderator's role)
6. Negotiation and decision on group roles
7. Standardization of rules for message handling
8. Face-to-face meetings in addition to CMC
9. Access to an array of communication tools

Inhibitors of implementation – to be avoided

1. Long start-up phase
2. Ill-defined costs, ignoring on-going charges
3. Unreliable communication connections
4. Lack of basic training
5. Support that is overwhelmingly technical
6. Infrequent usage by novice users
7. Lack of commitment to share ideas
8. Insufficient number in the online group
9. Duplication of messages in different media
10. High number of participants who have never met in person

Four Insights to the Future

Based on the implementation experiences of four novel and daring teams, who reported what they had learned through their daily collaborative problem-solving in a time-space spanning continents, these final thoughts provide some ripples for us to contemplate on the cresting wave of CMC applications.

The significance of collective memory

When teams used the conferencing facility of the software, rather than merely scattered e-mail memos, then the central message site, or host computer, maintained electronic copies of all messages, categorized and stored as the group saw fit, by any number of appropriate topics. Over time, this emerging textual database provided the group with a dynamic, searchable history of events, decisions and thoughts. The potential fruitfulness of such an electronic project archive was not foreseen when group members first began to work together. What they later discovered was that this collective memory could be searched to reconstruct and report on aspects of project activity, to trace the development of consensus on important issues, to introduce new staff to project ethos and to the way in which information flows among team members, to the type of decision-making that is characteristic of project activity, and to the communication styles of group members. The quality of group identity, historical self-awareness, and transmittable learning thus engendered was phenomenal.

The feasibility of inter-continental projects

Team members interviewed affirmed that the CMC medium allowed them to design and commit to the management of projects on a much larger scale than would have been conceivable otherwise. The Indonesian environmental development management project illustrated by its tripling and quadrupling budget, how a joint undertaking could efficiently and effectively escalate when a medium was available for comprehensive, immediate and uninterrupted consultation.

The orchestration of communications media

In the past, we have mistakenly assumed that an innovation in communications media would render earlier media obsolete: that television would replace radio, that videophones would replace voice-only telephones, and that Fax would replace postal services. What we have come to appreciate is the range of complementary benefits resident in an array of media. In the collaborative teams described here, the communications model which emerges shows CMC clearly serving as the communication core, with staff engaged in a continuing process of matching the communication task at hand with the appropriate transmission medium. Courier service was used to meet a sudden deadline, or scheduled on a regular basis to avoid the hazards of public mail. Computer floppy disks were often included in the courier bags in editing cycles that facilitated collaborative work. Fax and telephone were used as counterpoint when their distinctive features were called for.

The favourable exploitation of time zones

From a traditional perspective which casts distance between team members as a disadvantage, and therefore location on opposite sides of the earth as the most extreme barrier to communication, then CMC is viewed as a tool to cope with basically negative circumstances. But in fact, the medium may transform qualities of the time/space circumstances in which we work, to a revolutionary degree. What the Halifax-Jakarta teams discovered was that they could leverage the 12-hour difference between them to profitable advantage. The results of the day's work for the Canadian staff were filed at 5:00 p.m. and arrived almost instantly at what the Indonesian staff would experience as 5:00 a.m. of the same day. Conversely, shortly after the Jakarta staff left their offices, the Halifax group started work with the new information they had just received at the close of Jakarta's workday. Lag time on information gathering to answer each other's questions was reduced almost to nothing, given that each group had to go home to sleep. Task momentum was maintained due to the low turnaround time on requested information. Working via CMC allowed staff in all the cases studied to capitalize on geographic distances to some degree, in the extremes achieving what they referred to as the dual work day advantage.

References

1. Arkleton Trust (Research) Ltd.: Appraisal of the factors which influence evolution of agricultural structures in the community and contribute to the efficiency of the common agricultural policy at the regional and farm level. Second Report to the EC Commission on Rural Change in Europe: Research programme on changing farm structures and household pluriactivity. A Summary. Oxford: Arkleton Trust 1991.

2. Bryden, J. M. and Fuller, A. M.: New technology and rural development. Report of the Arkleton Trust seminar, 1986. Oxford: Arkleton Trust 1987

3. CIDA (Canadian International Development Agency).: EMDI Brochure. Hull, Quebec: CIDA 1989

4. CIDA (Canadian International Development Agency).: Environmental Management Development in Indonesia project, Phase 3: Management plan. Hull, Quebec: CIDA 1989

5. CIDA (Canadian International Development Agency).: Environment and Resource Management Project: Memorandum of understanding and management plan. Hull, Quebec: CIDA 1989

6. Keen, P. : Telecommunications and organizational choice. Communication Research, 14, 5 (1987)

7. Misener, B. and McCreary, E. K.: The Rurtel network in Scotland: An electronic highway for rural development. Proc. of the Third Guelph Symposium on Computer Mediated Communication, pp. 325-337. Guelph, Ontario: University of Guelph 1990

8. Mulyadi, P.: Keynote address. Proc. of the Sulawesi Regional Development Project Mid-term Review Conference, pp. 3-8. Guelph, Ontario: Sulawesi Regional Development Project, University of Guelph 1988

9. Quarterman, J. S.: The Matrix: Computer networks and conferencing systems worldwide. Bedford, MA: Digital Press, 1990

6
Collaborative Learning in a Large Scale Computer Conferencing System

Jesus Rueda
IBM International Education Centre, La Hulpe, Belgium

Abstract: Computer conferencing systems have been used for the last ten years by educational institutions at all levels, sometimes as an informal medium, sometimes as complementary, sometimes even as the only mechanism for delivering education. However, few educational organisations have used conferencing intensively for activities such as information exchange, brainstorming, project coordination, problem solving, and decision making. These uses are, in general, far less structured than the ones normally found in formal education settings; however in most of these activities a form of individual as well as collective learning emerges in a natural form, in particular when there are a large number of participants in the conferencing system. This paper describes some of the learning processes that take place within TOOLS, a family of computer conferencing systems used within the world-wide IBM internal network, with particular reference to the largest of them, the IBMPC conferencing system.

Keywords: collaborative learning, computer conferencing, computer networks, IBM, TOOLS, project coordination, information exchange, brainstorming.

The Environment

The IBM internal network

There are several computer networks operated internally by IBM to fulfil its different business requirements. Probably the largest and best known one is the commonly named VNET [6]. VNET originated in the late 1970's as an instrument to facilitate cooperation between different IBM research and development laboratories around the world. After a timid infancy period, the network was recognized as a strategic resource for the corporation and has experienced rapid growth since the mid 1980's, with more than 4300 interconnected computers, in all the countries where IBM operates, and with virtually all of its employees connected to it.

The software that runs the networks (Remote Spooling Communications Subsystem [3]) uses a store-and-forward mechanism: every message going through the network joins a queue on each of the intermediary nodes, is reprioritised depending on the other messages waiting in that particular node, and when its turn arrives is transmitted to the next node in the network. Despite this process, careful capacity planning of the communication lines, combined with high reliability and continuing enhancement of the network topology, makes it possible for short messages, like the ones used in computer conferencing, to travel between any location in the world in a matter of seconds.

The main uses of the network are for electronic mail and file transfer, in which the users are helped by tools offering directory services as well as user friendly interfaces to send, receive, file and retrieve mail. As is normally the case in large networks, there is not a single user interface used across the network, but the majority of the users have the standard IBM Office System (PROFS), which has promoted a dramatic increase in the use of electronic mail amongst users.

The operating system used by many of the computers in the network is the Conversational Monitor System [2]. Each user in this environment has control of an electronic work place (called a 'virtual machine'), and communications and data manipulation take place through this work place. For historical reasons, the user's data file storage area is called a 'minidisk', the incoming electronic mail box is a 'virtual card reader' (or just 'reader'), and the outgoing mail slot is a 'virtual card punch' (or just 'punch'). Files that are in the process of being transmitted from one user's work place to another are sometimes referred to as 'punch files'. Some minidisks are available for access to all users on the same physical computer (or at the same location). The network utilizes a flat type of addressing, in which a user is simply defined by the identification of the 'node' (the computer) to which he is connected and the name of his 'virtual machine'.

The TOOLS conferencing systems

The TOOLS software was originally conceived and written by M. Cowlishaw in 1981 as a relatively simple file server system, to allow secure and controlled shared access to collections of software tools. When the IBM Personal Computer was announced, internal interest in the product became highly desirable. A modification of TOOLS with some limited conferencing features was created to perform this function.

Each TOOLS system runs in a single virtual machine. The virtual machine has one minidisk used for the system itself and then one minidisk for each of the TOOLS 'disks' maintained by the system. In these disks information is organized into files. Because TOOLS does not impose any restriction on the information contained in the files, nor modifies them, it can be used for a large number of applications such as sharing documentation, programmes, digitised images or audio data and conferences or anything else that the host computer can store and transmit. TOOLS systems communicate with their users, and with each other, by sending and receiving messages and files through the virtual card readers and card punches. Communication between virtual machines resident on different computers is accomplished through the VNET network described above.

When TOOLS began to be used for conferencing, features were added to allow more than one person to update the same file. It is now possible to specify to TOOLS that files of certain types will consist of a series of items, and that any user satisfying certain criteria should be allowed to add a new item to the file (an action usually called appending). These files therefore consist of a series of items, making up a discussion among a group of people on some topic. Such files are often known as 'forum' files. When TOOLS is used primarily for computer conferencing, most of the files on the system are of this sort.

Making a comparison with terminologies used in other systems, what in TOOLS terms is referred to as 'conference disk' or simply 'disk' in other systems is the whole conferencing system, and what in other systems is known as a conference in TOOLS is known as a 'forum'. With these equivalences in mind, it is clear that TOOLS disks can indeed contain many different fora (the plural of forum), in the same manner that a conferencing system holds many conferences.

The addressing scheme for a conference is as follows:
- the node of the network where the TOOLS machine resides
- the name of the virtual machine that runs the TOOLS program
- the disk
- the conference.

For example for the Conference on C Language the address is:
- *Node*: YKTVMA (one of the computers in the IBM Research Laboratory in Yorktown Heights, New York)
- *Machine*: TOOLS (the name of the virtual machine that runs the TOOLS program in this computer)
- *Disk*: IBMPC (the conferencing system devoted to PC & PS/2 topics)
- *File*: C-LANG FORUM (the name of the file containing the conference about the C Programming language).

The structure of a conference file is very simple, as it just contains pieces of plain text with a separator record between them. This separator record includes attributes indicating the node and virtual machine name of the contributor, as well as the time and date (in GMT format) when the item was received and the file it belongs to. The text is kept exactly as the author wrote it, there is no separation between the different threads or subjects of the conference, and the whole file can be browsed or printed with the standard system utilities. Contributions to a particular forum are made by sending a message to the TOOLS machine that controls the disk (the conferencing system) where the conference resides.

The process of reading conferences varies, depending whether the required conference disk, or a copy of it, called a 'shadow', exists in the user's computer or not. If a shadow exists, the user is allowed to read the disk and explore the conference files as if they were his own. If no shadow exists, the user sends a message to the closest TOOLS virtual machine in the network with a shadow of that disk, asking to become a subscriber to the relevant conference; from that moment on, he will receive all the additions to the conference and can keep a copy of it in his own minidisks. All the shadowing processes are automatically performed by the TOOLS machines. Normally master-slaves relations are stipulated between a conferencing disk and its shadows.

The basic TOOLS commands for conferencing are shown below:

SUMMARY	gives a summary of the files in the conference disk
GET	sends the user the whole, or part of, a conference file
SUBSCRIBE	sends the user any new contributions to a conference
APPEND	adds a contribution to a conference
MODIFY	modifies a previously entered contribution.

Given the distributed nature of the system (the disk and its shadows) and the different ways a user can access it (by local access or by subscription) there is no way of knowing who are the readers of a conference. Details of the operation of TOOLS and more general aspects of its use in for conferencing can by found in Chess and Cowlishaw. [1]

User interfaces

Before participating in a conference, the user has to go through these steps:
– identify the appropriate conference disk from the different ones in the network, by matching an updated list of conference disk themes with the topic of interest;
– browse through the disk files/conferences or through a summary of it if a shadow does not exist locally;
– decide which is the most appropriate conference;
– browse through it;
– contribute to it, or create a new conference if no suitable one is found.

As previously mentioned, the communications between the user and the TOOLS virtual machines is made via messages. This, together with the size of the network, the different preferences of people in different countries and functions, and different support policies of the different computing centres, open the possibility of multiple interfaces for each of the above steps.

An example of one of the user interfaces that allows users to browse through the topics of the different conferencing systems is shown in Figure 6.1, where the name of the conferencing disk and a short description is given. The fact that they are described as a conference does not imply that it is a single conference, as we will see later when describing the IBMPC disk, each of them can hold several (even several hundred) conferences related to the same general theme.

```
        Viewing all of OMNIDISK LIST    A1                    Item 86 of 305
   ====>
   Place cursor next to a disk name and press one of the PF keys:
   'Show' to show files on disk, 'Tools' to issue a TOOLS request.

   Name        Access    Description
   -------------------------------------------------------------------------
   IBMAIARC    Master    IBMA conference archive
   IBMAPL      Master    APL Conference
   IBMARC      Master    IBM Amateur Radio Conference
   IBMDRAW     Master    DrawMaster Program Product Conference
   IBMIN       Master    IBM Information Network Conference
   IBMLAN      Master    IBM Local Area Network Conference
   IBMMVS      Master    MVS Conference
   IBMMVSB     Master    IBMMVS conference archive
   IBMOSI      Master    Open System Interconnection Standards & Projects
   IBMOSIC     Master    Open Systems Interconnection (restricted access)
   IBMPC       Link      IBM Personal Computer Conf.
   IBMPCARC    Master    IBMPC conference archive


   1= Help        3= Quit     4= Show      5= Tools     6= Tools-M
   7= Backward    8= Forward  9= Profile   10= All Disks
```

Figure 6.1 Browsing through the different conferencing systems

```
      IBMPC: C-LANG FORUM----------------------------------------Summary Mode

   Viewing appends summary                                  Append 205 of 258
      Line  4011: Append at 21:04:40 on 91/09/30 by JKESS at YKTVMH
      -> retrieving the name of a function
      Line  4019: Append at 22:07:56 on 91/09/30 by RLEUCKIE at HOUVMSCC
      -> Calling a routine at run-time
      Line  4061: Append at 22:16:03 on 91/09/30 by JKESS at YKTVMH
      -> Calling a routine at run-time
      Line  4073: Append at 22:26:41 on 91/09/30 by JKESS at YKTVMH
      -> Calling a routine at run-time
      Line  4086: Append at 02:02:04 on 91/10/01 by XXBGV12 at SYDVM1
      -> Insufficient memory
      Line  4100: Append at 13:43:36 on 91/10/01 by PERRY at TOROLAB2
      -> retrieving the name of a function
      Line  4121: Append at 15:08:51 on 91/10/01 by PERRY at TOROLAB2
      -> retrieving the name of a function
      Line  4132: Append at 04:27:49 on 91/10/02 by EKMANB at RCKVM1
      -> PL/I to C Translator ?
      Line  4140: Append at 09:04:22 on 91/10/02 by DUFFEE at WINVMF
      -> non echoed on screen chars
      Line  4150: Append at 09:18:32 on 91/10/02 by 8MANLEY at ASICVM1

   1= Help        2= View      3= Exit      4= Xedit     5= Bottom    6= Retrieve
   7= Backward    8= Forward   9= Repeat    10= Top      11= View all 12= Cursor
   ====>
```

Figure 6.2 One of the user interfaces showing a summary of a FORUM

```
┌──────────────────────────────────────────────────────────────────────────┐
│ IBMPC: C-LANG  FORUM------------09:10----------------------Line  462  of  4975 │
│                                                                              │
│  -- C-LANG  FORUM   at 20:04:51 on 91/09/04 GMT  (by JKESS  at YKTVMH)        │
│                                                                              │
│ Subject: Sample code for DLL's                                               │
│ Ref:      Append at 19:09:27 on 91/09/04 GMT (by V$IDWANN at BETVTVM1)        │
│                                                                              │
│  Exactly the same as sample code for a .LIB. The trick is creating a  DEF file which includes the │
│  right options to tell the compiler what | to import and export as DLL entry points, and compiling │
│  with the right  options. If you have Microsoft C, the Advanced Programming Techniques book │
│  has this info; see the chapter on Dynamic Linking With OS/2. If  you have C/2, it has a similar │
│  section (Chapter 6, OS/2 Multi-Thread and Dynamic Link Library Support). If you're using │
│  another C  compiler, check its manual.                                      │
│                                                                              │
│ * * * End of File * * *                                                      │
│                                                                              │
│                                                                              │
│                                                                              │
│                                                                              │
│ 1= To Ref      2= From Ref  3= Exit      4= Prev app    5= Next app    6=     │
│ Append                                                                       │
│ 7= Backward   8= Forward   9= Header   10= Last app   11= WhosWho   12=      │
│ Resume                                                                       │
│ ====>                                                                        │
└──────────────────────────────────────────────────────────────────────────┘
```

Figure 6.3 One of the user interfaces showing a particular entry

The task of browsing within a particular conference might seem a difficult one, considering the simple structure of the forum files. However, the programmes used to contribute to the fora take into account the entry to which they are commenting by automatically copying the same subject line and including a reference line to it. User interface programmes exist that take advantage of these subject and reference lines, allowing the user to navigate in those files, search for a specific subject, and follow its thread forward and backward in a full screen environment. An example of one such interface is shown in Figure 6.2, which displays a summary of the different entries in a forum, with information about the subject, author and date of each of them. On a terminal display, the lines containing the subjects are highlighted in a different colour, increasing its readability.

When the user has decided which entry he wants to read, this can be displayed as shown in Figure 6.3, and functions are supplied for the user to follow the thread back and forth (with the *To Ref* and *From Ref* keys or to follow the whole forum just with the *Next App* and *Prev App* keys. It is also possible to get a short curriculum vitae of the author of the entry (*WhosWho* key) as well as to comment on the entry (*Append* key). While preparing the text to be added to a conference, spelling checkers, dictionaries, and thesauri are generally available in the computers.

Use of the System

The users

Today, the majority of IBM's 380,000 IBM employees world wide have access to electronic mail facilities through their local office systems and, using country directories, can find the electronic address of, and communicate with, any other

IBM staff member around the world. However, computer conferencing, despite the fact that it is widely available, is still much less known than electronic mail to the average network user. One reason for this is that electronic mail has been considered strategic for the corporation, and a single user interface has been heavily promoted and supported, while this has not been the case with conferencing. There are also other, more psychological, reasons that inhibit users from participating in conferencing activities:
– some conferences were initiated by technical groups and still are considered by many people as being useful only for that constituency;
– conferences are, normally, international and conducted in English; language ability and preconceived attitudes to other cultures sometimes act as inhibitors to participation;
– the public nature of the conferences, where everyone can see the contents, means that formulating a question or giving an answer can expose the author to the scrutiny of the whole organisation.

The main users of the conferencing systems are people with technical backgrounds working in research, development, customer support or system engineering functions. They participate in the conferences on a voluntary basis, very often on top of their individual workload. The great majority of users do not know each other, live in different cities or countries, and often belong to different cultures. However, as will be seen later, they develop strong links that enable them to support each other and engage in extra work, to supply solutions to other peoples' problems.

The work

To understand the needs and motivation of the participants in the conferences, it is necessary to understand the nature of the work that those people are performing. The computer industry today, particularly the mini and micro computer segments, is characterised by fast technological change; newly emerging areas of application; new generations of productivity tools and methodologies; increasingly complex products, often conceived by multidisciplinary and multiorganizational teams; and tougher market conditions. These market conditions require faster solutions to customer requirements, characterised by a large number of companies bringing products into the market place at an accelerated rate, accompanied by customers interested in getting the best solution to their problems, independently of who can supply it; this implies a trend towards mixed, multi-vendor environments.

The real problem is the management of a new and ever changing environment. Because of the mixing and inter-relation of products and the increasing pressure for total customer satisfaction, computer professionals are confronted, more and more frequently, with unique situations. Whereas ten years ago, uniformity dictated by a single supplier was the rule, today this situation is the exception, and multiple supplier environments, highly customized to specific customer needs, are the norm. In such environments, in-depth knowledge of the most important components of the system is not enough to provide the right solutions, as every case is different, and it is the performance of the total system that counts. No single person has all the answers, and therefore exploratory and team work skills are acquiring renewed importance. It is in this context that computer conferencing plays an important role, expanding the technical expertise and practical experience of the professionals far beyond geographical and departmental borders. Although in this chapter we are focusing on a particular network and on the particular subject area of Information Technology, it is important to realise that such a situation is not unique to this environment, and that, increasingly, we can find similar situations in other industrial sectors such as finance, insurance, chemicals, and transport.

Usage

At this moment, there are more than 280 different disks controlled by TOOLS machines in a network of over 4000 computers, accessible to the 380,000 potential users in IBM. Most of the disks are used as software and documentation repositories, but around 100 are used mainly for conferencing. In this sense we can say that there are more than 100 TOOLS-based conferencing systems in the network.

The largest of these is the IBMPC disk, which was started in 1981 as a mechanism for sharing information on the then just announced IBM PC computer; the majority of its conferences still deal with different aspects of the PC and PS/2 world, but due to its popularity, this disk also hosts other conferences on more general topics. The IBMPC disk hosts more than 1600 conferences, which receive more than 1500 entries in each working day. Each of these entries is copied to the more than 240 shadows of the IBMPC that exist in other computers around the world. Although it is not possible to know exactly the number of readers of its conferences, in 1987 they were estimated to be between 20,000 and 90,000 people.

There are no restrictions on the creation of conferences and the contribution of new material. Any user can create a conference or append new information to existing ones on any of the public systems. However, use of conferencing, as of any other corporate resource, is restricted to activities related to the company's business and is done with management approval. A banner indicating this is shown on every terminal before accessing any computer in the network. It is commonly accepted that information to be placed in the conferences should comply at least with one of the following criteria:

– it helps some employees do their jobs better;
– it improves job-related knowledge and/or skills;
– it can contribute to improvements of the company's products and processes.

This might explain why the socialising type of conferences that are so popular in some other conferencing systems do not exist here.

Although there is no significant formal use of conferencing for in-company training, it is important to realise that the second criterion for selection of material, together with the freedom to set up new conferences, creates a powerful tool for individuals to discover the skills gaps and knowledge needs that they have, and to take the initiative of opening discussions on them. This is reflected in the wide range of themes in the conferencing systems (e.g. Photographic Laboratory Techniques, Publishing, Artificial Intelligence, Image Processing, Personal Computers, etc). Within the IBMPC Disk the conferences can be grouped into the following categories:

– discussion of software products
– discussion of hardware products
– specification of new products
– individual programming languages

– applications of computers in sectors like avionics, meteorology, disabilities
– general topics (e.g. electronics, mathematical problems, reliability of magnetic materials, virtual reality, artificial intelligence, expert systems, electrical batteries, reviews of books and magazines, use of computer networks, industry news, etc.).

The Analysis

It is not clear how to set about looking for learning patterns within discussions that, in principle, do not have learning or teaching as a primary purpose. However it helps to recall some of the basic principles of adult learning [4,5] in particular the following:
– adults prefer to focus on current, real, problems rather than on abstract concepts, and are more problem-centred than subject-centred;
– adults clearly view learning as a benefit when they can find an immediate application to real world problems;
– adults learn best when they are involved, and when they can learn by doing;
– adults already have a vast reservoir of experience and knowledge that should be capitalised on.

We can try to identify some of the activities described by these principles within our conferences, and if we succeed in finding them, we might then assume that learning is taking place, even if the initial, formal, purpose of the discussion is not explicitly pedagogical. To carry out such an analysis over the 1600 conferences in the IBMPC disk is a huge task outside the scope of this chapter. For this analysis, five partial conferences (on general problems with the C programming language, virtual reality issues, mathematical problems, and discussions on keyboards and display screens) have been selected and analysed. The details are given in Table 6.1.

Table 6.1 Details of the analyzed Fora

	Period	Lines	Entries	Dialogues	Contributors
C-LANG	21/6/91-13/9/91	6400	333	73	118
VREALITY	15/8/91-13/9/91	4800	191	80	67
MATPROB	22/8/91-12/9/91	1973	89	28	43
KEYBOARD	28/8/91-13/9/91	5000	314	130	150
DISPLAYS	4/12/90-11/9/91	4549	322	124	165
Totals		22722	1249	435	

The introductory questions

Most of the discussions within a conference start with an entry containing a question. By analysing these questions, we can discover whether the discussion has been initiated merely out of curiosity, or whether the initiator is facing a real problem that he is trying to solve.
We can classify the questions as follows:
– questions asking for information, where it is difficult to know if the person formulating it is dealing with a real problem or is just interested in the subject (I)
– questions asking for information concerning a concrete problem (O)

– questions asking directly for help, where it is clear that the person who formulates them has a real problem that he is trying to solve (H)

– questions asking for improvements to an existing solution, which tell us that the person who formulates them not only is dealing with a real problem, but he already has a solution which he is trying to optimise (X).

– questions which are conscious expressions of the person engaged in a problem and his attempts to solve it (S).

An analysis of the 200 or so different dialogues in the fragments of the C-LANG and DISPLAYS conferences under examination, lead to the following summary of question types:

– **Type I**: 12 categories (How do I do it? What is it? Does it exist? Is there...? What do I need? What is the difference between...? Can I do that? What should I do? Is it possible to do ...? and, if so, how? What would happen if ? Anyone have any cute ideas? Does anyone have ...? Would someone be nice enough to provide that information here?)

– **Type H**: 3 categories (Can anyone help me? Can someone help me with this one? I would very much appreciate some help, suggestions, guidance with this dilemma)

– **Type S**: 6 categories (Is there something about ... that I do not know? Is there something that I am not doing? Am I doing it correctly? What am I doing wrong? What am I missing ? Am I on the right track with this?)

– **Type O**: 8 categories (Has this been tried? Has anyone any experience in this area? Has someone just developed something like this? Has anyone been in that situation before? Is this normal? Any ideas why this happens? What currently exists to do this? What is the best approach to this problem?)

– **Type X**: 3 categories (Is there a better way? Is there any way to do this easily? Is this a reasonable way to approach it?).

This analysis shows that 62% of the question types (20 out of 32) express, in an implicit or explicit manner, that the person is dealing with a real problem. What is not clear from this analysis is whether the questions are answered at all in the fora, or left in the air without any reply. However, the fact that the IBMPC conferencing system has been in existence for ten years now implies that the participants are getting some replies, so let us try to quantify them. Table 6.2 shows the results of an analysis undertaken of five fora, showing the percentage of dialogues with replies. The figures are not an absolute measurement of the replies that the people formulating questions obtain, since they can also receive a personal reply by e-mail instead of through the conference. However, we can try to identify some trends, bearing in mind that the sample is very small compared with the total number of conferences, and that a much larger analysis is necessary to get definitive conclusions. With these reservations, the data indicates that there is a large dispersion in the range of the results, but, on average, more than half of the questions get replies. Furthermore, the rate of responses increases with the concreteness of the subject and with its relevance to the immediate work of the participants (VREALITY, the conference with the lowest rate of responses, is of little relevance to the current work of most of the participants).

The correlation with the first three principles of Adult Learning mentioned above is clear. There is evidence that most of the questions presented in the conferences refer to real problems that users are actually dealing with at the moment of submitting the question and most of them get a reply.

Table 6.2 Replies to questions in the analyzed fora

Fora	Dialogues	Number with replies	Percentage with replies
C-LANG	73	52	71%
VREALITY	80	30	37%
MATPROB	28	16	57%
KEYBOARD	130	68	52%
DISPLAYS	124	69	55%
Totals	435	243	55%

Patterns of user behaviour

To illustrate some of the trends in user patterns, a conversation that took place over four days in September 1991 on the C-LANG FORUM has been analysed and summarised below:

(1) 21:11, Sept 9th John from Lexington, Kentucky, asks what would be an elegant method of branching in C language over the value of a character string. In fact, a simple problem that most of the beginners will not doubt can be solved using a sequence of "if" statements.

(2) 00:06, Sept 10th Mark from Austin, Texas, gives a solution based on converting the character strings to numbers using certain functions of the language. He recognizes that this solution is compiler dependent.

(3) 00:19, Sept 10th Mark also asks if some of the functional that can be used in his solution had any chance of becoming standards in the C language.

(4) 00:41, Sept 10th Dave from Toronto, Canada replies to the question formulated by Mark.

(5) 09:40, Sept 10th Mathew from Warwick, UK, gives a solution to the problem presented by John based on a "table look-up" algorithm.

(6) 13:14, Sept 10th John, the originator of the dialogue seems satisfied with the the proposed solutions; he plans to use Mark's solution and thanks the group for it.

(7) 14:01, Sept 10th David from Toronto, Canada, points out that Mark's solution will not work for long strings.

(8) 4:45, Sept 10th Ian from Boulder, Colorado, gives another solution to the original problem.

(9) 15:04, Sept 10th Russ from Toronto, Canada, comes up with another solution to the problem based on the use of the "strstr" function.

(10) 16:13, Sept 10th Andrew from Burlington, Vermont spots a mistake in Russ's solution.

(11) 16:54, Sept 10th Peter from San Jose, California, suggests that a possible solution could be based in a "perfect hashing" algorithm, although he does not know how to code it.

(12) 17:06, Sept 10th Russ alters his solution with the input from Andrew.

(13) 17:25, Sept 10th Gary from Winchester, UK, criticizes Mark's solution because it is not portable and suggests an elegant solution based on use of the "if" statement.

(14) 18:00, Sept 10th Tony from Yorktown Heights, New York, brings yet another solution to the problem based in "parallel index and enumeration tables".

(15) 18:53, Sept 10th Frank from Raleigh, North Carolina, detects another problem with Russ's solution...

(16) 11:45, Sept 11th ...that Gary rapidly fixes although it was not his solution.

(17) 17:59, Sept 11th Derek from Endicott, New York, also dismisses Mark's solution because it is "not portable and confusing". He favors solutions based on "well known" algorithms such as "linear search and perfect hashing".

(18) 18:24, Sept 11th Andrew again finds mistakes in Russ's revised solution.

(19) 19:38, Sept 11th Mark reacts over Derek's comment on the ground that the other solutions are too theoretical and that few people are aware of those algorithms. He ask for theoretical background.

(20) 12:45, Sept 12th Bob from Toronto, Canada, gives a further solution to the problem based on individually analysing each character of the string.

(21) 13:31, Sept 12th Liu from Raleigh, North Carolina, suggests new developments based on the "Finite State Machines" theory.

(22) 13:51, Sept 12th Andy from Rochester, Minnesota, objects to Derek's comment because "perfect hashing" is not portable either.

(23) 13:56, Sept 12th Nicolas from Gatherisburg, Maryland, elaborates on the Liu suggestion and suggests a code already available to implement it.

(24) 14:52, Sept 12th Patrick from Yorktown Heights, New York, asks Liu for some clarification of his comments.

(25) 15:32, Sept 12th Derek goes to the library and comes back armed with more theoretical ammunition to defend his position.

(26) 16:07, Sept 12th Liu now offers not a suggestion, but a complete new solution to the original problem based on "Finite State Machines".

(27) 16:13, Sept 12th Liu responds to Patrick's criticisms.

(28) 16:26, Sept 12th Andy is not convinced by Derek's library research and he reiterates his criticisms.

29) 16:42, Sept 12th Lars from Raleigh, North Carolina, suggests an improvement to Liu's solution.

(30) 19:07, Sept 12th Tony tries to mediate in the discussion between Derek and Andy indicating that the solutions under discussion will work in most of the cases.

(31) 20:58, Sept 12th Finally Derek recognized that Andy's criticisms can be valid...

(32) 21:53, Sept 12th ...but Andy is in a very critical mood and even criticizes Tony's mediation.

33) 22:10, Sept 12th Finally Andy favours Liu's solution.

(34) 22:28, Sept 12th Tony supports the last comment from Derek...

(35) 13:01, Sept 13th ...and Patrick refers to a good bibliography, which seems to close the discussion.

This particular dialogue motivated 19 people from 13 different places to write 35 entries supplying 9 distinct solutions which required background knowledge ranging from simple C programming skills to the third year of a university Computing or Mathematics degree course. From the conference discussion, there is no doubt that the fourth principle of adult learning listed above (the application of personal knowledge and experience) is manifest. To better visualise the relations between the entries in the discussion, Figure 6.4. shows a graphic representation, with the time along the horizontal axis, and indicating each of the entries with a character related to its semantic nature. Except for the Q and S types of contributions, all the others have an arc associating them with the prior contribution to which they refer. Such an analysis leads us to make the following observations, which can be said to be typical of many conference discussions.

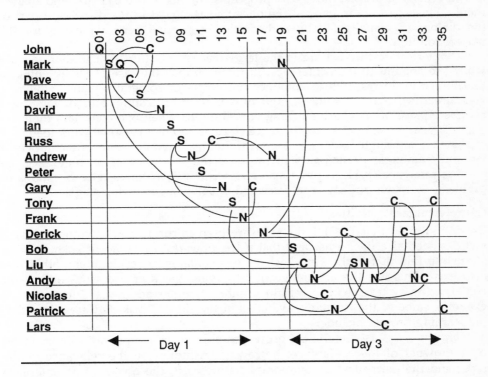

Figure 6.4 Message map for the C-LANG Forum

Key S : a solution (ones without an arc refer to the initial question)   Q : a question
       C : a positive, encouraging or constructive comment   N : a critical comment

Clearly, there was a very fast response to the initial question, with seven solutions being supplied in the first 24 hours. The Forum owner kept a relatively low profile (in this case it was Dave, who only made a positive contribution at the beginning of the debate). Interestingly, the role of the dialogue initiator is often very marginal. He is just the trigger that activates the minds and willingness of colleagues around the world, not merely to solve his problem, but to dig deep into implications and potential solutions. In this example , if the only motivation had been to provide a solution to the initiator's problem, the whole debate would have finished after entry (6), where the originator declares himself satisfied.

There were two distinct parts to the debate – a creative part, and a discussion part. The creative part, which occurred over the first day in the example above, is characterised by a succession of solutions to the initial problem, provided by quite a number of people, with little or no criticism of them. Because, as a rule, different people supply different solutions, this part appears in Figure 6.4 as a 'downhill' trend. The second, discussion part, of the debate often occurs towards the end. In general it has fewer participants and either they argue amongst themselves, as in this example, or they speculate on more theoretical approaches to the problem. In the graphic representation, this second part appears more or less as a horizontal trend. The two parts of the debate seem to reflect the existence of two groups of people: those who propose solutions, and the critics who analyse them. The second are in general the ones that take part in the discussion part of the dialogue, normally led by a theoretically minded person looking for the perfect solution.

Another interesting feature is the large amount of effort that individuals are willing to commit to the conference. In this example, the case of Derek going to the library to do research to convince the others of something about which he was already convinced himself, and of Liu writing, testing, and debugging a complete piece of code, are amazing contributions when one considers them for what they are – voluntarily accepted activities on top of a personal work load.

Finally, although it does not appear in this example, one often notices a tendency amongst participants to improve the efficiency of a conference, by making references back to previous entries when newcomers raise questions or problems that have already been discussed or solved at an earlier stage.

Complementary activities

Bearing in mind that TOOLS, the software used to run these conferences, was in fact designed as a file server, and that it has powerful functions as such, it is not strange to find that in the same disks where conferences reside, many other files also exist. This has the advantage of supplying the user accessing one of the conferencing systems with a certain number of other additional functions. For example, some of the functions available in the IBMPC disk that are relevant to the learning process include:

Fora archiving: as conferences grow, the old entries are periodically removed by the owner of the conference; however, depending on the relevance of the topic and the permanent or temporary nature of it, the owner of a conference might decide to archive old entries, so that they can be retrieved in the future if needed. An example is the C-LANG FORUM for which archive files exist dating back to July 1984. Although the archived fora are no longer distributed to all the 'shadows', any user can request and get a copy of them.

Fora indexing: as a complement to the archiving process, some of the archived fora are indexed. Files exist indicating which are the subjects that have been discussed within each of the archived files of that particular forum.

Subroutine libraries: some conferences in the IBMPC disk are devoted to storing small subroutines that solve very specific problems. In these conferences every entry is a piece of well documented code. Given that software development is an almost natural activity in IBM, these conferences hold valuable knowledge for a great number of readers. Additionally, the owner of the conferences also creates indexes for them, which makes it far easier to find the subroutine needed in solving a particular concrete problem. In a way, this resource can be compared to the collection of problems with solutions widely used in certain technical training manuals (e.g. the Schaum series).

Q & A programmes: recently, a special format of conference has been created and is starting to be used. These are the ANSWERS conferences, where each entry has the format of a question and its reply. This, together with a simple user interface that shows an index of the questions, is enough to allow some forum owners to create conferences that are summaries of their experiences in the general conferences and that take the form of 'The most common questions on subject X'.

General documents: descriptions of products, evaluation reports, articles related to the general topic of the conferences are just other types of files that exist within each of the conferencing systems.

Conclusion

A system of the size and characteristics of the one described in this chapter has many different aspects, and obviously calls for a much more detailed and exhaustive study in order to obtain more precise conclusions. However, a certain number of important conclusions can be drawn from the present analysis.

Firstly, despite the fact that there are no formal training or learning activities organized in the system, patterns that are characteristic of adult learning are clearly recognisable within it. If we look at these as part of a learning process, then this process can be considered highly productive, since it is totally initiated by the learner when he has a real problem to solve – in other terms, when he has the motivation to learn and the possibility to put immediately into practice whatever he learns. It is also a learning process on a very large scale, considering the potential number of readers of any given conference.

Secondly, the aspect of timeliness – getting the training when it is needed – is highly supported by the fact that the questions posed get replies in a very short period of time (normally less than 12 hours), which is a direct consequence of the large numbers of readers and potential participants using the system.

Finally, our analysis shows that, in a network of this size, there are skilled individuals ready to commit considerable amount of extra effort to help and share experiences with colleagues around the world. In other words, the system encourages, and the participants are already creating, mechanisms for a sort of collective memory than can be the basis for a form of true organisational knowledge.

References

1. Chess D. and Cowlishaw M.: A large scale computer conferencing system. IBM Systems Journal, 26, 1. pp. 138-156 (1987)

2. IBM: VM/ESA CMS User's Guide: IBM order # SC24-5460 1990

3. IBM: VM RSCS Networking V.2, R.1 Library: IBM order # SBOF-3226 1991

4. IBM Education Europe: A systems approach to education, A compendium. Denmark: IBM order # GR19-5074 1991

5. Knowles, M.S.: The adult learner: a neglected species. Houston,Tx: Gulf Publishing 1984

6. Quaterman J. and Haskins J.: Notable computer networks. Communications of The ACM, 29, 10 (1986)

PART II

Ways of Understanding Online Collaboration

The five papers in this part of the book present a variety of perspectives on the analysis and evaluation of the nature of collaborative activities in the online environment, ranging from detailed content analysis of conference messages, at one extreme, to the examination of the social and organisational implications of providing people with access to computer networking facilities at the other extreme.

To some extent, any given research methodology will only reveal information and understandings of a particular kind about the processes and interactions taking place in a specific situation. It is important to ensure that the methodologies used in our research do not mask important aspects of what is happening in the CMC environment. For example, message maps can reveal the existence of extensive and complex webs of interactivity through the plotting of comment links amongst conference messages, but have only a limited significance without information about the content of the messages and the perceptions and intentions of the users at the time they emitted the messages. User statistics on connect times are meaningless, other than for accounting purposes, without information on individual differences in preferences for off-line and online working. Controlled experiments under laboratory conditions comparing, say, completion of a group task under different forms of mediation, provide useful micro-level analyses, but the conditions prevalent in real-life applications are so different from the laboratory situation that it is often difficult to draw meaningful comparisons – the very notion of a 'group' may even need redefining in the context of a large distributed networked organisation or community.

The first chapter in this Part, by Robin Mason, reviews evaluation methodologies that have been applied to computer conferencing interactions, and analyses the strengths and weaknesses of particular evaluation strategies for trying to gain an understanding of the nature of online collaboration in computer conferences. She makes a case for putting more focus on content analysis of the transcripts of conferences, in an attempt to pin down the indicators of truly collaborative interactions – such as messages which, instead of merely exchanging information, build one on another and add new meanings to a discussion (e.g. the message sequences analysed by McConnell, and by Rueda, in Part I of this book).

In the next chapter, France Henri develops some specific proposals for content analysis techniques, which could provide tools to help educators and learners benefit from the richness and efficiency of CMC exchanges, through identification of indicators of higher-level cognitive and meta-cognitive skills in message exchanges. This level of analysis is perhaps the most fruitful direction for progressing beyond simplistic indicators of 'interactivity' (such as numbers of comments or commenters per message) towards measures of *collaborative* interactivity which might indicate that individual learning is happening as a result of message exchanges.

The chapter by Michael Waggoner argues the advantages of a case study approach to evaluation of the complexity of interactions within the educational CMC environment, integrating both quantitative and qualitative methods. He reviews the main elements in the collaborative learning process, and relates these to the system characteristics of computer-mediated communication, and to individual and group characteristics.

Sara Kiesler's paper moves the analysis to the organisational and social level, through a review of research findings from the social sciences relevant to the potential impact of computer networking on traditional educational structures, hierarchies, and organisations. For example, the growth of access to networking facilities could create – indeed already is creating – new market places for education which could, in some circumstances, provide more flexible and cost-effective provision than can, say, local schools or colleges – but these new opportunities may well lead to the creation of new problems, particularly in the re-definition of the roles of teachers and of educational providers. Kiesler also stresses the need to re-examine conventional concepts of the 'group' and of 'collaboration' in the light of the diversity, fluidity, and scale of networked communities, whether they are operating in educational or corporate settings.

The final paper, by John Gundry, tries to identify the nature of networked collaboration, and collaborative learning, in the corporate context, and to indicate how experience gained from the long-standing practice of networking in an organisation such as Digital might help the educational world to develop 'collaborative cultures'. In particular, he emphasises the values which seem to underlie the successful use of CMC in the organisational context; these include mutual support, openness of communications, informality, authority based on knowledge rather than position, personal responsibility, and self-judgement.

7
Evaluation Methodologies for Computer Conferencing Applications

Robin Mason

Institute of Educational Technology, The Open University, United Kingdom

Abstract: This chapter is a review of evaluation methodologies for computer conferencing applications. It focuses on major practitioners: the work of Roxanne Hiltz, the Ontario Institute for Studies in Education, the Institute for the Future, the Open University, and the University of Stockholm. The advantages and disadvantages of a wide range of evaluation strategies – survey questionnaires, laboratory experiments, case studies and user interviews – are discussed as they apply to conferencing applications, and particularly to collaborative uses of computer conferencing. The chapter makes a case for evaluators to focus on content analysis of conference messages as the key methodology for establishing the educational value of this medium.

Keywords: evaluation methodologies, conference interactions, survey questionnaires, user interviews, laboratory experiments, case studies, user statistics, content analysis, participant journals, educational value of conferencing.

Current Trends in Educational Evaluation

The use of computer conferencing in educational applications has grown in the last few years to such an extent that there is a real need to devise evaluation methodologies to assess the value of this new teaching medium. The purpose of this chapter is, therefore, to examine existing approaches to evaluation, draw out the relevant strategies and propose techniques unique to the nature of computer conferencing.

The field of educational evaluation has developed very rapidly over the same period that computer conferencing has been used in educational settings. The 'state of the art' of educational evaluation has recently been described as:

> ... a multidimensional, pluralistic, situational, and political activity that encompasses much more than simple application of the skills of the empirical scientist. [29, p. 5]

Three alternative paradigms could be said to have emerged from the evaluation debates of the last 20 years:

Postpositivism: an experimental, quantitative core buttressed by critique from varied analysis, theoretical perspectives, and value frameworks, combining the use of survey and observational data, with regression and cluster analyses.

Interpretivism: based on the social constructions of meaning being inherently time and place dependent; therefore, relies heavily on qualitative methods, especially interviews and observations, and acknowledges and legitimates the value-laden nature of inquiry.

Critical Theory: seeks to illuminate the historical, structural and value bases of social phenomena and to catalyse political and social change – not through particular methods, but through awareness of one's situationally-located standpoint.[1]

Although there are examples of Critical Theory applied to computer conferencing [3], the most extensive evaluations of conferencing applications are either broadly Postpositive [9, 12] or Interpretive [4,17].

Focus of Conferencing Evaluation

There are many motivations for conducting an evaluation: it may be a required component of the funding source; it may be an institutional request; it may be the interest and enthusiasm of the proponents and participants. The focus of the evaluation will inevitably reflect the primary motivation – to show levels and spread of use, or to assess value of investment and user acceptance, or to analyse the quality of learning and nature of educational interactions. All of these are aspects of the success of the application, but some are much more difficult, time consuming and expensive to evaluate.

The published literature on educational computer conferencing consists, to a very large extent, of application-oriented descriptions. The work of Hiltz [9] is a notable exception, but her studies are primarily oriented to determine the exchangeability of the outcomes of students using computer conferencing with those obtained in the traditional classroom. Very few researchers tackle the difficulties of analysing the educational quality of conference interactions. The

---

[1] I am indebted to the authors of *Evolution of Evaluation Methodolgy* [5] for this analysis of the current trends in educational evaluation.

reasons for this are not hard to find: there are no tried and tested methodologies for assessing educational value, and, despite the growing acceptance of qualitative approaches to research, there is still strong pressure to measure in some way the elements of 'success' or 'learning' or even 'educational exchange'. The taint of subjectivity is so threatening, that most computer conferencing research stops with quantitative analyses of messages sent and by whom, number and time of logons, and message maps showing the number of replies and message chains. The consequence is that those aspects most susceptible to evaluation are often taken to define the whole. Presenting technical, statistical data of an application is not an 'innocent' act justified by lack of funding, time or skill to carry out a full evaluation – slowly but surely, the statistical data (quantity of messages, the number of logons, and the extent of participation) comes to signify the value of the educational transaction. Conclusions as to the revolutionary potential of computer conferencing are often drawn with scarcely a mention of the actual content, much less the value of the interactions.

Most conferencing systems provide automated user statistics, or else these can be compiled by systems operators relatively inexpensively. This data normally includes number and time of logons, number and length of messages sent per user, and activity traces so that student and tutor use can be monitored during the course. This data can easily be manipulated in spread sheets to produce diverse statistical results: the relation of student to tutor messages, the identity of key messages which received the most comments and sparked off the most chains of interactions, and the pattern of logons by day over the period of the evaluation. This information gives a useful framework for any evaluation, but as the only data for an evaluation, it is not only inadequate, but actually misleading. As Critical Theory has established, the methodological choices evaluators make are never value-free.

Evaluation Techniques

Many of the standard evaluation techniques have been applied to conferencing applications – survey questionnaires, interviews, empirical experimentation, participant observation and case study methodology. A number of in-depth evaluation studies have been carried out, by the Institute for the Future and by the New Jersey Institute of Technology in the USA, the Ontario Institute for Studies in Education in Canada, Stockholm University in Sweden and the Open University in Britain. These studies will form the basis for the following analysis, but other published work will be referred to as well.

Survey questionnaires

Although many evaluators have surveyed their conference users, three major studies have been carried out using extensive and innovative survey techniques. The most notable is that carried out by Roxanne Hiltz at the New Jersey Institute of Technology, primarily on the EIES system.

> Pre- and post-course questionnaires completed by students are the most important data source. The pre-course questionnaire measures student characteristics and expectations. The post-course questionnaire focuses on detailed evaluations of the effectiveness of the online course or course segments, and on student perceptions of the ways in which the Virtual Classroom is better or worse than the Traditional Classroom. [9, p. 77]

Using questionnaires, Hiltz studied both the technological determinants affecting use as well as the social-psychological characteristics of the users and the human interactions which might determine success. One of the most striking outcomes of this approach was the discovery that the single significant predictor of subsequent use of the conferencing system was the prospective users' estimate of the amount of time they would spend online. Age, typing ability, attitude to and previous use of computers all had no significant effect on subsequent usage. Hiltz's extensive surveying of many users across a number of systems involved with a variety of conferencing applications has provided valuable data for all evaluators in the field.

The Open University (OU) in Britain has been using computer conferencing since 1988 on a large population course in Information Technology. Each year over 800 students fill in and upload a questionnaire consisting of 60 questions about their background, attitude to conferencing and use of the system. This extensive database of information, showing changes over time with successive cohorts of students, can be interrogated by gender, by educational background, by location throughout Britain, and attitudes to use can be compared with actual use. In fact, a number of questions from Hiltz's pre-use questionnaire were used in the OU example in order to test whether her results would replicate amongst British OU students. Using the 1988 survey, it was discovered that OU students expected computer conferencing to be much more difficult to learn and impersonal to use than Hiltz's students reported, yet a more productive use of their time [17]. The survey questionnaire technique, when used with large numbers, over time, or in a variety of settings, can be a very powerful tool for exploring aspects of computer conferencing applications. The possibility of replicating and refining results from one study to another, especially by using the same questions, is another significant advantage of this methodology.

The COM system, developed by the Swedish National Defence Research Institute, has also been extensively evaluated by questionnaire. In addition to addressing many of Hiltz's concerns about user acceptance, satisfaction and system attributes, Adrianson [1] and Adrianson and Hjelmquist [2] have studied the usefulness of work-related conferences by people in the Swedish National Defence Research Institute and in other commercial, governmental and academic settings. They were interested in discovering whether, and in what way, the work-related and general discussion conferences were considered useful or not.

The results were quite clear. For both types of conferences the possibilities of obtaining information and getting opinions were considered to be the top priority. Equally important are the reasons for usefulness which were mentioned infrequently. Again, the pattern was very similar for both types of conferences, viz. 'decision support', 'take decisions', 'increased co-determination' and 'documentation' were all mentioned infrequently. These results are important in relation to previous discussions about COM as a possible means of equalization and co-determination. It is still possible that COM could be useful for these, but they are not mentioned as the most salient assets of the conferences. [2]

This is another example of the kind of result obtainable by survey questionnaire, which perhaps could not be so easily determined by other means.

The disadvantages of surveys are well known: the wording of the questions is critical, the accuracy is dependent on respondents' subjective impressions and memory of events, and the pre-formatted answers or number scales are confining and annoying to many respondents.

As a method for evaluating group processes online, the survey is less than ideal. Group interactions are complex, whether electronic or face-to-face; they thus make poor subjects for pre-structured answers. A variation of the survey questionnaire more appropriate for evaluating collaborative interactions is the open-ended questionnaire. Typically this consists of a number of issues on which the participant is invited to comment (for example, "How would you compare your online collaborative experience with working in face-to-face groups?"). Although this method allows participants much more scope to convey their attitudes and experience, it does not allow the evaluator to question and clarify their comments. The data is also less appropriate for simple quantitative analysis. A half-way house – combining a mix of open-ended and pre-structured questions – is a method often used on survey questionnaires generally.

User interviews

Although many studies and evaluations of conferencing applications use some form of direct contact with users – either by telephone, by computer or face-to-face – the most extensive analysis of interview data is that by Burge for her doctoral dissertation at the Ontario Institute for Studies in Education (OISE). With 56 hours of face-to-face interviewing covering around 60 questions relating primarily to the nature of online learning, this work makes a significant contribution to the understanding of conferencing as a pedagogical tool, as well as exploiting the potential of this methodology.

Burge set out to examine many of the unsubstantiated claims made by conferencing enthusiasts in the literature:

> When I looked into the CMC-in-higher-education literature, it became obvious that the writing shows the somewhat isolationist but enthusiastic attitudes and assumptions of the technologically enlightened who believe that CMC is equivalent in impact to the Gutenberg printing press. I became tired of reading some of the early literature on CMC in education that assumed, for example, system-wide advantages of CMC without much evidence or knowledge of the learner's actual behaviour. [4]

By extensive questioning of adult learners studying an online course, she investigated a number of typical claims made about educational computer conferencing: the benefits of simultaneous discussions, the focus on the message rather than the writer, the value of the recorded transcript of discussions, and the asynchronous nature of participation. This data and her analysis of it makes an obvious contribution to the field.

The importance of this methodology lies in its grass-roots nature – asking those who live the experience to report their reactions. The contact with real users is invariably satisfying to evaluators, and the results of the study are often surprising. Nevertheless, carrying out face-to-face interviews is a very time-consuming process and the subsequent analysis of the transcripts requires even more care and attention. This leads to the inevitable disadvantage of interviewing: the resource implications of interviewing a wide enough sample to be able to make significant generalisations.

An interesting variation of the personal interview is the 'group interview'. A new study of the impact of high-speed networks on scientific communication and research, sponsored by the US Congress, Office of Technology Assessment, used this technique of 'focus groups':

Focus groups are group discussions that center on topics of particular concern to both the participants in the group and the researcher. The researcher typically takes the role of moderator, and participants discuss a particular topic among themselves. Focus groups are currently used most often to conduct market research, although the technique has its origins in sociology. [16]

The advantages of group interviewing are that the participants interact amongst themselves rather than with the interviewer, thus leading to a more open, spontaneous, participant-led discussion. It may also be less time consuming, easier to conduct and less costly than single, face-to-face interviewing. In terms of collaborative learning, its use is even more appropriate. If students of an online course, or members of an online business team or research team, who are accustomed to electronic group working, meet in a physical location, a group interview would provide very valuable data to use in triangulation with conference transcripts and individual questionnaires.

Empirical experimentation

The work of Kiesler and her associates at Carnegie-Mellon University is the most prominent use of empirical approaches from social psychology applied to computer-mediated interactions. In a number of controlled experiments conducted in laboratory conditions, Kiesler explored the impact of computer communication on group decision processes, for example, the ability to reach consensus on a choice-dilemma problem. One of the main findings from the studies was that groups show significantly higher choice shift and uninhibited behaviour in computer communication than in face-to-face settings [12]. The tentative explanations given for these results involved the lack of social cues, the break-down of normal social restraint, the difficulties of coordination online, the depersonalised atmosphere and the etiquette associated with the computing subculture.

Lea and Spears have continued and refined these studies using the same methodological approach.

In our design we manipulate what we see as two critically important social psychological variables independently of each other, namely whether the group or individual identity of participants is made salient, and whether participants are de-individuated by virtue of being isolated and anonymous as opposed to being co-present. [14, p. 289]

The findings of this research lead to the conclusion that the role of social contextual factors and normative processes in computer-mediated interactions is greater, not less than, that in face-to-face interactions.

The advantages of controlled, laboratory evaluations of computer-mediated behaviour are that particular issues or controversies can be investigated very directly. All the variables and contextualisation of other methods can be controlled, and results can be replicated and refined. Because of this ability to focus and control the environment, empirical experimentation is particularly appropriate for investigating group working online. However, the disadvantages of the method lie in the limitations imposed by laboratory conditions, both for the participants, and also for the type of issues and situations which are susceptible to study in this way. Researchers at the Institute for the Future commented further on the use of laboratory experiments in this field:

In the case of communications research, the problems of control have been magnified. In even the most 'simple' instances of interpersonal communication, multiple complexities are always present. A researcher must attempt to isolate the effects of a communications medium from the interrelated effects of such things as group dynamics, personal attitudes, and topical content of the communication. In a situation such as this, there is the constant danger of simplifying the 'real world' to meet the limitations of the laboratory. [28]

Vallée describes his group's work at the Institute as 'field experimentation with limited controls'. One aspect of this work was the generation and classification of hypotheses or statements about conferencing, and subsequently the use of purposive and open-ended tests to examine them. Now nearly twenty years later, it is apparent that this pioneering work of the Institute led to the identification of the major elements in group communication through computer conferencing, as well as the initial use of almost all the evaluation techniques still being applied to conferencing applications. The Institute's work, stretching over five volumes [26, 27, 28] merits much greater use by evaluators than it generally receives.

Another problem occurs in applying experimental methodologies to educational settings – randomly assigning students to matched courses is neither ethical nor possible in many instances. Consequently, a number of conferencing evaluations involve quasi-experimental conditions.

At the University of Jyvaskyla in Finland, quasi-experiments are taking place to find ways in which conferencing can increase the awareness among students and teachers in a campus university setting of their membership in an academic community. In one experiment, four groups of eight students were formed: tutor-led, student-led, seminar-based, and conference-based. Results from this study have led to further experiments in the design of online communities to support academic argumentation and to improve term paper writing [13].

A similar kind of study was conducted at the University of California, San Diego, by Quinn *et al*, this time to compare the instructional interaction among students using an electronic message system with those in a conventional class discussion [23]. The analysis of the results showed that students' responses in the electronic situation were on average, longer and more complex than in the face-to-face class. Furthermore, the structure of electronic discussion differed from the typical 'Initiation, Response, Evaluation' pattern of classroom interactions, in that there were multiple student responses but less evaluation by the teacher.

Quasi-experiments of this kind are commonplace in educational evaluation generally. They often provide very 'usable' results with obvious applications. However, they rarely indicate *why* results have happened, and the real complexities of educational issues are not addressed.

Case study methodology

It is primarily the aim of case study methodology to seek a more holistic view of educational outcomes.

Case study research, and in particular the qualitative case study, is an ideal design for understanding and interpreting observations of educational phenomena. [20, p.2]

Case study methodology, though it often uses survey questionnaires and interviews, has unique characteristics: it is unashamedly particularistic and descriptive, concentrating on a specific case or cases and aiming to present the experience of the individual's world. Unlike empirical experimentation, it is inductive, allowing hypotheses, concepts and generalisations to emerge from the study.

One major case study in the field of computer conferencing has been carried out by Mason at the Open University [17]. Participant observation was a significant tool used to collect data on students, tutors and course designers.

> While interviewing gives a secondhand account of actual experience, observing as a participant gives firsthand experience of the event being studied. In terms of this study, participant observation took a variety of forms: students were observed over-the-shoulder as they attempted various procedures on CoSy, and tutorial and self-help group meetings were attended. In addition, full participation in course team meetings and in the preparation of course materials was an integral part of the research methodology. [17, p. 94]

The advantages of this method are that it is possible to give a rich and wide-ranging picture of a conferencing application, providing multiple points of view and to develop standards and theory which can be tested by other methods and applications. The disadvantages are that the results, which are rich in process, cannot easily by generalised to other instances and contexts. It is often difficult to isolate the most important factors amongst such a wealth of detail.

Computer-generated statistical manipulations

The methodology most often employed by evaluators of online activities is that which is unique to the medium – computer-generated statistics about logons, messages sent and read, levels of participation, and number and length of entries in conferences.

Levin, in conjunction with a number of other colleagues, has carried out the most extensive work in this field. Inter-message reference analysis is a technique for tracing the multiple threads in an online discussion. Each message is coded according to whether it refers explicitly or implicitly to another message. By representing the information graphically, a message map can be drawn, showing the extent to which the conference contains multiple threads of interwoven discussion [15]. Levin sees the benefit of this technique as an initial approach to a full content analysis.

Harasim, while at OISE, used computer-generated statistics to plot the percentage of messages by hours in the day and by days of the week, thereby showing the extent to which access is time-independent. She has also prepared boxplots showing usage by participant over each segment of the course. These have shown that students participate regularly and that the distribution of communication among members of her course was relatively equal [7].

This kind of analysis has the advantage of the data being 'self-transcribed'. It can be collected without intrusion of any sort, and is relatively accurate and reliable. The danger of it, as alluded to above, is that student *activity* may be mistaken for student *learning*. Applied to cooperative work online, group *interaction* could be mistaken for group *collaboration*.

A variation of computer-generated statistical research has been carried out by Palme on the COM system, by using specially written programs to collect and process user traffic.

> In one investigation, I wanted to find out if the usage of a conference system was mainly new communication, or if it was a replacement for communication which previously took place using other means of communication. The normal way to investigate this might be to make a query to the users of the system. However, such a query would tell how many users believe that the communication is new communication, and users' beliefs might not be correct. Instead, I wrote a program which randomly selected contributions written in the system

(both personally addressed mail and conference contributions). For each contribution the program sent a question to the writers of the contribution, asking them to what extent they believed they would have communicated the same information by other means if the conference system was not available. They were also asked how many people they would have communicated this information to if the conference system had not been available. The answers were then weighted by the number of readers of the contribution. For example, if a contribution was read by 20 users, and the writer said that without the conference system, he would have communicated this to only 3 people, this was counted as 3 replacement communications and 17 new communications. Thus, the figure which came out of the investigation was not how many of the users believed that conferencing replaces or does not replace other communication means, but rather what percentage of the actual communication going on in the system was a replacement for previous communication by other means. [22]

In another example of this method, Palme wanted to find out to what extent computer conferencing influenced the organizational distance between the sender and the recipient of the information. To investigate this he had a programmer modify the conferencing system so that every time anyone read a message or contribution, the organizational position of both the author and the reader was noted in a file. In analysing the data, he showed that while e-mail was used most often within a single department of an organization, conference entries were most often read by users outside the organization altogether. Thus conferencing can be seen as a medium which encourages contacts between people at a larger organizational distance [21].

Participant journals

One of the methods from the qualitative evaluation stable to be applied to computer networking is the keeping of a diary or journal by participants of the 'significant events' of their online experience [24]. Records might be kept of a typical online session, or of particularly notable occurrences – technical frustrations, serendipitous findings, new online friendships or encouraging responses from others. An 'up-dated' version of this method is the audio cassette journal. This consists of sending participants a blank audio cassette with a variety of questions or issues which they are invited to address, preferably at several points throughout the online period. Such a self-made tape was used to gather the ideas of an online tutor in an analysis of moderating skills [19].

Participants can be asked to focus on any particular aspect of their online experience with these techniques, and therefore are very appropriate for investigating collaborative online experience. Used in combination with other evaluation techniques, these participant-structured methods provide valuable data to explain and enhance other evidence, particularly quantitative. Of course, the obvious drawback is that, like open-ended questionnaires, comments cannot be queried nor can interesting points be followed up.

Content analysis

The most obvious data available to conferencing evaluators – the transcript of all conference interactions – is paradoxically the least used. There are astonishingly few comments, let alone analyses, in the literature of this central core of the whole enterprise.

The early work by the Institute for the Future again stands out. By studying conference transcripts they established three simple categories for a basic analysis: problem-solving messages, information exchange and general discussion.

In these preliminary investigations, we noted that the early portions of a conference were frequently dominated by 'information exchange' comments, usually involving learning about the system. Later in the conference, more 'problem-solving' entries occurred, as the substantive purpose became the focus of attention [28, p. 71]

Their study of the threading capabilities of conferences – tracing specific themes as they weave their way through messages – led them to discover three types of roles emerging:

In some cases, for instance, particular persons tend to introduce many new ideas, while others function as idea-developers, and still others as synthesizers of previously developed ideas. These roles could vary greatly among persons and conferences. Thus, by examining the overall patterns for a FORUM conference, one can see both key persons (roles) and key ideas. [28, p. 74]

A number of evaluators have attempted to categorise conference messages according to basic types. Haile [6] uses four: organisational issues, technical help, social and content-specific. Kaye [11] uses three: technical, social and content-specific. He finds that content-specific messages predominate.

Henri has taken content analysis further in order to study the nature of online interactivity:

Most authors equate the interactive process with participation: when they report on an experiment in training with CMC, they imply that to measure participation is to measure interaction. Thus it is presumed that any and all messages recorded in a teleconference are interactive. [8]

She discovered in one particular course that the percentage of truly interactive sequences initiated by students was relatively low. Their messages were content-specific and included questioning, reasoning and personal comments:

However, the analysis of the teleconferences did not indicate that the learners participated collectively in the reconstruction of knowledge, as the majority of the messages were independent. [8]

Mason has pursued a different line in content analysis, attempting to draw up a typology of conference messages related to the educational values they display [19]. This method involves a thorough reading of a set of messages with a view to discovering what, if any, skills and abilities the participants are displaying or developing. Some of the questions the educational analyst would want to bear in mind during such a process are:
– do the participants build on previous messages?
– do they draw on their own experience?
– do they refer to course material?
– do they refer to relevant material outside the course?
– do they initiate new ideas for discussion?
– does the course tutor control, direct or facilitate?

This kind of questioning would lead to a typology of messages which focuses on the independence and initiative of the student, and would provide a means by which evidence of these attributes in students can be sought in the conferencing medium. By using other educational goals, such as collaborative learning, critical thinking, deep understanding of course material, or broad awareness of issues, and by breaking these down into examples of behaviour or written work which display these characteristics, it is possible to analyse conference content and draw conclusions about the educational value of the particular online activity. Quantitative data can be used to show to what extent all students took part, or what percent of the total activity the educationally valuable interactions represent.

By using a strategy such as the one suggested here, we can, as a community, progress beyond description to analysis. We should not be afraid of making value judgements about what is educational interaction. The educator/evaluator can go beyond description and explanation of conferencing interactions, and actually interpret them according to educational criteria. This stance represents a view of evaluation as 'construction' of knowledge rather than 'discovery' of knowledge.

> As a practice, its characteristic is neither the innocent gathering of facts not the revelation of their supposed causes. Research is the more or less systematic and critical accomplishment of meaning - the active conferral of sense upon the world. [25, p. 158]

This approach to evaluating educational conferencing seems appropriate for a number of reasons:
– There are presently no methodologies from within the Postpositivist or Interpretative paradigms which have emerged for tackling this important area.
– Conference interactions are particularly appropriate for a situationally-based approach in which value is determined by the context.
– The process of defining the educational aims of the conference and analysing the conference transcripts is circular, each one continually illuminating and reinterpreting the other.

Conclusions

This review of evaluation methodologies for computer conferencing applications has focussed on the major practitioners and on the advantages and disadvantages of each method. A plea is made for evaluators to take up the challenge of content analysis both as the key to increasing the professionalism of the field and as the essence of the educational value of the activity.

References

1. Adrianson, L.: Group communication via computer: Social psychological aspects of the COM-system. Goteborg Psychological Reports, 4, 15 (1985)

2. Adrianson, L and E. Hjelmquist: Users' experiences of COM – a computer-mediated communication system. Behaviour and Information Technology, 7, 1, pp. 79–99 (1988)

3. Boyd, G.: The life-worlds of computer-mediated distance education. In: Mindweave: communication, computers and distance education (R.D. Mason, A.R. Kaye, eds.). Pergamon: Oxford 1989

4. Burge, E.: unpublished PhD Thesis. Toronto: Ontario Institute for Studies in Education 1992

5. Greene, J. and C. McClintock: The evolution of evaluation methodology. Theory Into Practice, 30, 1, pp. 13–21 (1991)

6. Haile, P.: An analysis of computer conferences supporting the distance learner. Paper presented at the Annual Conference of the American Educational Research Association. San Francisco, April 18, 1986

7. Harasim, L. and R. Wolfe: Research analysis and evaluation of computer conferencing and networking in education (Final Report). Toronto: Ontario Institute for Studies in Education 1988

8. Henri, F.: Distance learning and computer-mediated communication: Interactive, quasi-interactive or monologue? In: Computer supported collaborative learning (C. O'Malley, ed.). Heidelberg: Springer-Verlag (in press)

9. Hiltz, R.S.: Learning in a Virtual Classroom. Final evaluation report. Research Report 25. Newark, N.J.: Computerized Conferencing and Communications Center, New Jersey Institute of Technology 1988

10. Johansen, R., R. DeGrasse and T. Wilson: Group communication through computers, Vol. 5: Effects on working patterns. Menlo Park, CA: Institute for the Future 1978

11. Kaye, A: quoted in Mason, R: Use of CoSy on DT200, 1989. CITE report no. 99, Institute of Educational Technology. Milton Keynes: The Open University 1990

12. Kiesler, S., J. Siegel and T. McGuire: Social psychological aspects of computer-mediated communication. American Psychologist, 39, 10, pp. 1123–1134 (1984)

13. Konttinen, R and S. Kari: Computer-mediated communication in higher education. Based on an article in Life and Education in Finland, 1, 1, pp. 48–54 (1990)

14. Lea, M. and R. Spears: Computer-mediated communication, de-individuation and group decision-making. International Journal of Man-Machine Studies, 34, pp. 283-301 (1991)

15. Levin, J., H. Kim, and M. Riel: Analyzing instructional interactions on electronic message networks. In: Online education: perspectives on a new environment (L. Harasim ed.). New York: Praeger 1990

16. McClure, C., A. Bishop, P. Doty and H. Rosenbaum: The National Research and Education Network (NREN): Research and Policy Perspectives. Norwood. New Jersey: Ablex Publishing Corporation 1991

17. Mason, R.: A Case Study of computer conferencing at the Open University. PhD Thesis. CITE Thesis No. 6, The Institute of Educational Technology. Milton Keynes: The Open University 1989

18. Mason, R.: Computer conferencing: An example of good practice from DT200 in 1990. CITE Report No. 129, Institute of Educational Technology. Milton Keynes: The Open University 1990

19. Mason, R.: Moderating educational computer conferencing. Electronic Networking: Research, Applications, and Policy. 3 (1992)

20. Merriam, S.: Case study research in education. A qualitative approach. San Francisco: Jossey-Bass 1988

21. Palme, J.: Experience with the use of the COM computerized conferencing system. Stockholm: Stockholm University Computer Centre 1984

22. Palme, J.: Use of conference systems for research on them. Personal communication 1991.

23. Quinn, C., H. Mehan, J. Levin and S. Black: Real education in non-real time: The use of electronic message systems for instruction. Instructional Science 11, pp 313-327 (1983)

24. Thorpe, M.: The tutor perspective on computer-mediated communication in DT200. CITE report no. 76, Institute of Educational Technology. Milton Keynes: The Open University 1989

25. Usher, R. and I Bryant: Adult education as theory, practice and research. The captive triangle. London: Routledge 1989

26. Vallée, J., R. Johansen, H. Lupinski, K. Spangler and T. Wilson: Group communication through computers, Vol 3: Pragmatics and dynamics. Menlo Park, CA: Institute for the Future 1975

27. Vallée, J., R. Johansen, H. Lipinski and T. Wilson: Group communication through computers, Vol. 4: Social, managerial, and economic issues. Menlo Park, CA: Institute for the Future 1978

28. Vallée, J., R. Johansen, R. Randolph and A. Hastings: Group communication through computers, Vol. 2: A study of social effects. Menlo Park, CA: Institute for the Future 1974

29. Worthen, B. and J Sanders: The changing face of educational evaluation. Theory Into Practice, 30, 1, pp. 3–12 (1991)

8
Computer Conferencing and Content Analysis

France Henri
Télé-Université, Université du Québec, Montréal, Québec, Canada

Abstract: The chapter presents a framework and analytical model that could be used by educators for a better understanding of the learning process and of the riches available in the content of CMC messages. The analytical model was developed to highlight five dimensions of the learning process exteriorized in messages: participation, interaction, social, cognitive, and metacognitive dimensions. These dimensions were chosen because they pertain to the work of an educator in dealing with a group of distance learners, and because of their connection with the cognitive approach to the learning process. The point is that CMC messages are polysemic, and that content analysis helps us to understand the learning process and offers data useful to improving the efficacy of interaction with students. The analytical model appears capable of promoting and supporting a collaborative learning process.

Keywords: computer conferencing, learning process, content analysis, method of analysis, student's skills, interactivity, participation, cognitive skills, metacognition, qualitative method of analysis.

The Underlying Meaning of Messages

Computer-mediated conferencing (CMC) is proving to be a gold mine of information concerning the psycho-social dynamics at work among students, the learning strategies adopted, and the acquisition of knowledge and skills. An attentive educator, reading between the lines in texts transmitted by CMC, will find information unavailable in any other learning situation. Telephone conferencing in distance education imposes as many time limitations on interaction as does conventional, on-campus classroom work – the time limit on all encounters making it physically impossible for all the learners to have their say, and focusing the content of interaction on the subject matter, rather than on the learning process itself. On the other hand, computer conferencing, freed of the constraints imposed by time and space, allows all participants to express themselves. The social network, group cohesion and interactive process characteristic of CMC enter into play as well. Here the social aspects of virtual groups are no disadvantage; they contribute, rather, to the richness of the interactive process. An in-depth study of the meaning of messages will teach us much of interest and importance about the richness of their content, and allow us to pinpoint the information which tells us about learners and learning processes.

Studies of the pedagogical uses of CMC have shown that the dynamics of group communication within the learning process must be taken into account [16, 13], and also that the content of interaction itself is perceived by learners as a source of learning [23]. These studies have not, however, yielded the tools for the in-depth analysis of message content which now seems so crucial to the learning process.

Why this focus on content analysis? What is there in the content of computer conferences which warrants looking beyond the surface meaning of the exchanged messages? What further meanings can such analysis reveal? The role of an educator in CMC learning goes beyond understanding what is said about the subject under discussion; the social and cognitive processes at work in and among the learners must also be understood. Content analysis, when conducted with an aim to understanding the learning process, provides information on the participants as learners, and on their ways of dealing with a given topic. Thus informed, the educator is in a position to fulfil his main role, which is to offer immediate support to the individual and the collective learning process.

What methods allow us to analyse and understand message content? So far we have only applied the same reading methods and techniques of analysis as those we use when confronted with a newspaper article, a memo, an essay, a novel, or a philosophical treatise – methods not specifically adapted to this new mode of communication, nor to the analysis of the learning process. CMC-generated messages may belong to the class of print, but they have little in common with texts as we know them. The chronological sequence of the messages does not partake of the logic of spoken or written discourse: CMC messages follow upon each other without immediate continuity of meaning, issuing from several authors who do not usually consult one another before transmitting. The results, and the meaning to be derived from a session of computer conferencing, are the fruit of a collective endeavor. In addition, each message, each person's contribution, has its own meaning and can be considered on its own. The social dimension of CMC gives rise to elements of meaning which find expression in varied patterns of interaction and in the use of various levels of discourse. We cannot analyse a CMC text as we might a 'constructed' text, one featuring a structure and a content on which its authors had agreed beforehand: a participant's contributions must be considered both singly and in relation to those of the others if the processes and strategies used by each of the learners are to be identified.

At present, educators are not making use of the content of CMC exchanges to further the learning process. This is due to the fact that we have no means of dealing with the abundance of information contained in the messages, nor of interpreting the elements of meaning which have significance for the learning process.

Researchers studying the pedagogical applications of CMC are confronted with the urgent task of developing these means. Educators must be provided with the tools to draw the marrow from the bones – to find in the exchanged messages those elements which best reveal the learning process. And a means must also be found of ensuring that the new understanding afforded by this analysis is in fact used by educators to support the individual and group learning process.

The Problem of Analysis

We do not know how to make use of the riches provided by CMC content, nor how to optimise CMC efficiency. Experiments with CMC in learning situations[1] attribute the richness and efficiency of exchange to factors inherent in the technology, and to the phenomenon of group functioning in a virtual environment, for example:

– the exactness of expression possible with written messages;
– the direct, informal style and brevity demanded by limited screen space;
– the asynchronicity allowing persons separated by time and space to be linked;
– the flexible access allowing multiple and varied collaboration, unhindered by time and space;
– the multiple inputs made possible by group exchanges;
– the reduction of social pressure due to the virtual quality of the group;
– the feeling of belonging coming from collaborative effort.

The richness of exchange

Like many other authors, Harasim [12] states that interactivity, CMC's most striking characteristic, is the factor with the greatest influence on learning. She is of the opinion that CMC encourages a collaborative process which alters the nature of learning and increases its quality. For McCreary [25], the value of CMC lies in its use of the written word – the form of communication which, more than any other, demands exactness, coherent organisation of thought, and clear, restrained and authentic expression. Yet the statements and observations of researchers concerning the richness of exchange do not in fact tell us what additional elements are expressed by students when they use CMC. Wherein lies the value unique to CMC, and how can it assist the learning process?

---

[1] For example, to quote only a few : [10,13,16,18,23,24,25]

Efficiency of exchange

The literature shows that this richness leads in turn to efficiency. In numerous reports of the efficient use of CMC by groups of scientists, politicians, managers, professionals and teachers [20, 17, 21], the efficiency of CMC communication is attributed to the very factors which indicate its richness – i.e., the possibility of group interaction unhindered by time and space restrictions. Group work, which involves reflection, decision-making, and problem-solving, has its own laws of energy: it consistently yields results of a higher calibre than those attained by the average group member [20]. This is due to the greater amount of information available within the group, the greater diversity of interpretations of fact and the opportunity to test individual ideas. The dynamics of the group rid the individual of the insecurity linked to intellectual endeavors and frees him or her to propose and experiment with new ideas. Not only does the work of the group improve, but the individuals involved also learn more than those of comparable skills working alone. In terms of content, then, the combination of social osmosis, the circulation of ideas, and the links established among the participants all contribute to increase the efficiency of CMC group exchanges.

It would appear that the group itself is a factor in the increased efficiency of CMC learning environments. The group allows a collective process wherein the knowledge and experience of the learners are put to use [36]. The interactive structure of the group leads the users to deal with learning in a co-operative mode, which places value on collective knowledge [26, 14]. The content to be learned is built up collectively, with the exchange of interventions and interactions.

Yet though findings confirm the efficiency of CMC, the means whereby educators can use this efficiency to support learning have not been identified. Hiltz [16, p.10] asks this very question from the point of view of the learner, observing that to prove the effectiveness of CMC would be to demonstrate that learners do benefit from the interactive nature of the CMC exchange – which is recognised as the very source of the richness and efficiency of this new means of communication. This question applies to educators as well: it is essential that we examine the ability of the educator, as well as that of the learner, to make use of the advantages for learning provided by this medium. It is up to us to make specific suggestions about how each might best do this.

And in questioning the ability of educators and learners to profit from the richness and efficiency of CMC, it is essential that we be more specific, in a strictly pedagogical perspective, as to the nature of this richness and efficiency. At present, our knowledge is rather superficial: our descriptions so far either have been quantitative (number of participants, number of messages, number of interactive messages, number of conferences, length, etc.) or have used indirect indicators (user perception, level of satisfaction, attitudes, etc.). We do not yet possess a body of knowledge concerning the pedagogical characteristics of the content of computer conferences, the scenarios of how the learning occurs, or the elements which give rise to learning.

Only when we have a better understanding of computer-mediated learning, will we be in a position to say that we are making the best use of CMC – using its full potential. We believe that this understanding can come only from a finer-grained content analysis.

In Search of a Specific Methodology

Is there a method specifically suited to the analysis of CMC messages? Certainly, there is no lack of analytical methods for studying communication patterns. Psychology and linguistics, among other disciplines, have devised methods and models for the semantic interpretation of spoken or written messages. But these have been designed as research tools; their complexity makes their application difficult for non-specialists. Furthermore, the aims of such methods make them useful only for a study of CMC's pedagogical aspects: propositional analysis, for example, concentrates on phenomena which are not fully relevant to the study of computer-mediated learning processes. Therefore these methods are not truly useful to educators who wish to gain a better understanding of computer-mediated exchanges.

Educators working in computer-mediated learning situations, often unable to develop an appropriate framework of response, are ill-equipped to deal with the mass of on-screen messages and to guide learners through the process. Understanding and interpreting the content of computer conferences can become an acute problem. Educators must be able to interpret the messages rapidly, to identify the strategies the learners are using, to recognize the strengths and weaknesses of the learners, and to offer adequate pedagogical support. If the educators fail in this, then they are not in a position to conduct successful teleconferences, and they are not using the full potential of this mode of communication to respond to the needs of learners.

Understanding and interpreting message content is a demanding, time-consuming task, and CMC software does not provide specialised functions in this connection. The organisation and retrieval of information are basic functions of message content analysis – yet the current software merely organises the teleconferences by theme, and then divides them into sub-themes[2], or into a branching structure[3], and information retrieval within these sub-themes and branches is limited to keyword searches, either through indexation of the message titles or linking of inter-referential messages. Such functions do not fill the need. Rather, they seem quite inadequate to the task of extracting the significant aspects of a set of messages. They deal only with the more superficial aspects of content, which often have little or no meaning in terms of the overall learning process.

It is our opinion that the solution lies in setting up an appropriate analytical method and in developing tools for the better understanding of messages, and for distilling the useful elements of their meaning. An appropriate analytical method would identify the learning processes and strategies selected or developed by learners. The results of this analysis would constitute a basis for the development of a framework to guide interventions and support the learning process.

---

[2] Messages are classified according to an *a priori* organisation of the theme, with a top-down structure, as in CoSy, for example.

[3] Progressive organisation of messages: conferences are organised into a branching, top-down, structure, as in Participate.

Issues in Content Analysis

Since the introduction of CMC, on campus as well as in distance education, research has sought to prove that this technology is as efficient as face-to-face education. Hiltz states that

> ... effectiveness was conceptualized as being related to four dimensions: course content, characteristics of the teaching, course outcomes, and comparisons of process in the virtual and online formats. [19, p.157]

The research has mainly explored the last three of these elements; the question of 'content' is generally laid aside. The reason for this, says Hiltz, is that:

> ...the content coding proved to be extremely time-consuming and expensive, and not very fruitful for our purpose. A very rudimentary kind of content analysis employed the automated counts of the number and length of comments in class conferences by each participant. [19, p.161]

Research in computer conferencing content is usually restricted to the gathering of quantitative data on participation. The volume of messages thus becomes an implicit measure of the efficiency, success and fruitfulness of exchanges. Participation is measured by the number of messages transmitted, the number of server accesses, the duration of consultations and even – for Hiltz and some other researchers – the number of lines of text transmitted. Some studies distinguish between the messages of educators and those of learners. Such methods of dealing with content may have been legitimate in the early days of this technology, when the aim was to demonstrate that teaching using computer conferencing was as efficient as traditional classwork. But proof of this is no longer lacking. It is time to give up strictly quantitative approaches for qualitative approaches, to analyse the interactive exchanges of CMC and to demonstrate the effects and advantages of interactive exchange in learning.

Some very interesting efforts in the area of content analysis, by Ellis and McCreary [5] and by Waugh *et al* [37], have shown that qualitative analysis could be of use in understanding conference content. The methods they propose are incomplete, but useful nevertheless. Waugh proposes to analyse messages in terms of their impact on the pattern of exchanges, a method which makes it possible to identify the messages which trigger interaction in the group. Unfortunately, Waugh *et al* do not tell us how they conducted their analysis. Ellis and McCreary's approach to interactive process looks at the various levels of linkage between messages – e.g., actually linked, apparently linked, unlinked. By tracing these connections, the authors give a visual representation of the organisation of teleconference content.

These two qualitative approaches show not what was said about the topic of the teleconference, but how it was said. For us, this is the proper focus of content analysis. Such an analysis will allow an identification of the particularities of CMC, and an understanding of how learners use the medium to work out and transmit their ideas, and how capable the learners are of communicating in interactive patterns. This approach can analyse the social, psychological and cognitive dimensions of the exchanges. To continue to analyse the content of exchanges only in terms of the theme under discussion, ignoring the other aspects of content, would be to forgo real knowledge of the richness and efficiency in learning situations of which CMC is capable.

A Proposed Method of Content Analysis

The method we propose has three main components: a framework defining the dimensions of the analysis; an analytical model corresponding to each of these dimensions; and a technique for the analysis of message content. These components are described below, after the following account of the rationale under which the method was developed.

Rationale

The method was developed for the purposes of a recent study [15], in the hope of providing educators with a tool for understanding the content of computer conferences aimed at learning. The method of analysis used a qualitative approach and had two characteristics: *a priori* criteria, and a cognitive view of learning.

Following a suggestion made by Miles and Huberman [27], we chose to develop an analytical method working from criteria established *a priori*. This allowed us to concentrate on a single aspect of CMC – the learning process as revealed in the messages. An attempt to analyse all dimensions of CMC would have led to the collection of an abundance of data and information, much of it irrelevant to the learning process.

We also wanted our analysis to be consistent with our cognitive conception of learning, which focuses on the 'process' of learning rather than on its 'product', on what and how the learner understands, rather than on what should have been understood. Learning can be said to be significant when the learner seeks information actively, uses it to produce knowledge, and integrates these into his or her cognitive structures.

Our view of the learning process also follows cognitive theories in that it stresses the process of metacognition, which deals with the knowledge and skills the learner brings to bear on the overall cognitive activity – i.e., how he or she manages and controls this activity. It is widely acknowledged that the development of metacognitive knowledge and skills has positive long-term effects on learning. Several studies have indicated that for students and learners at university level, academic achievement is linked to metacognition [32, 34, 29]. This is why the cognitive and metacognitive dimension of message content is so important in our analysis.

In a CMC learning situation, the educator can offer input at three levels: what is said on the subject or theme under discussion; how it is said; and the processes and strategies adopted in dealing with it. Each of these levels of content will in turn be subjected to the three levels of analysis. The educator may favour one or another level, according to his or her pedagogical aims and intentions.

What is said on the subject

The first analysis is the one which is spontaneously applied. It allows us to extract from messages the ideas which have been presented, so that what has been said about the subject may be understood. Exactitude, logic, coherence, relevance and clarity are the main variables in understanding and judging the quality of what is being said.

How it is said

The second level of analysis is a result of the CMC process which structures the content of teleconferences and shapes its patterns. Three elements comprise this analysis : the nature of participation, the social presence and the interactivity factor. This analysis allows us to measure how actively the learner acquires information and uses it to produce new knowledge.

Processes and strategies

The third level of analysis is less obvious: it deals with the processes and strategies adopted by the learners, as they reveal them in dealing with the subject. Processes are rendered tangible in strategies, which depend on and reveal the varying degrees of mastery of the learner's skills. The educator will carry out this third analysis according to his or her vision of the learning process. Our own preference, the cognitive approach, translates well into the analytical framework we have developed. Cognitive psychology sees two types of strategies[4] underpinning the learning process: cognitive and metacognitive [4]. Cognitive strategies allow the student to fulfil a task; metacognitive strategies have to do with the management and control of the learning situation. Content analysis should be designed so as to identify the indicators of these strategies and the skills connected with the use of them.

The Analytical Framework and Model

The first of these three possible levels of analysis deals essentially with the 'product' of learning. The latter two we believe reveal more of the 'process' of learning, and we have chosen to use these to establish the framework of the content analysis. Our framework has five dimensions: participative, social, interactive, cognitive, and metacognitive.

In order to make use of these dimensions, we established operational definitions of each, and then identified indicators which would allow us to recognize their expression in the text (see Table 8.1). Each dimension was used in developing the tools to identify the occurrences of these elements.

We now present each dimension in turn, explaining the theoretical foundation of each, and proposing interpretations of the data.

The participative dimension

Theoretical foundation

As we have pointed out above, it is not sufficient merely to count the number of messages if we are to give an accurate picture of student participation. However, such quantitative data can be useful in content analysis if it is not the only factor considered, and if it is analysed in conjunction with data from the analysis of the other dimensions as we have defined them.

We have found it useful to distinguish between two categories of quantitative data: data covering the totality of the messages issued by all participants, and data concerning the participation of the learners and educators in the learning activity.

---

[4] The literature also covers 'affective' strategies, which refer to the motivation, level of interest and emotional state of learners, in connection with the task at hand or with the learning situation in general. We agree with Deschênes [4] in including these strategies in metacognitive territory.

Table 8.1 The Analytical Framework

Dimension	Definition	Indicators
Participative	Compilation of the number of messages or statements transmitted by one person or group	Number of messages Number of statements
Social	Statement or part of statement not related to formal content of subject matter	Self-introduction Verbal support "I'm feeling great..."
Interactive	Chain of connected messages	"In response to Céline..." "As we said earlier..."
Cognitive	Statement exhibiting knowledge and skills related to the learning process	Asking questions Making inferences Making inferences Formulating hypotheses
Metacognitive	Statement related to general knowledge and skills and showing awareness, self-control, and self-regulation of learning.	"I understand..." "I wonder..."

It is well known that CMC environments give rise to various types of conferencing, not all of which are concerned with learning activities *per se*. For conferencing can focus on socialisation and the exchange of general information and management tasks, as much as on the subject of study. The analytical model dealing with participation allows us to collect data on both overall participation (participation in all conferences), and active participation in the learning process (participation in conferences directly related to the subject of study).

In compiling the data, we propose to distinguish between learners' messages and educators' messages (see Table 8.2).

Table 8.2 Analytical Model: Participation

Category	Definition	Indicators
Overall	Total number of messages and accesses; duration of connection for educators and learners	Quantitative data supplied by server
Active participation in learning process	Number of statements directly related to learning made by learners and educators.	Statements related to formal content of lesson

The usual approach in studies of this kind – a straight count of messages – could not be used here to arrive at a quantitative measure of participation, since the message as a unit of measure is a highly variable one: some messages contain very little information, others contain several paragraphs dealing with numerous ideas, and set out complex arguments which may be broken up into several messages. Messages of such unequal length cannot serve as precise measures of active participation. What then were we to count? What is the significant measure of active participation? Our proposal is to divide messages into statements corresponding to units of meaning, and to use these, rather than messages proper, as the counted units measuring active participation.[5]

Some results and possible interpretations

A first look at the quantitative data provides a breakdown of educator messages and learner messages, and shows the relative importance of the educator in the exchanges and in the learning process. The data also tells us how many of the exchanges are directly related to the learning process, and how many are not. The number of messages and statements for different conferences tells us in which type of conference the students are most active, and, maybe, which they prefer.

The data on participation, when combined with other data, can corroborate or correct interpretations based on message content analysis. Comparative numbers of learner and educator messages, for example, would tell us how much the learning process – or the learners themselves – are centred on the educator,and what levels of collaboration and autonomy are at work in the learning process. Lastly, the quantitative data on the numbers involved in various conferences can tell us how satisfactorily the virtual environment is set up and if it meets the needs of the students.

The social dimension

Theoretical foundation

Many studies have offered in-depth analyses of the social dynamics of conferencing exchanges. The results suggest the importance of this aspect of communication for participation, social cohesion within the group, and the feeling of belonging. Not wanting to replicate these studies, we limited our inquiry to identifying the occurrences of the expression of the social factor. We based our model on that of Berger [1], who proposes (pages 51–52) that social presence or interaction is at work in any statement not related to the formal content of the subject matter (see Table 8.3).

Table 8.3 Analytical Model: Social

Dimension	Definition	Indicators
Social	Statement or part of statement not related to formal content of subject matter.	Self-introduction Verbal support "I'm feeling great..."

---

[5] A description of the division of messages into statements is given below in the section on Analytical Method.

Some results and possible interpretations

The frequency of socially oriented statements in computer conferences which deal exclusively with the subject under study allows various interpretations which can be supported by other data – for instance, by data concerning the cognitive dimension. The frequency might indicate the level of learner focus on the task, or the level of social cohesiveness established in the group, or that affective support plays a greater or lesser role in the learning process. The high levels of socially-oriented messages may sometimes be a disruptive element, distracting learners from the purpose of the communication; in other cases, these messages can be supportive of the learning process. Interpretation must take into account the overall results of the content analysis.

The interactive dimension

Theoretical foundation

Although users and researchers are in full agreement that CMC is essentially an interactive process, nowhere does the literature provide a full theoretical or operational definition of what we are to understand as 'interactive process'.

Table 8.4 Analytical Model: Interactivity

Category	Definition	Indicators
Explicit Interaction	Any statement referring explicitly to another message, person, or group	
Direct response	Any statement responding to a question, using a direct reference	"...in response to Denis's message 16"
Direct commentary	Any statement taking up and pursuing an expressed idea, using direct reference	"...I share Nicole's opinion absolutely"
Implicit Interaction	Any statement referring implicitly to another message, person, or group	
Indirect response	Any statement obviously responding to a question, but without referring to it by name	"I think the solution is..."
Indirect commentary	Any statement taking up and pursuing an expressed idea, but without referring to the original message	"The problem under discussion will need the assistance of..."
Independent Statement	Any statement relating to the subject under discussion, but which is neither an answer nor a commentary and which does not lead to any further statements	"After examining the problem, I think that..."

The importance of the concept of interactivity in CMC made it imperative that we give it some in-depth analysis. Our first task was to arrive at an operational definition of interactivity. We used a definition provide by Bretz [2], who defines interactivity as a three-step process :
– Step 1: communication of information
– Step 2: a first response to this information
– Step 3: a second answer relating to the first.
The process can be represented schematically in the following manner:

$$A=======>B=======>A=======>B$$

The conceptual approach adopted for studying computer conferences must allow for interactivity, and for its absence as well. A conference without interactivity would comprise a series of statements linked only by the theme or subject under discussion – we would be faced with a collection of monologues and one-way statements. Our model qualifies non-interactive messages or statements as 'independent'. The distinctions made are as follows: interactive *versus* non-interactive, and explicit *versus* implicit interaction (see Table 8.4.).

Among exchanges made up of interactive statements, we distinguish between explicit interaction, expressed as one or more ideas referring specifically to one or more messages, and implicit interaction, the content of which refers obviously to one or more messages or ideas, but does not specifically mention the connection.

Some results and possible interpretations
Analysis of interactivity allows us to describe the actual structuring of teleconference content. It progresses on a basis either of interactive contributions or of an accumulation of monologues. An analysis of interactivity will reveal where the process occurs: if learners react only to the educator's messages, for example, this tells us something about the educational process, and about the vision of learning entertained by the learners. It might indicate that the learners value the educator's messages above all others, so that his or her interventions must be dealt with; it might mean that learning can only happen in the 'presence' of an educator; that learners lack initiative, and must be constantly called on to react – or perhaps they do not have the skills to understand, comment, criticise and incorporate ideas expressed by other learners. Together with other data, the analysis of interactivity can lead to an evaluation of the levels of collaboration at work among learners, of their active participation in the accumulation of knowledge, and of their skills in structuring the information presented on-screen.

We cannot automatically interpret the absence of interactivity in CMC learning situations as a failure. A study conducted by Guertin [9] reveals that learners participating in low-interactivity conferences consider themselves to have learned a lot from reading co-learners' messages. The interpretation of results should not lead us to a judgement concerning the success or failure of a conference, but only to a description of the learning process, as it reveals itself in conferences, and of learners involved.

The cognitive dimension

Theoretical foundation
Two questions had to be answered before a model for the cognitive dimension could be established: which cognitive process was to be analysed, and how should

this process be defined? Since our interest lies in the learning process, it made sense to try to identify the elements within messages which would tell us something about the ways people learn. To clarify what we meant by 'ways of learning', we used the tendencies and orientations of North American teaching programs as a foundation. A large number of cognitivists go beyond the usual objectives of knowledge acquisition research, seeking information on the development of the cognitive potential of learners – the mastering of the skills needed to learn how to learn and to learn how to think [8, 30, 33, 11]. According to these programs, cognitive skills supporting a significant learning process are connected with understanding, reasoning, the development of critical skills, and problem resolution.

Table 8.5 Analytical Model: Cognitive Skills

Reasoning Skills	Definitions	Indicators
Elementary clarification	Observing or studying a problem identifying its elements, and observing their linkages in order to come to a basic understanding	Identifying relevant elements Reformulating the problem Asking a relevant question Identifying previously stated hypotheses
In-depth clarification	Analysing and understanding a problem to come to an understanding which sheds light on the values, beliefs, and assumptions which underlie the statement of the problem	Defining the terms Identifying assumptions Establishing referential criteria Seeking out specialised information
Inference	Induction and deduction, admitting or proposing an idea on the basis of its link with propositions already admitted as true	Drawing conclusions Making generalisations Formulating a proposition which proceeds from previous statements
Judgement	Making decisions, statements, appreciations, evaluations and criticisms Sizing up	Judging the relevance of solutions Making value judgements Judging inferences
Strategies	Proposing co-ordinated actions for the application of a solution, or for ollowing through on a choice or a decision	Deciding on the action to be taken Proposing one or more solutions Interacting with those concerned

In setting up our model, we chose to focus on the skills connected to reasoning which uses critical thought. Quellmalz [31] states that this type of reasoning calls upon a higher level of cognitive skills, on a par with those at work in problem resolution. The taxonomy developed by Ennis [6] includes fourteen aptitudes and twelve cognitive skills related to critical reasoning activities. We concentrated on the skills used in this taxonomy, grouping them into five categories to facilitate analysis: elementary clarification, in-depth clarification, inference, judgement and the development of strategies (these are defined and exemplified in Table 8.5).

It seemed to us insufficient to identify the cognitive skills at work only as they are indicated by message content – we found ourselves with superficial results telling us only of the presence and frequency of use of these skills. Therefore we developed a second model, which would allow us to evaluate the skills identified. The elements of this model were drawn from the work of Schmeck [35], Marton *et al* [22], and Entwistle and Waterston [7]. These studies indicate that the learning process is influenced by the level at which information processing occurs. Schmeck defines 'in-depth-elaborative' treatment thus: "it is the process whereby learners critically evaluate information, organise it conceptually, and compare and oppose it to previously-held information". This is accomplished only when the learners translate newly-acquired information into their own terms, connecting it, for example, with their lived experience. Entwistle and Waterston distinguish between a 'surface' and an 'in-depth-elaborative' treatment of information, which are seen to be opposite ends of a continuum.

Table 8.6 Analytical Model: Processing Information

Surface Processing	In-Depth Processing
Repeating the information contained in the statement of the problem without making inferences or offering an interpretation	Linking facts, ideas and notions in order to interpret, infer, propose and judge
Repeating what has been said without adding any new elements	Offering new elements of information
Stating that one shares the ideas or opinions stated, without taking these further or adding any personal comments	Generating new data from information collected by the use of hypotheses and inferences
Proposing solutions without offering explanations	Proposing one or more solutions with short-, medium-, or long-term justification
Making judgements without offering justification	Setting out the advantages and disadvantages of a situation or solution
Asking questions which invite information not relevant to the problem or not adding to the understanding of it	Providing proof or supporting examples
	Making judgements supported by justification
Offering several solutions without suggesting which is most appropriate	Perceiving the problem within a larger perspective
Perceiving the situation in a fragmentary or short-term manner	Developing intervention strategies within a wider framework

Table 8.6 presents the criteria for distinguishing surface processing from in-depth processing, which is more complex. This model is employed after the identification of the cognitive skills in message content.

Some results and possible interpretations

The proposed analysis of the cognitive dimension makes it possible to identify the skills linked to critical reasoning and then to evaluate the level of information processing applied by learners in each of the skills. The results of this analysis do not comprise an exhaustive description of learners' cognitive activity, but despite its limitations, the analysis offers valuable information which can help educators give their learners appropriate cognitive support.

The results of such an analysis must be interpreted in relation to the cognitive tasks assigned to the learners. If knowledge acquisition is the aim, we can expect to find high levels of clarification and inference activities; if problem resolution is the aim, we can expect the whole range of skills to surface. If only a superficial processing of information is occurring, it might be due to the task at hand, or to a lack of relevant knowledge – or even to the inability of learners to carry out in-depth processing of the information.

The metacognitive dimension

Theoretical foundation

The metacognitive process is difficult to observe within a traditional teaching/learning situation, as it is rarely manifested or intentionally expressed by the learner. When studying this process, researchers usually invite subjects to think out loud or to describe, in speech or writing, the operations they would normally accomplish mentally. These techniques allow for the identification of mental processes, and of cognitive mistakes or weaknesses; thus strategies for increasing the metacognitive skills of the subjects may be elaborated. These means of collecting information about the mental activities of learners are simply not available to educators in the course of their daily practice. In a CMC environment, however, the examination of transmitted messages can be a valuable source of information on metacognitive activities. These messages cannot be expected to reveal the totality of the metacognitive process, but they do offer information well worth an educator's consideration.

In the elaboration of the metacognitive model, we used a definition proposed by Deschênes [3], which makes a theoretical distinction between metacognitive knowledge – declarative knowledge concerning the person, the task, and the strategies (see Table 8.7), and metacognitive skills – procedural knowledge relating to evaluation, planning, regulation and self-awareness (see Table 8.8). This breakdown has the advantage of simplicity, while encompassing the important research on metacognition. Identification of manifestations of metacognitive activity exteriorized in messages may thus be carried out using the definitions of metacognitive knowledge and skills.

Some results and possible interpretations

As was the case with the cognitive dimension, the analysis of results should allow us to identify the characteristics of the learning process and the manifestations of metacognitive activities and skills in learners. We might, for instance, arrive at the following observation: "learners use task evaluation and strategy planning, but fail to evaluate themselves as cognitive agents in connection with the task". A description like this can be used diagnostically, to orient the educator's approach in support of the learning process.

Table 8.7 Analytical Model: Metacognitive Knowledge

Knowledge	Definitions	Indicators
Person	All that is known or believed about the characteristics of humans as cognitive beings	Comparing oneself to another as a cognitive agent Being aware of one's emotional state
Task	All information acquired by a person in terms of the task or different types of tasks Appreciation of the quality of available information	Being aware of one's way of approaching the task Knowing whether the task is new or known
Strategies	Means chosen to succeed in various cognitive tasks	Strategies making it possible to reach a cognitive objective of knowledge acquisition Metacognitive strategies aimed at self-regulation of progress

Table 8.8 Analytical Model: Metacognitive Skills

Skills	Definitions	Indicators
Evaluation	Assessment, appraisal or verification of one's knowledge and skills, and of the efficacy of a chosen strategy	Asking whether one's statement is true Commenting on one's manner of accomplishing a task
Planning	Selecting, predicting and ordering an action or strategy necessary to the accomplishment of an action	Predicting the consequences of an action Organising aims by breaking them down into sub-objectives
Regulation	Setting up, maintainance and supervision of the overall cognitive task	Redirecting one's efforts Recalling one's objectives Setting up strategies
Self-awareness	Ability to identify, decipher and interpret correctly the feelings and thoughts connected with a given aspect of the task	"I'm pleased to have learned so much..." "I'm discouraged at the difficulties involved..."

The results of any such analysis must be interpreted in light of the learners' task. Even if no metacognitive activity was noticed, one could not conclude that the students are weak in this area: previous research [15] suggests that metacognitive activity is more perceptible when the task at hand is to understand ideas or remember past learning, than it is in cases of problem resolution.

Analytical method

The final task is the actual analysis of the messages. It might seem logical that we analyse each message in turn, respecting the structure and organisation of the conference, but for several reasons we sought another solution, and did not use the message as the unit of analysis.

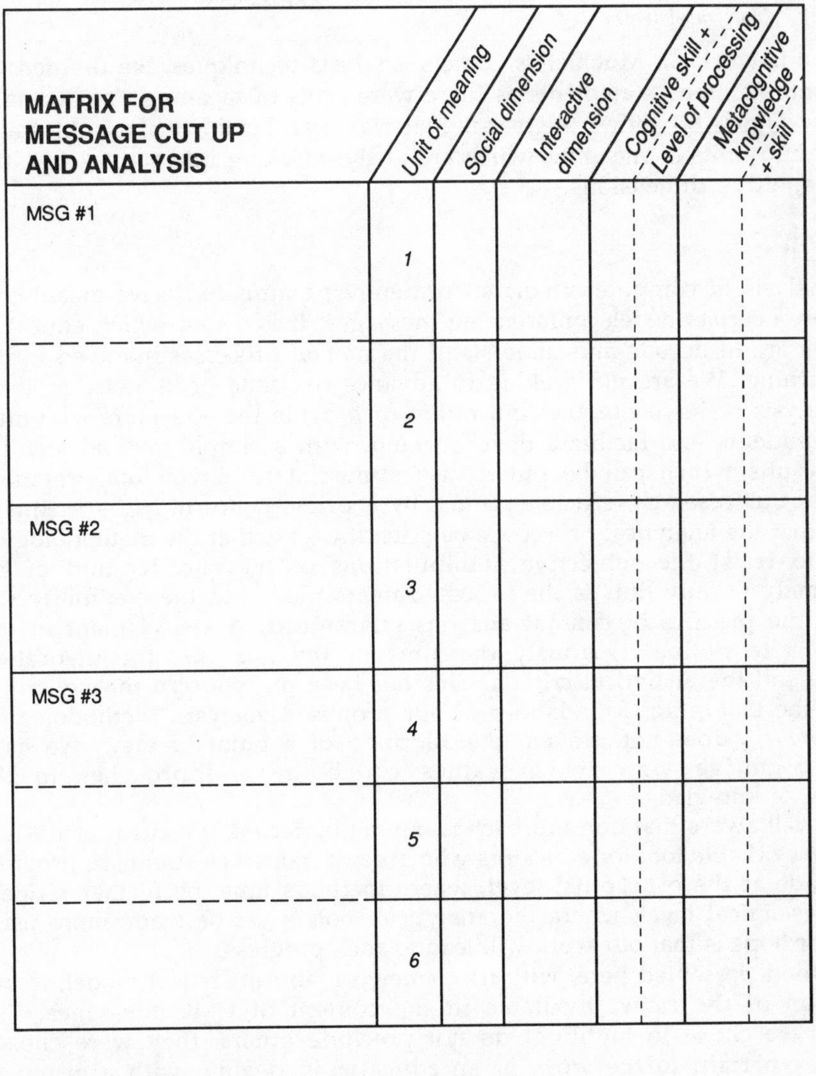

MATRIX FOR MESSAGE CUT UP AND ANALYSIS	Unit of meaning	Social dimension	Interactive dimension	Cognitive skill + Level of processing	Metacognitive knowledge + skill
MSG #1	1				
	2				
MSG #2	3				
MSG #3	4				
	5				
	6				

Figure 8.1 Matrix for Message Cut Up and Analysis

CMC-generated messages harbour more than one unit of meaning. According to Muchielli [28], the choice of the unit of analysis proceeds from the objective of the content analysis: the analysis must break up the content into units of meaning according to the analytical objectives. Each analysis will define its own relevant unit of meaning, entailing a distinct breakup of the material. But which analysis is appropriate – by word, by group of words, by proposition, by sentence or by paragraph? Muchielli believes it is useless to attempt an objective determination of the unit of meaning and a lexicological or linguistic definition. For content analysts, the essential factor is not form but meaning.

> .... It is absolutely useless to wonder if it is the word, the proposition, the sentence or the paragraph which is the proper unit of meaning, for the unit of meaning is lodged in meaning [28, p. 32] ....It is the intelligence of the text, which rests upon a logical decomposition (as in a detailed table of contents) which will make the appropriate divisions apparent. [28, p. 33]   (our translation)

Basing our work on Muchielli's content analysis techniques, we divided the messages into as many statements as there were units of meaning, "as in a table of contents." Figure 8.1 shows the matrix that was used for the analysis. Messages are cut up into units of meaning which are analysed along interactive, cognitive and metacognitive dimensions.

Conclusion

Content analysis of computer-mediated conferencing aims to derive meaningful objects from a *corpus* of teleconferencing messages. It is a tool which educators need if they are to decode and understand the mental processes involved in this kind of learning. We are not seeking to advance the state of knowledge about content analysis or its techniques, but rather to provide the educators who must coach the students and facilitate their learning, with a simple method yielding practical results which can be put to use immediately. Given the pragmatic approach of our research, efficiency must be a prime concern. We are equally concerned that the analytical procedure be scientific – i.e. that the methodology is equipped to resist the subjective manipulations of the encoder and of the educator/analyst. Only thus is the process safeguarded, and the credibility and validity of the practice of content analysis guaranteed. A key element in this protection is to define rigorously the aims of the analysis, the theoretical framework, and the analytical criteria. This has been our concern throughout in presenting the theoretical foundations of our proposed analysis. Methodological rigour, however, does not prevent the adoption of a point of view; we have chosen a cognitive view which values collaborative approaches to the construction of knowledge.

We are well aware that our approach is not yet perfected; if content analysis is to become a workable tool for educators who are not trained as scientists, progress must be made at the conceptual level, where methods must be further refined, and at the technical level, where the analytical tools must be made more user-friendly. Our hope is that our work will lead to such progress.

The method presented here, with its framework and analytical model, is but an indication of the riches available in the content of CMC messages. The dimensions we chose to highlight do not preclude others; they were chosen because they pertain to the work of an educator in dealing with a group of distance learners, and because of our own view of the learning process. The point is that CMC messages are polysemic, and that content analysis helps us to understand the learning process and offers data useful to improving the efficacy of interaction with students.

Our analysis appears capable of promoting and supporting a collaborative learning process. If this type of learning does indeed rest on a collective process of content construction, on truly interactive activity, and on the cognitive and metacognitive skills capable of an in-depth processing of exchanged information, then our work will serve to further genuine collaboration among learners.

References

1. Berger, D. E., Pezdek, K., Banks, W. P. (eds.): Applications of cognitive psychology: Problem solving, education and computing. London: Lawrence Erlbaum Associates 1987

2. Bretz, R.: Media for interactive communication. London: Sage 1983

3. Deschênes, A.-J.: La métacognition. Mimeo. Québec: Télé-université, Université du Québec 1983

4. Deschênes, A.-J.: La lecture: une activité stratégique. In: Actes des entretiens Nathan sur la lecture, 10 et 11 novembre. Paris: Nathan 1990

5. Ellis, M. L., McCreary, E. K.: The structure of message sequence in computer conferences: comparative Study. Paper presented to the Workshop on Computer Conferencing and Electronic Messaging. Guelph: University of Guelph 1985

6. Ennis, R.H.: A taxonomy of critical thinking dispositions and abilities. In: Teaching Thinking Skills: Theory and Practice. (J.B. Baron, R.J. Sternberg eds.) New York: W.H. Freeman 1986

7. Entwistle, N., Waterston, S.: Approaches to studying and levels of processing in University students. British Journal of Educational Psychology, 58, pp. 258–265 (1988)

8. Glaser, R.: Enseigner à penser – le rôle de la connaissance. In: L'art et la science de l'enseignement (M. Crahay, D. Lafontaine eds.) Brussels: Edition Labors 1986

9. Guertin, E.: Rapport des entrevues téléphoniques avec les agents conseils réalisées à la Télé-université du 5 au 9 décembre 1988. Projet de recherche subventionée par le CEFRIO, la Télé-université et le Mouvement Desjardins, Montreal: Télé-université 1988

10. Haile, P. J., Richards, A. J.: Supporting the distance learner with computer teleconferencing. Paper presented at the 15th Annual Convocation of the Northeastern Educational Research Association, Ellenville, New York 1984

11. Halpern, D. F.: Analogies as a critical thinking skill. In: Applications of Cognitive Psychology: Problem Solving, Education, and Computing (D.E. Berger et al. eds). Hillsdale, NJ: Lawrence Erlbaum Associates 1987

12. Harasim, L.: Online education as a new domain. In: Mindweave: communication, computers and distance education (R.D Mason, A.R. Kaye eds), pp 50–62. Oxford: Pergamon Press 1989

13. Harasim, L.(ed.): Online education: perspectives on a new environment. New York: Praeger 1990

14. Harasim, L., Wolfe, R.: Research analysis and evaluation of computer conferencing and networking in education. Toronto: OISE, Ontario Ministry of Education 1988.

15. Henri, F.: La téléconférence assistée par ordinateur dans une activité de formation à distance. Thèse de doctorat. Montreal: Concordia University 1989

16. Hiltz, R.: The Virtual Classroom: Initial explorations of computer-mediated communication systems as an interactive learning space. Newark, N.J.: New Jersey Institute of Technology 1985

17. Hiltz, S. R.: Online communities: a case study of the office of the future. New Jersey: Ablex 1985

18. Hiltz, R.: The Virtual Classroom: using computer-mediated communication for university teaching. Journal of Communication, 36, pp. 95–104 (1986)

19. Hiltz, R.: Evaluating the Virtual Classroom. In: Online education: perspectives on a new environment (L.Harasim, ed.), pp. 133–184. New York: Praeger 1990

20. Hiltz, S. R., Turoff, M.: The network nation: human communication via computer. Reading, MA: Addison-Wesley 1982

21. Johansen, R., Vallée, J., Spangler, K.: Electronic meetings: technical alternatives and social choices. Reading, MA: Addison-Wesley 1979

22. Marton, F., Hounsell, D.J., Entwistle, N.J. (eds.): The experience of learning. Edinburgh: Scottish Academic Press 1984

23. Mason R. and Kaye, A.(eds.): Mindweave: communication, computers, and distance education. Oxford: Pergamon Press 1989

24. McCreary, E., and Van Duren, J.: Educational applications of computer conferencing. Canadian Journal of Educational Communication. 16, 2, pp. 135–166 (1987)

25. McCreary, E.: Eliciting more rigorous cognitive outcomes through analysis of computer-mediated discussion. Paper prepared for Improving University Teaching, Fifteenth International Conference, Vancouver 1989

26. Meunier, C., and Henri, F.: Recherche en télématique et formation à distance. In: Actes du Premier Congrés des Sciences de l'Education de langue française du Canada, Quebec 1987

27. Miles, M. B. and Huberman, A. M.: Qualitative data analysis. London: Sage 1987

28. Muchielli, R.: Méthodes actives dans la pédagogie des adultes. Connaissance du problème, applications pratiques. Paris: Librairie Technique/Entreprise Moderne d'Edition 1984.

29. Nightingale, P.: Understanding processes and problems in student writing. Studies in Higher Education, 13, 3, pp. 263–283 (1988).

30. Perry, W. G. Jr.: Cognitive and ethical growth. In: The Modern American College (A.W. Chickering ed.). Washington: Jossey-Bass 1981

31. Quellmalz, E.S.: Needed: better methods for testing higher-order thinking skills. Educational Leadership, 43, 2, pp. 29–35 (1985)

32. Rembold, K., Yussen, S.R.: Interaction of knowledge, learning, and development. Report from the Project on Metacognitive Aspects of Prose Comprehension, Program Report 86-8. Madison: Wisconsin Centre for Education Research 1986

33. Sadler, W. A.: Thinking about learning: redefining liberal education through skill development. Journal of Learning Skills, 4, 16 (1983)

34. Salomon, G.: AI in reverse: computer tools that turn cognitive. Journal of Educational Computing Research, 4, 2, pp. 123–139 (1988)

35. Schmeck, R.R.: Learning styles of college students. In: Individual difference in cognition (R. Dillon, R.R. Schmeck eds.). New York: Academic Press 1983

36. Shapiro, H., Møller, M., Nielson, N.C., Nipper, S.: Third generation distance education and computer conferencing in Denmark. Paper presented at the Second Symposium on Computer Conferencing. Guelph: University of Guelph 1987

37. Waugh, M., Miyake, N., Levin, J., and Cohen, M.: Problem solving interactions on electronic networks. Paper presented at the Annual Meeting of the AERA. New Orleans: AERA 1988

9
A Case Study Approach to Evaluation of Computer Conferencing

Michael Waggoner

Schindler Education Centre, University of Northern Iowa, USA

Abstract: The use of computer conferencing in collaborative learning involves a complex interplay of three sets of conditions: the basic elements of a planned collaborative learning experience; the characteristics of the computer conferencing system; and individual and group characteristics. The understanding of such complex interactions among the numerous variables involved does not emerge from a particular analytic approach, be it statistical manipulation, content analysis, or other single quantitative or qualitative technique. Rather, an encompassing approach is needed to provide a comprehensive view and broader insight into the multifaceted phenomenon that occurs when a group of individuals, embarking on a collective task, mediate their communication through a computer conferencing system. A case study approach is proposed that combines selected quantitative and qualitative techniques.

Keywords: computer conferencing, evaluation, case study, collaborative learning.

Interacting sets of conditions

Elements of collaborative learning

Collaborative learning has occurred as long as groups have attempted to work together toward a common goal. It has been during the the last twenty years, however, that collaborative learning as an intentional teaching and learning strategy has seen increasingly formal development, study and evaluation. Pioneered in the elementary and secondary education environments, the technique has found its way into college, university, and corporate settings in undergraduate, graduate, and continuing education applications. The technique, as described by its leading proponents and practitioners is characterized by five basic elements: positive interdependence, face-to-face interaction, individual accountability, interpersonal and small group skills, and group processing [5,10,11,12,13,22].

Positive interdependence

Fostering a positive interdependence among group participants has been found to be a key element in a successful collaborative learning experience. Group members need to feel that they need each other to accomplish the task at hand. This can be done through establishing goals mutually conceived, negotiated, and agreed upon by the group. Establishing joint rewards to be received by all members is another aspect helping to create an environment of positive interdependence. Shared information and materials are equally important to the group in so far as this provides a basis for members to have insight into the overall task and to be of assistance to each other. The final aspect contributing to positive interdependence is the assignment of individual roles. Each person must understand the part they play and their relationship to the whole project. The presence of these aspects are important to insuring a successful collaborative learning experience.

Face-to-face communication

As traditionally conceived, collaborative learning involves face-to-face communication. Verbal interactions taking place among students and leaders of the experience are important. Similar to the conduct of effective discussions, periodic synthesizing and summarizing are necessary, as are explanation and elaboration. This is the element of collaborative learning that obviously incurs the most substantial transformation when moving into a computer-mediated environment. Communicating in a typewritten medium where interaction is disembodied from nonverbal cues and, most often, delayed due to members interacting from different places at different times, can be expected to significantly impact the group's work [8,16]. Interventions will have to be designed and evaluated during the collaborative learning experience to ameliorate the negative effects of this changed medium as well as to exploit the opportunities that this medium provides.

Individual accountability

Though the focus in this experience is on the life and work of the group, individual accountability is a key to the group's effectiveness. In the traditional application of this technique, much of the group's interaction takes place out of view of the instructional leader, making aspects of individual assessment difficult. In a computer-meditated environment, much of the individual's performance and interactions are captured in text and are available for closer analysis and feedback.

Interpersonal and small group skills

Students often do not come to school or college with the social skills they need to be effective in collaborating with others in a task. Consequently, instructional leaders often need to teach these skills, which include: communication, leadership, trust, decision making, and conflict management. Further, they need to motivate the members of the group to use these skills in order that the group function effectively. This teaching task is complicated when the activity is taken into a computer-mediated environment. The nonverbal aspect of communication, heretofore so important to teaching these skills, is absent. New strategies for teaching these skills in an online environment must be developed along with methods for evaluating their success in facilitating the collaborative learning activity.

Group processing

The final element essential to constructing and to implementing a successful collaborative learning experience is group processing. Closely related to the previous element – interpersonal and small group skills – group processing provides the members with the time and procedures for analyzing the functioning of their group and their own use of interpersonal and small group skills. This helps alter the focus of the individual to the larger group and to make judgments about overall effectiveness and his or her relative contributions to the achievement of the group goal [1,2]. Central to the success of this is the oversight and timely intervention of the teacher. Again, the change in communication environment will require alteration of monitoring and intervention strategies that may differ significantly from a conventional face-to-face setting.

In any teaching situation, attention to the characteristics of the students is critical to selecting the appropriate teaching strategy, to structuring the material to relate to their prior knowledge, and to engaging their attention [2]. As individuals come together in groups, they form a collective identity as well. These realities of a given teaching situation take on added importance when the learning experience is taken in to a computer-mediated context.

System characteristics

The literature on individual and group characteristics in the context of computer-mediated communication derives from the research on user interface concerns in information retrieval in libraries. Bennett [3] underscored the importance of attending to the user as the key in interactive computer systems. He argued that a human engineering approach must be taken where trade-offs are made among design possibilities, system capabilities, and human use capacity and alternatives.

In work from the same period, Katter [14] introduced a concept of a user's 'line of credit' that is extended to a new system or task involving interactive computing. During this time, the system must deliver the expected benefits before the patience of the user is exhausted. He goes on to suggest that within the 'line of credit' period, the user may pass through three stages of development: 1) uncertainty, during which he gains a comfort level about technical competence to effectively operate the system; 2) insight, at which point he sees the underlying systems and principles and sees how to apply the system to accomplish useful tasks; and 3) incorporation, the point at which the use of the system becomes second nature and part of normal work behavior. These findings constitute important guidance for the successful use of computer-mediated communications within collaborative learning contexts. Although there may be increasingly sophisticated software design options available, there seems to be some limit to what a user will undertake and a time within which it must demonstrate a payoff. This is an additional layer of complication to the design of the collaborative learning situation. The novelty inherent during the 'line of credit' period must be used to engage the motivation of the learner to proceed with use of the system and the academic task.

In addition to these broad system considerations are two other major factors that must be acknowledged and accommodated: the narrowed communication channel deriving from the exclusive use of typewritten communication and the delay in interaction that is inherent to asynchronous systems. The constriction of the communication channel to typewritten text eliminates nonverbal cues from the interaction process. This phenomenon has been widely studied and commented upon by practitioners [8,16,17,24]. The essence of these studies suggest that compensating mechanisms need to be developed and employed to offset the nonverbal dimension that is so integral to most communication in group work. It is particularly important in a teaching situation where learner progress is often monitored by observing nonverbal behavior and where some teacher feedback is given nonverbally. The delayed interaction inherent in most asynchronous systems likewise requires intervention strategies to compensate for the momentum that may naturally develop from the immediacy of face-to-face communication.

The design and implementation of a computer conferencing system in a collaborative learning experience, then, may be said to have two aspects: the design of the technical software system, and the design of the teaching-social system. Software system features are addressed elsewhere in this volume (notably in Part 3). The second aspect, the teaching-social system, requires a close look at individual and group characteristics.

Individual and group characteristics

In a 1982 study, Kerr and Hiltz [16] identified categories and characteristics of individuals and groups that may influence the acceptance and use of a computer conferencing system. The individual variables are in five categories: attitudinal variables; skills and characteristics; demographic characteristics; environmental variables; and psychological variables.

Attitudinal variables include attitudes toward the task. What is the relative importance or priority given the task among the individual's other commitments? What is the attitude of the individual toward the media to be used? This can include not only feelings about computers, but expectations regarding specific systems as well, such as anticipated usefulness, impact upon productivity, and difficulty of use. Further, views toward alternative media need to be considered here; these include telephone, conventional mail, and travel to face-to-face meetings.

Attitudes toward the group also come into play. For example, are the other group members liked, respected, or considered to be an important reference group? Finally, there will inevitably be expectations about how the system will effect relationships within the group.

Some basic skills figure importantly in the evaluation of the use of computer conferencing in collaborative learning. Kerr and Hiltz cite personal communication skills, previous related experience, and physical or intellectual disabilities as such factors. Personal communication skills include reading speed, typing speed, preference for speaking or writing, and general writing ability. Among the previous related experience factors are use of: computers, terminals, other computer-based communication systems. Physical or intellectual disabilities are those that become factors due to the requirements of the computer interface to the communication process.

Demographic characteristics may impact the acceptance and use of the system. These include age, gender, level of educational attainment, and ethnicity, nationality or subculture.

Environmental variables may, likewise, figure importantly. Available resources, including secretarial support, may affect system use, as might position of the individual in the organization or their relative status in a more informal group. The amount of pressure to use the system from superiors and peers can also be an important factor.

Finally, psychological variables may influence participation. Personality characteristics and basic values are two dimensions suggested that may interact with the other variables above to affect an individual's acceptance and use of a system in a collaborative learning situation.

Attitudinal and psychological variables characterize the mental set that an individual will bring to the learning activity. These will need to be anticipated and accommodated in order for the collaborative learning experience to be effective. Motivations for participation will vary and early identification of incentives and the establishment of mutual expectations will set the tone for the individual's participation. Personal communication skills, previous related experience with the technology, technique, or topic, as well as physical or intellectual conditions may require careful individual attention to insure full participation. Since each individual in a collaborative learning activity has specific responsibilities, this aspect of preparation and monitoring becomes increasingly important. Similarly, demographic and environmental characteristics should provide important information in designing and implementing the teaching social system aspect of the collaborative learning activity in a computer conferencing environment.

Into this complex milieu, another set of variables must be introduced. While individuals possess distinctive characteristics, they also acquire characteristics as they become part of a group. Here too, Kerr and Hiltz [16] have elaborated factors that may affect the work of a group in the context discussed here. The major factors affecting the work of the group are the structure, leadership, and cohesiveness of the group. Significant among the structural factors are the size of the group, its degree of geographic dispersion, whether control is centralized or decentralized, and the extent to which there have been pre-existing communication ties among the group members.

Leadership has proven to be an important quality in the effectiveness of groups in a computer-mediated environment. The style of the leader and the level of activity figure importantly [15]. This is another parallel to the face-to-face collaborative learning activity. Leadership by the teacher is a key variable in the effectiveness of that teaching and learning strategy.

The cohesiveness of the group can play a key role in the effectiveness of the group. An analysis of sociometric ties can determine whether members: have ever met face-to-face, know each other prior to the activity, have worked together previously, exist as a collection of cliques, have many individualists, or are an integrated group. In addition to the sociometric ties, the relative competitiveness, and degree of trust or openness can affect the work of the work in this collaborative computer-mediated communication environment.

The composition and commitment of the group to the task is important in a structured application of computer conferencing like collaborative learning. Pre-existing ties among group members is an influential favorable variable, as group formation has already taken place to a certain extent and movement of the group into the electronic environment may be facilitated as a consequence. Additionally, Kiesler *et al* [17] found that electronic groups were as task oriented as face-to-face groups, but because of keyboard entry time, took more time. They also found that groups participated more equally in an electronic context and were more uninhibited in their remarks than in face-to-face groups. These findings may suggest that this medium may be conducive to use in a collaborative learning activity. Further, because group activity is observable through this medium and other participation variables can be identified with some predictive value, the possibility exists for a comprehensive evaluation of a collaborative learning activity conducted in a computer conferencing environment.

A framework for evaluation

The case study

As can be seen from the preceding sections, there are numerous variables that interact to influence the processes and outcomes of a collaborative learning experience taking place within a computer-mediated communication environment. While a number of the variables are directly observable and lend themselves to quantitative analysis, others do not. In order to gain the encompassing view and broad insight desired regarding the effectiveness of this kind of experience, a comprehensive evaluation strategy is needed [19]. A case study approach is recommended to accomplish this.

The single case study can accommodate a wide variety of quantitative and qualitative information that impact upon and that emerge from the examination of a contemporary phenomenon is its real-life context. The approach is similar to historical research except that due to the contemporaneity of the event, additional collaborating sources of information become available, including direct measurements, interviews, and other 'midstream' observations. Since Campbell and Stanley [7] attempted to discredit the case study approach, Campbell [6] has mollified his position, now defending the method as a useful research approach, particularly in the search for explanation through a pattern matching process. According to Yin [26], this "process can be applied even if there is only a single case because the pattern must fit multiple implications derived from an explanation or theory."

The case study enables explication of events and occurrences surrounding a case for the more general understandings that may be derived and subjected to further analyses. The information from a case study can, thereby, add to the cumulative knowledge about a class of phenomena. The key to the explanatory power of the case study is the systematic presentation of a cogent and compelling argument, supported by credible evidence, that demonstrates a consideration of the alternative points of view and explanations of facts and circumstances.

Evaluation framework components

There are four components of a case study framework for evaluating a collaborative learning activity that is mediated by computer conferencing: the integration of technical and teaching-social subsystems, that is, the presence of key elements of a collaborative learning experience adapted to the computer-mediated communications environment; member participation analysis, both observed and self-reported; outcome measures analysis related to knowledge attained and the efficacy of the activity design; leadership activity analysis. All four aspects then need to be viewed as a whole to recognize interaction effects. Further, those conducting the evaluation need to take cognizance of the impact of their own relationship to the activity.

Integration of technical and teaching-social subsystems

Research and practice in teaching has shown that certain elements must be in place to assure the opportunity for an effective collaborative learning experience. As elaborated above, they involve the design of the teaching strategy and facilitation of individual performance in the context of group work. The replacement of the face-to-face component with computer-mediated communication adds the technical complications of a new communication system to the instructional milieu.

The first step in evaluating such a collaborative learning activity is simply to check to see the extent to which the five basic elements of a collaborative learning activity – positive interdependence, face-to-face-communication (changed to a computer-mediated medium), individual accountability, interpersonal and small group skills, and group processing – are present and the extent to which measures have been taken to account for the foreseen effects of the computer conferencing medium on the process.

Experience has shown that the process of bringing a group together in an online activity, particularly where the group members had not previously known each other, may be significantly aided by beginning with more traditional forms of communication using the telephone, conventional mail, and written explanatory material [24]. This may be important in collaborative learning, where shared materials and individually tailored assignments figure prominently. In The University of Michigan's Interactive Communications Simulations (ICS), an exemplary use of collaborative learning through computer conferencing, teams of students receive extensive written material that assist them in preparing for their online experiences. There is also substantial reference material online [9].

The analysis of the extent to which the technical and teaching-social subsystems have been integrated will involve considered judgment by the evaluator and may be informed by data from the other essential components of the case study evaluation framework.

Member participation analysis

The analysis of participation by group members is a multifaceted and potentially rich data source for evaluating the efficacy of the collaborative learning experience. There are two main dimensions to this analysis: information related to participation as observed, and as self-reported. The first can include data collected by the computer system regarding frequency and duration of participation, as well as the content analysis of the text of the participants' interactions. A number of techniques have been developed for this kind of analysis. Quantitative analysis has been done since the advent of these systems; content and discourse analysis has come along more recently. [1]

The second dimension is self-reported information. This is an important part of the analytic process as well, since it involves comment from the participant about many aspects of the process. For example, some assessment of psychological type may be made through administration of the Myers-Briggs Type Indicator instrument. Other instruments exist or may be developed to ascertain attitudes towards use of various kinds of communication media. Still others elucidate learning styles that may suggest important information to the teacher regarding strategies to employ. Special instruments have been designed to solicit perceptions about efficacy of group function within the computer-mediated process [24]. Taken together, these methods of collecting self-report data can contribute to the overall picture of what took place and how effective it appeared to be.

Outcome measures analysis

In a planned collaborative learning activity using computer conferencing, knowledge attainment measures may be constructed and taken. Also, measures related to the efficacy of the design may be implemented to provide feedback for refinement of the model in subsequent applications.

Knowledge attainment can be measured through standard classroom evaluation procedures like examinations, papers, participation in group discussion, among others. The advantage of group discussion online is, of course, that a verbatim transcript is created that may be reviewed at a later time by the instructor for a closer reflection on the quality of knowledge exhibited by a group member. Outcome measures related to the design of the technical and teaching-social system may be highly idiosyncratic due to the wide variety of conferencing systems in use combined with the unique implementation that may be designed by the instructor. Nevertheless, this aspect of analyzing outcomes for knowledge and system design is important. In both cases, an assessment should be made regarding intended versus actual consequences of implementing a collaborative learning activity using computer conferencing.

Leadership activity analysis

Leadership has been cited as a crucial element in collaborative learning activities in conventional face-to-face settings [11,12]. It has also been cited as crucial in the successful functioning of computer-mediated communication systems [15]. When combining the activity and the medium, leadership is clearly critical. Evaluation of leadership, however, is elusive. Is it to be judged in light of the results, i.e., knowledge attained, or in light of the perceptions of the participants regarding a productive learning experience? Again, a combined reading of these example measures along with others can provide a more complete picture than any single one. In this case, an interview with the activity leader may be appropriate, even essential. For with the leader resides the knowledge of the technical system,

---

[1] See Chapter 8 in this volume for a discussion of content analysis.

knowledge and assumptions about the group members, and assumptions about the relative utility of given teaching strategies in this context. It would seem productive to probe the leader for insights into these and other questions, since these assumptions guided the implementation of the activity.

Many of the variables within these four categories potentially interact with each other. The person conducting the evaluation must occasionally step back from the data within each category and look for the larger connections. Many of the variables discussed above may be quantified and even benefit from multivariate and factor analysis. Others, however, do not yield to such treatment and must be the subject of a more gestalt reflection on the potential meaning of the interacting aspects of the activity.

The literature of social science and qualitative research provides helpful guidance for this aspect of the evaluation process where the evaluator may be participant as well as observer [4,18,21,23].

Conclusion

Evaluating the use of computer conferencing in a collaborative learning activity involves the analysis of many interacting variables. Many of these may be measured using quantitative techniques, but others require qualitative analysis. A case study offers the most comprehensive approach to understanding this complex process. While more research and evaluation needs to be conducted based upon models of these interacting measures, this is not practical for a typical instructional use. A teacher with considerable experience in both collaborative learning techniques and computer conferencing should be able to construct and assess an implementation of collaborative learning using computer conferencing that will be a productive learning experience if short of a complete, highly disciplined research study.

References

1. Ausubel, D.: The psychology of meaningful verbal learning. New York: Grune and Stratton 1963

2. Bandura, A., Ross, D. and Ross, S.: Social learning and personality. New York: Holt, Rinehart, and Winston 1963

3. Bennett, J. The user interface in interactive systems. Annual Review of Information Science Technology, Vol. 7, ASIS Press 1972

4. Bellah, R.,Madsen, R.,Sullivan, W., Swidler, A., and Tipton, S.: Appendix: Social science as public philosophy. In: Habits of the Heart: Individualism and Commitment in American Life. Berkeley, CA.: University of California Press 1984

5. Budin, H. Computers and cooperative learning: A background for teachers. In: Technology and Teacher Education Annual 1991 (D. Carey, R. Carey, D. Willis, J. Wills, J. eds.). Society for Technology and Teacher Education 1991

6. Campbell, D.: Degrees of freedom and the case study. Comparative Political Studies, 8 (1975)

7. Campbell, D. and Stanley, J.: Experimental and quasi-experimental designs for research. Chicago: Rand McNally 1966

8. Feenberg, A. The written world. In: Feenberg, A.: The written world. In: Mindweave: communication, computers and distance education. (R.D. Mason, A.R. Kaye, eds.), pp. 22–39. Oxford: Pergamon 1989

9. Goodman, F.L.: Instructional gaming through computer conferencing. In: Empowering networks: computer conferencing in education. (M. Waggoner, ed.). Englewood Cliffs, N.J.: Educational Technology Publications 1992

10. Harasim, L.: Computer-mediated cooperation in education: group learning networks. In: Proceedings of the Second Symposium on Computer Conferencing. Guelph, Ontario, Canada: University of Guelph 1987

11. Johnson, D. and Johnson, R.: Learning together and alone: Cooperative, competitive, and individualistic learning. Englewood Cliffs, N.J.: Prentice-Hall 1975

12. Johnson, D., Johnson, R., Holubec, E., and Roy, P.: Circles of learning: Cooperation in the classroom. Alexandria, Virginia: Association for Supervision and Curriculum Development 1984

13. Johnson, D. and Johnson, R.: Computer-assisted cooperative learning. Educational Technology, January 1986

14. Katter, R.: On the on-line user of remote-access citation retrieval services. Santa Monica, California: System Development Corporation 1970

15. Kerr, E.: Electronic leadership; a guide to moderating online conferences. In: IEEE Transactions on Professional Communication. Vol. PC-29, 1 (1986)

16. Kerr, E. and Hiltz, S.: Computer-mediated communications systems. New York: Harcourt Brace Jovanovich 1982

17. Kiesler, S., Siegel, J. and McGuire, T.: Social psychological aspects of computer-mediated communications. American Psychologist, 39,10, pp. 1123-1134 (1984)

18. Lincoln, Y. and Guba, E.: Naturalistic inquiry. Beverly Hills, California: Sage Publications 1985

19. McClure, C., Bishop, A., Doty, P. and Rosenbaum, H.: Research on computer-mediated communication and its significance for the NREN. In: The National Research and Education Network (NREN): Research and Policy Perspectives. (C. McClure, A. Bishop, P.Doty, H. Rosenbaum eds.). Norwood, NJ: Ablex Publishing Corporation 1991

20. McKeachie, W.: Teaching tips: A guide book for the beginning teacher. Lexington, Massachusetts: D.C. Heath and Company 1986

21. McMillan, J.: Designing ethnographic research. In: Research in Education (J. McMillan, S. Schumacher eds.). New York: Scott Foresman 1989

22. Slavin, R.: An introduction to cooperative learning research. In: Learning to cooperate, cooperating to learn (R. Slavin, et al eds.). New York: Plenum Press 1985

23. Schon, D.: The reflective practitioner. New York: Basic Books 1983

24. Waggoner, M.: Explicating expert opinion through a computer conferencing delphi. Unpublished dissertation. Ann Arbor, Michigan: University of Michigan 1987

25. Waggoner, M.: Explicating expert opinion through a computer conferencing delphi. In: Empowering networks: computer conferencing in education (M. Waggoner ed.). Englewood Cliffs, NJ: Educational Technology Publications 1992

26. Yin, R.: The case study as a serious research strategy. Knowledge: Creation, Diffusion and Utilization, 3 (1981)

10
Talking, Teaching, and Learning in Network Groups: Lessons from Research

Sara Kiesler

Department of Social and Decision Sciences,
Carnegie Mellon University, Pittsburgh, Pennsylvania, USA

Abstract: Using empirical research findings, this chapter describes what we know about electronic groups and how electronic groups may change education. Electronic groups are not just long-distance traditional groups. Electronic groups can transform computer and people resources, both for informal and formal learning. Among these changes are qualitative changes in social contacts and group dynamics. A major structural change would be a shift from traditional classroom organization to more group or team centered collaborative learning in education and training. This transformation may benefit many students and educators but also will create new complications, such as the possibility of further centralization of school institutions, of new 'free' markets for education, and of changing roles of teachers and students.

Keywords: educational resource, technological change, groups, communication technologies, process loss, ARPANET, electronic mail, distribution list, bulletin board, electronic group, Internet, electronic archive, social information, social context cues, school, market, hierarchy, trans-organizational collaboration, student role, teacher role.

Introduction

Computers, which used to be female clerks, today are electronic technologies of astonishing mental power. Among the most important of these achievements is communication based on computers and computer networks. Networked environments can make a difference in education because they give access to two kinds of educational resource: computers and people. Computer resources accessible on networks include computer tutors, online library catalogs, encyclopedic databases, and graphics programs. People resources increase through links to more people in more places. Also, as we shall see, networks give social and psychological access to more kinds of people.

In this chapter I will focus mainly on changes in people resources. I will argue that these changes potentially increase not just the quantity of educational access but can change the nature of education. A major qualitative change would be a shift from traditional classroom organization to more group or team centered collaborative learning. This transformation may benefit many students and educators but also will create new complications for education and training.

Framework of analysis

In thinking about technological change, we can consider two levels of potential impact. Some technological change is primarily amplifying, making it possible for people to do what they have done before, but more accurately, quickly, or cheaply. Historically, many important technological innovations have had amplifying effects. The vacuum cleaner, for example, itself a modest social innovation, was a significant part of the revolution in household technology that vanquished servants from the middle class home. Cleaning was something that people had done, but the new device was so much more efficient that a special class of cleaners was no longer required. Similarly, amplifying technological change can lead to the rare and esoteric becoming a commonplace part of human existence. Travel as a widespread leisure pursuit, made possible by improving transportation technologies and greater wealth, is an example of this kind of change.

When technology is more than just amplifying and brings about qualitative change in how people think about the world, in their social roles and institutions, in the ways they work, and in the political and economic challenges they face, we say it has transformative effects. Technologies such as printing, mass production using interchangeable parts, electrification and mechanization of the farm, and the automobile, show this transformative characteristic.

Computer resources accessible on networks can have transformative effects because these resources can create educational settings people encounter nowhere else – rapid interactive triggering of new text, vivid graphics, infinite patience, no criticism or status games, personal control over the pace of learning. Many people find learning by computer approachable and intrinsically motivating. Online computer programs can allow for the explicit and developmentally-graded presentation of problems and exemplars, with interactive feedback on the learner's progress. Detailed, individualized record-keeping also can be incorporated, and this in turn allows theorists to test whether learners can progress to higher skills levels without building on some intermediate levels specified by theory as prerequisites. The network makes it possible for groups of children or adults anywhere to have access to these special resources.

People resources on networks also may have transformative effects. History shows that most new communication technologies, ranging from papyrus to the telephone, have had far-reaching transformative consequences. These occur because by making information more portable and by increasing opportunities for social contact, communication technologies also change thinking and social relations. The telephone had amplifying effects when it replaced the telegraph in business communication; for instance, it improved the efficiency of international trade. Its transformative effects were to bring rural areas in closer contact with cities, to extend peoples' psychological neighborhood, to create new social and occupational roles, and to aid the geographic dispersion of families and organizations. New information flows and contacts among people can lead to significant organizational change. Researchers studying computer networks are already seeing early evidence of organizational changes in firms.

Social scientists must use a variety of techniques to see beyond a new technology's immediate problems and amplifying effects. Some fundamental questions can be studied through laboratory experiments. For instance, how do people respond emotionally to different forms of communication? What skills are best learned by watching experts or talking with them? Other questions, particularly those concerning worklife and organizational change, are not amenable to laboratory experiments. Therefore, researchers turn to real organizations that have been using computer networks for some time, where employees access remote databases and communicate by electronic mail routinely. From field studies and experiments, we gradually construct a body of evidence on amplifying and transformative effects. This research is often a disorderly process as we see people using new technology in surprising ways. Often paradoxical effects show up that contradict previous theories.

Groups and learning

In order to think about the implications of network communication for education, particularly about the implications of the people resources on networks, we must first review some principles of how people learn. At the outset, much of what we learn depends on solitary listening, study, and practice. Yet learning with other people has some tremendous advantages for increasing motivation and achievement of learners. Young children learn by imitating and interacting with adults and older children. Once in school, students working as a group stimulate planning and active learning, and they contribute to one another's motivation and social skill development [1]. Children and adults in groups also make cognitive gains: they help one another remember, they correct one another's mistakes, they exchange experience-based knowhow; they expose each other to different perspectives on issues. I will use the term collaborative learning to describe the process of learning in groups. Since in collaborative learning, people learn from one another, more than one person is talking. Also in collaborative learning, learners are teachers, and teachers, learners. Talking, teaching, and learning are intertwined processes in groups.

Collaborative learning is not a pure good. One cost of working in groups is that some resources must be invested in group coordination. For instance, planning as a group takes time and effort, and may have psychological costs. When a group member is listening to others, he or she is not writing. When a group member is talking to others, he or she is not listening. Social psychologists who study small groups have called the transaction costs of being in a group 'process losses' [22].

The quality of the individuals who are members of a group is a major constraint on the value of collaborative learning. A group of competent individuals often produces strong group performance – learning far better than would be predicted on the basis of the individuals' average ability. A group of incompetent individuals results in an even weaker group [23]. Over time, competent groups get better at what they do well and gain more from interventions that increase coordination, individual competency, and inter-member learning, so the gap between excellent and poor groups grows.

The value of collaborative learning also depends upon the kind of task or skill to be learned. Beethoven doubtless would not have written better symphonies working in a group. To examine task differences, social psychologists have constructed experimental tasks that call on different skills and then permit an artificial but theoretically useful comparison of a group's achievement with the sum of what individuals would have done without the group [19]. In these experiments, task differences often determine whether the group product is worse than, equal to, or better than the sum of individual efforts. An example of a positive effect is found in groups given a problem that is hard to solve or information that is hard to remember. If the group has a discussion, the group will be more likely to solve the problem or remember the information than will the same people working alone [3,11,13]. Group members contribute valuable non-overlapping skills and cancel one another's errors, so, at least in the short run, group interaction bestows benefits.

Process losses reduce the benefits of collaborative learning most when the task requires creativity and a finely-tuned chain of logic or argument. When engaged in group interaction, groups expropriate their members' valuable time and thinking. This is a major reason why brainstorming is actually more effective when done individually rather than in a face-to-face group [5]. Also, groups produce conformity. Suppose a group spends considerable time talking about a foolish idea because it is promulgated by a member who has high status. This group would have been better off working as individuals. A fair summary of the experimental research is that for most kinds of intellectual problem solving and decision making, and when the group has a mix of competencies, process losses result in group achievement that is somewhat above the level of the average group member but below the level of the most competent member.

Electronic Groups and Collaborative Learning

In the United States, the technology for today's network communications began with the development of time sharing computers and the ARPANET, a packet switching network that connected universities and research institutions conducting computer science research. The ARPANET was meant to permit more efficient allocation of scarce computer resources by allowing researchers to log on to remote computers unavailable in their own institutions. The initial conception of the ARPANET was of researcher-to-computer interaction. Then another facility called 'electronic mail' made possible researcher-to-researcher communication and soon a blizzard of electronic mail eclipsed the initial purpose of the network.

Once electronic mail was available on the ARPANET, computer scientists around the country started to exchange ideas spontaneously and casually on topics ranging from system design to programming bugs to movie reviews. Graduate students consulted professors and other students who could offer interesting problems and skills without regard to where these colleagues were located physically. Principal investigators used electronic mail to coordinate the work of multi-person research projects and to stay in touch with other projects and funding agencies. A large network community formed, filled with friends who didn't know each other and collaborators who rarely met in person. Starr Roxanne Hiltz and Murray Turoff developed a way for scientists to have electronic conferences [12]. When I and my colleagues first began to monitor computer networks systematically in 1982 [21], we documented that the most used programs were those for human communication.

The rise of groups on the networks

Electronic mail transmits messages to people by copying messages to their personal electronic mailboxes. To communicate with a group, a sender can explicitly list the name of each recipient or can deliver the message simultaneously to many mailboxes by sending the message to a group name or distribution list – for example, *All_Staff* or *Privacy_Issues*. The sender does not need to know the names and addresses of group members. The software uses a file that contains the names and addresses of all group members to mail a copy of the communication, which is addressed to the group as a whole, to the personal mailbox of each group member.

Electronic bulletin boards (bboards) and conferences are common variants of group electronic mail. Like distribution lists, they have names that identify their topic or audience. Bboards display messages in a publicly accessible file as they are received. Computer conferences sort messages by topic and display grouped messages together. Whereas distribution lists send messages to recipients' personal mailboxes intermixed with personal communications, people have to 'visit' conferences and bboards. As software becomes more sophisticated, the distinctions among these forms of group communication are diminishing. Already some software allows people to forward bboard posts to their personal mailbox or to receive distribution list mail separately from personal mail. As these changes occur, transitional problems occur too. Employees today may find it hard to know where or how to look for different kinds of group activity. Creating new groups whose members use different computers and networks still can be awkward.

Many electronic groups on today's computer networks were created for fun or because people's interests converged on some topic. If company policy permits, extracurricular electronic groups can range over every conceivable topic, from restaurant reviews to child raising tips to motorcycle riding. In many organizations there are electronic forums for buying and selling goods, for giving tips about local businesses, for trading information about professional affairs, and for discussing current news events. Several years ago the Fort Collins city government set up an electronic 'classified ads' to encourage employees to use the new computer network. An organization can be connected to BITNET, to the Internet (heir of the ARPANET), or to one of the commercial networks; its employees can belong to groups whose members come from many different organizations. Brian Reid of Digital Equipment Corporation monitors Internet use. In 1991, some 37,000 organizations were connected to it. One group forum accessible through the Internet, called *Newsgroups*, consisted of over 1500 different groups. Many of them focus on topics of professional interest; others center on current issues; still others are just for fun. Today more than 1.5 million people read at least one newsgroup and that number is growing rapidly.

Unlike what is true in traditional institutions, people having access to a computer network are likely to belong to a raft of electronic groups. Because physical location is unimportant and conversation can be asynchronous, these groups can span time zones and countries. Some electronic groups are extensions of existing workgroups. They provide a convenient way for members to communicate between meetings. Others consist of people who do not know one another personally and rarely or never have the opportunity to meet in person. Unless organizations deliberately restrict access, networks do not have borders defined by department, job category, or hierarchical position in the organization. Therefore, they provide access across social categories as well as physical access. For instance, at Hewlett Packard, the human factors engineers in different departments might get together at one conference a year. By forming an electronic conference group, they had an ongoing forum for discussing professional and company issues [8]. Electronic discussions are usually informal and egalitarian. In some ways these groups are like friendship groups in the non-electronic world: they have norms, sustained interaction, and peer pressure. But unlike non-electronic friendship groups, they often have a hundred members or more of people who do not know one another but who are bound together electronically.

Electronic group organization

Some researchers believe that transformative effects of computer networking will emerge from the proliferation of electronic groups. Today's educational organizations, for example, have a structure that reflects the constraints and traditions of the non-electronic world. Physical locations usually put teachers and students in proximity – in the same classroom in the same school. Science teachers in U.S. high schools rarely talk with their peers at other schools and districts. New teachers often have very limited access to expert, experienced teachers. Traditional formal organization also shapes and reinforces talking, teaching, and learning – who discusses what with whom, who has influence, the degree of information sharing, the number of levels information must climb before reaching its recipient, interconnectivity, and most social relationships. These constraints could change significantly when we introduce a communication technology – the computer network – that allows people to freely create working relationships and groups to talk across physical, temporal, social, and organizational boundaries.

Informal groups are common on networks, promoting a shift to more collaborative learning. A defining characteristic of today's organizational form is the formal system of training, record keeping, and routines for information distribution. Much important organizational information that could be exchanged remains in personal experience and never makes it into the formally-authorized distribution system – the war stories told by service reps that never appear in the official repair manuals, the folklore about how the experimental apparatus really works that never appears in the journal articles, the gossip about what good teachers do that isn't described in any personnel policy. This information travels by word of mouth and, in the past, its spread has been strongly influenced by physical proximity and social acquaintance. As a result, local expertise is unavailable to people in other locations and represents an untapped organizational learning resource. Electronic groups provide a forum for sharing war stories, expertise, and gossip independent of proximity and acquaintance.

A unique institution we have studied is the "Does-anybody-know...?" message, which appears frequently on computer networks. In this case, the electronic 'group' receiving the question can be the entire organization. Or, the sender might broadcast a request for information to a particular distribution list or bulletin board. Anyone who sees the message and knows the answer can reply. In a study of this phenomenon on the network at Tandem Computers Inc., [21, p. 135] we found that employees broadcasted an average of about 6 "Does-anybody-know?" messages every day to the company-wide distribution list. Typically, requests are from people who work directly with customers, usually in far-flung locations, and solicit personal experience or knowledge that could not be easily found in formal documents or in the sender's own workplace. At Tandem, the average question received about eight replies. Less than 15% of the people who answered a question were personally acquainted with the question asker or were even located in the same city as the asker.

The "Does-anybody-know?" message benefits a question asker by yielding information that otherwise would be unavailable to him or her. The technique allows others to benefit as well because question askers can redistribute the answers they receive electronically, by putting them in a public computer file on the network. About half of the Tandem question askers made their reply files publicly available over the company network to other employees. Tandem takes this sharing process one step further and maintains an electronic archive of questions and reply files that is itself accessible over the corporate network. The firm has thereby created a repository of current information and working expertise that is accessible internationally. That archive is accessed over 1000 times a month by employees seeking information.

The discretionary information sharing we discovered at Tandem and other networked organizations would puzzle social scientists if it occurred outside an electronic environment. The askers are admitting ignorance publicly, perhaps to hundreds or thousands of people. People are responding to requests for help from strangers with no expectation of any direct benefit to themselves. We think it is a combination of technology attributes and organizational norms that supports this kind of behavior at low cost to participants. The result is an electronic altruism quite different from prognostications that networks would destroy the social fabric of organizations.[1]

Group dynamics

Research suggests that interaction within groups differs in networks from that in traditional educational settings. For example, a field experiment conducted by the Rand Corporation suggests that networked groups have more flexible structures than has been traditional. Tora Bikson and J. Eveland formed two task forces in a

---

[1]See the paper by Jesus Rueda in Part 1 of this book for a documented example of the use of IBM's worldwide computer conferencing network for handling "Does-anybody-know?" questions. (ed.)

large utility firm, each assigned to analyze employee retirement issues and produce a report [7]. Each task force had 40 members, half of whom had recently retired from the company and half who were still employed but were eligible for retirement. The only difference between the two groups was that one was provided with networked computer terminals and software and the other was not. Both task forces created subcommittees, but the task force with electronic communication created more of them. Also, unlike the task force without electronic communication, the task force with electronic communication assigned people to more than one subcommittee. The task force with electronic communication also organized their subcommittees more complexly in an overlapping matrix structure. New subcommittees were added during the course of that task force's work. And that task force decided to continue meeting even after its official one-year life span had ended.

Research suggests that an electronic discussion is unique. Though people 'talk' using text, it is not the equivalent of a fast letter. Nor is it a transcribed face-to-face discussion, which has social rules and requires turn taking. In an electronic exchange, the social and contextual cues that usually regulate and influence group dynamics are missing. Electronic messages lack such social information as senders' and receivers' job titles, social importance, hierarchical position, race, age, and appearance. The context is undifferentiated too, since formal and casual exchanges look about the same. People have information about senders, receivers, and situations from other sources, but there are few cues in the computer interaction itself to remind people of that knowledge.

In a series of experiments at Carnegie Mellon University, we compared how small groups would make decisions using computer conferences or electronic mail as against face-to-face discussion. In one experiment, we looked at how people got to know one another by computer as compared with face-to-face. In another, we examined risk-related decisions of administrators and executives. All of the experiments showed that using a network slowed up decision making but also made the participants talk more frankly and more equally. Instead of one or two people doing most of the talking, as happens in many groups, everyone had a say. On the dark side, people also expressed extreme opinions and anger more openly in electronic communication than when they talked face-to-face. Computer scientists using the ARPANET had called this phenomenon 'flaming'.

We took the idea of deregulation further to see if electronic communication could influence people's status, which is one of the most pervasive and strongest regulators of group interaction. Previous research had shown that group members defer to people who have higher status, adjust the tone and content of their communications, and are more obedient to their direction. Their speech and demeanor become more formal in the presence of people who have high status. (One manager calls this the social Heisenberg effect – the conversation changes when he walks into the room.) Higher status people act differently too: they talk more and try to influence group discussion more than do lower status people. We reasoned that if cues indicating group members' statuses are absent, as would be true of electronic conversations, then status differences among group members might be reduced. In an experiment at Clarkson University by Vitaly Dubrovsky, Sara Kiesler, and Beheruz Sethna, groups whose members differed in social status were asked to make decisions both face-to-face and by electronic mail [6]. The results showed that the proportion of talk and influence of higher status people was reduced when group members communicated by electronic mail (even though the higher status members weren't aware of the change). This research indicates that electronic discussions are likely to be more egalitarian than discussions held face-to-face. Is this a good thing? If higher status members don't know what they are talking about, more democracy could improve decision making. If higher status members are truly smarter, the result will be less good.

Researchers have put forth alternative explanations for the openness and democracy one finds in electronic talk. One hypothesis is that the types of people who use computers are peculiarly asocial, but this hypothesis doesn't explain our experimental results, which show that the very same people talk more openly on a computer than face-to-face. Another hypothesis is that text messages require strong language to get one's point across; this hypothesis could explain flaming but not the reduction of social and status differences. The most promising theory is that when social context cues are absent or weak, people notice their social surroundings less and cease to care how others evaluate them. Hence they spend less time in social posturing and social niceties. Social scientists who advance this theory have proposed we use computers to carry on counseling, surveys, and interviews on sensitive subjects, situations in which people are anxious and cover their true feelings and opinions.

Greist and his colleagues at the University of Wisconsin, in taking patient histories, discovered that patients reported more undesirable symptoms in a computerized patient history interview than did patients who gave their histories to a doctor [9]. We conducted true experiments by randomly assigning respondents to two forms of survey administration – an interoffice mail pencil and paper questionnaire or an electronic mail version of the same questionnaire [16]. People randomly assigned to reply electronically reported significantly more socially undesirable behaviors, such as sometimes telling a fib and using illegal drugs.

The results of these studies show that people will report undesirable symptoms or behavior on a computer, but are these reports truthful? Without objective data on the true incidence of reported behavior, we might be measuring only negative self-presentation rather than honesty. A study by Waterton and Duffy, in Glasgow, Scotland, clears up this matter somewhat. They compared a computer interview with a personal interview in a survey of alcohol consumption and then compared their results to actual sales of alcohol. People who were randomly assigned to the computer survey reported higher alcohol consumption in the previous week than those who were randomly assigned to the human interviewer. Furthermore, the computer reports of consumption extrapolated more accurately to alcohol sales than did the face-to-face reports [25].

The experimental studies of electronic interaction show that, at least in a controlled setting, people can work collaboratively in computer-mediated groups. Paradoxically, talk in these groups seems impersonal because it lacks social and individual cues, but this lack can make people feel more comfortable than they might otherwise be. More playfulness, more opinions and unusual ideas, and even more anger may surface in group discussions on the network. Because of these responses, many group learning activities are being done at long distance on computer networks people didn't think would be possible. These range from group discussions of sex, to health counseling, to training new employees, to huge electronic project groups. Just as an electronic message isn't merely a fast letter or transcribed conversation, an electronic group is not just a traditional group whose members use computers.

Questions and Complications

The earliest literature about computer technologies was largely speculative, for there were few computer systems to study in the 1950's and early 1960's. Writers took established theories of rationalistic Weberian bureaucracies, industrial democracy, or economic task systems dominated by a legitimate administrative hierarchy, and deduced from these images how technologies should change business, communities, and education. These early reflections often polarized around utopian or Orwellian visions, both visions assuming the changes would be unidirectional and uniform – the same for all institutions, for all computer technologies, and for all time periods.

These applications of theory crumbled as empirical research accumulated. I now review some of these debates to show how theory has progressed, to show how current knowledge suggests networks might change the process of education, and to show the kinds of new complications that may ensue. I have chosen to discuss three debates about the organization of education and three about individual experience.

Structure of schools

Hierarchy throughout society is an established fact. Most social science explanations posit hierarchy as a consequence of underlying fundamental processes. Class theories usually explain hierarchy as a powerful instrument for elite control over the masses and preservation of the status quo. Alternatively, theories of cognitive limitation such as bounded rationality and axioms about the limits of effective span of control usually explain hierarchy as a response to the practical requirement for specialization and division of labor in large social undertakings. In these theories, growing size and changes in technologies and tasks set the parameters of hierarchy.

Networks might be of no consequence for hierarchies in education under the class politics theories, because the elites will aggrandize whatever instruments of social control are provided by the new technologies, and suppress those technologies that work against their interests. However, if prevailing organizational structures are artifacts of limits to cognition and control, computer-based technologies could change conditions in striking ways. Harold Leavitt and Thomas Whisler published an influential paper in 1958 which argued that by the 1990's computer information systems would radically restructure organizations and make them much more centralized. They saw computers as tools that would collect, aggregate and communicate information about organizational activity from the lowest level to upper management and would effectively bypass middle managers [26].

By the mid-1960's others argued that computers would decentralize organizations. Computer communications would encourage administrators to delegate some of their decisions downwards since administrators could be assured that they could catch emerging problems and monitor success. Therefore, increasing investments in computing would lead to a cascade of decision-making and authority downwards in organizations. Networks are already being heralded as powerful enabling instruments for 'de-layering' organizations, that is, to allow significant increases in effective spans of managerial control and reduce the layers of middle management. In education, students and teachers could co-organize classes and decide for themselves what to learn and how to learn it.

In the 1970's scholars began to study empirically the organizational consequences of computer-based information and communication systems. Danziger, Dutton, Kling, Kraemer, King, Bjorn-Anderson, and Robey [4,17,18] among others showed that organizations that were already somewhat centralized tended to use computers in ways that led to further centralization. Organizations that were already somewhat decentralized introduced computers in ways that further decentralized their decision-making procedures. This finding, essentially of amplifying effects, has significant import for any goal we might have to reorganize traditional educational institutions. School organization usually entails hierarchy and role boundaries for decisions about curriculum setting, testing, teaching, and learning, and traditional educational organizations have a history of resistance to change. Group-centered and collaborative learning designs may be hard to introduce except cosmetically.

Network technology itself poses some barriers to new organizational forms in education. Because of the organizational resources required for networks – for hardware, for experts to specify or customize software, for authority to collect new data or reorganize existing data, and for money to support network maintenance – significant organizational influence is often a prerequisite for building and effectively using these networks. This requirement creates a selection bias, helping mainly the organizationally powerful and those who prefer centralization to adopt technology and to install computing designs and policies that reflect their desires.

Experience in the manufacturing sector [20] suggests that networks will have no impact on existing school organization. We may have to deliberately create special 'greenfield' organizations whose structure is consistent with the potential of networks. Some prototypes already exist – Hiltz's networked classes in New Jersey, the University of Lancaster's computer-mediated management courses[2], and in my town of Pittsburgh, a new organization that has been created to give teachers and students in the school system accounts on the Internet.

Education markets

Education is not just a social institution; it is an industry and as such can be examined from the perspective of economics. From this perspective, hierarchy is not only an important feature of organization structure, but also of industry structure. Hierarchies in the form of regulatory agencies are seen as necessary for coping with imperfections in markets. A major imperfection is that an essential condition for perfect competition, the condition of availability to buyers at zero cost of perfect information about products and prices, is seldom met in markets. Networks provide, in the view of some theorists, the means to greatly reduce this constraint. The infrastructure of computer-based communication technology could provide 24 hour access at exceedingly low cost to almost any kind of information desired. Moreover, this infrastructure could provide the means for effecting real-time transactions based on such information. This could eliminate

---

[2]See the paper by David McConnell in Part 1 of this book . (ed.)

whole classes of intermediaries (e.g., schools) whose whole function is to provide an essential information link between 'buyers' of expertise and 'sellers' of expertise. With these intermediaries would go the existing hierarchies that pervade most forms of education and training.

Market changes based on networks could go the other way, providing essential information and transaction capabilities to sellers of expertise. A powerful example in another domain can be seen in the rapid growth in mail order distribution. This phenomenon has grown enormously, brought about through a hybrid mix of technologies and systems infrastructure. These include the bulk mail postal system for distribution of catalog advertising, 800 number catalog order lines, credit data and payments systems for credit-card ordering on voice approval, specialized shipping via UPS or other carriers that depend heavily on computer systems, and finally on computerized analysis of buying and credit characteristics of individual customers to better target catalog advertising. This hybrid system has become so interlinked and sophisticated that major new financial product releases (e.g., the AT&T Universal Card) have been distributed initially through highly selected 'profile' mailings in which credit data systems are used to provide the names and addresses of highly desirable customers. Further elaborations of the electronic links between sellers and buyers can be seen in the *Télétel* videotex system in France, which now provides over 15,000 services to French telephone users. And in a slightly different manner, the heavily computerized warehouse department stores in the United States such as Walmart and Price Club have stolen significant business from traditional department stores by capitalizing on the cost-saving advantages of direct computer ordering from suppliers, computerized inventory and point-of-sale, and low hands-on service that makes possible very low product prices for consumers.

Network technologies provide new organizing opportunities far upstream from the education or training consumer marketplace, offering the potential for drastic changes in the 'production' sector. For example, it has been suggested that widespread use of electronic data interchange technologies could eventually create a kind of 'spot market' for tutoring, individualized training, or support services for apprentices, and greatly reduce students' dependence on their local schools. A company desiring training for its workers could electronically send complete digital curricula specs to a collection of possible expertise providers, each of whom would load the specs into their own computerized planning and training systems. Bids to provide training would be transmitted back to the firm, which would choose and provide the desired trainers with an electronic order for the desired program. The traditional social linkages between learning and schooling would be all but eliminated in this vision, and networks of highly efficient and responsive 'suppliers' of education would grow up around sophisticated networked industries.

Hierarchy under the visions articulated above retains its traditional usefulness in coordination, and there is no reason to assume that hierarchy would be altogether displaced. The crux of the arguments favoring markets over hierarchies here revolves around the powerful attractor of reduced transaction costs and the possibility of greater innovation in transactions than is possible under the constraints of hierarchy. The mail-order companies and computerized warehouse outlets in the U.S. have already stolen significant market share from older retail establishments. Educational organizations predicated on ongoing auction, negotiation, and coalition building, without the overhead and conservatism of hierarchy, could unleash an unprecedented wave of innovation.

Before we speculate too much, the evidence to date has not demonstrated the withering of hierarchy in economic organization much less in educational organization. Indeed, many networks are used to forge more stable and long-lasting relationships among selected economic partners: quite the opposite expectation of the fluid and impersonal 'spot market'. In fact, the ecology of changes found in these networks can be quite complicated. For example, travel agents, while in theory able to move freely among various computerized reservation systems, tend to lock into one system as their primary reservation aid, and build their business around that system. This is precisely the desire of the reservation companies, which are owned by airlines and have in many cases been used as powerful competitive weapons against other airline companies. These reservations companies strive to keep a tight hierarchical hold on travel agents through various incentives. And it is precisely this behavior that has brought larger hierarchy of the federal regulatory system into play by promulgating rules to make reservation systems 'neutral' with respect to airline advantage. These experiences suggest it is not clear that the powerfully seductive visions of the move from hierarchies to networks in educational organization is comprehensive in its consideration of what must change.

Trans-organizational collaboration

The appearance of nationally and internationally accessible computer-based communication networks has produced a number of new and surprising social interactions. Paramount among these are the strengthening of existing distributed work groups and the creation of new such groups. In some cases, these groups have become sufficiently powerful and influential to exert significant and concentrated pressure on established organizations and institutions. In a few instances, these distributed groups have evolved features of size, hierarchy and operating norms common to organizations. These are fundamentally new kinds of social organization, not anticipated or explained by existing social theory. Moreover, they show promise of being a major form of social organization in the coming years.

The central feature of electronic groups is that they can exist completely within computer-based telecommunication networks, and their members can function as members of one or more formal organizations at the same time as they are active participants in the electronic groups. A common situation is that of a university faculty member or a researcher in a corporation with access to one of the major national/international networks (e.g., BITNET, or Internet). Although the person has normal organizational duties and responsibilities in the organization of his or her employment, these duties can extend through the networks to people in other such organizations. Collaboratively authored documents flow back and forth through the networks, residing in different versions here or there in various host machines, eventually wending their way to dissemination or publication. Also, there can be extensive discussion via private person-to-person electronic mail, broadcast electronic mail from one person to many, or via posting to public bulletin boards or news groups or conferences.

The astonishing growth in use of these connections, as measured by both numbers of users and message traffic, is crude but powerful testimony to their significance among their users. At minimum, they are a great convenience for those with access to them. The import of these networks, however, may go far beyond that of just another way of communicating. Among other things, these networks have been used several times as instruments for mobilization of major social actions by distributed and institutionally disconnected individuals. This is particularly true in the case of the newsgroups described above, available through various networks such as Internet and BITNET. Two instances of newsgroup activity for political organization are worth noting.

One instance was during the Tiananmen Square confrontations in June of 1989, in which the newsgroup *soc.culture.china* became a highly interactive communications device among Chinese students in the United States and Europe for sharing information and plans for action in response to the crisis. This was not simply an electronic version of Tom Paine and the pamphleteers; it was a powerful organizing modality that permitted nearly real-time mobilization and coordination across vast distances. The fact that postings to this newsgroup could not be anonymous meant that participants identified themselves as protestors in a way not common to mass physical demonstrations. Records of the transactions were lasting and widely available.

Another incident occurred in 1991, with extensive discussion of the new Lotus Development Corporation's product 'Households' (a 'profile' advertising database) on the *comp.risks* newsgroup. This discussion began when an individual close to the development of the product but not working for Lotus leaked a detailed description of the product to his own company's bulletin board. This was read by another person, and re-posted with a few keystrokes to the *comp.risks* bboard with its thousands of readers. The subsequent discussion on *comp.risks* precipitated an electronic protest message writing campaign directly to the e-mail address of Lotus CEO Joe Manni that produced thousands of e-mail messages decrying the new product. It is reported that this message campaign had a pronounced effect on the Lotus leadership, who subsequently scuttled the product.

In quite a different vein, these networks have been used to conduct professional work among widely distributed actors concerned with common issues. Some of these activities are discrete and one-time-only. For example, mathematical computer scientists at Bell Communications Research and Digital Equipment Corporation used the network as a coordinating mechanism for organizing a distributed work project to factor a very large prime number, Fermat's 9th Number. In this case, the distributed computing resources of many organizations were contributed to the project using the network as the analytical coordinator. In other cases, the collaborations are ongoing and have become embedded work routines of whole cadres of professionals. For example, physical oceanographers have been using electronic network distribution lists to coordinate large projects, such as the World Ocean Current Experiment. The network is used to report results to colleagues, solicit advice and help for doing the work of the experiment at various locations, and to obtain access to large databases. These activities all occurred in oceanography before networks were available, but use of the network has significantly increased participation overall, and especially by those scientists located in remote locations.

Who benefits?

The potential spanning of physical, organizational, social, and psychological boundaries by networks raises important intellectual and theoretical questions about effects on individuals. For instance, who are the people who join and leave electronic groups? How do they establish and maintain group cohesion, and deal with minority viewpoints? What kinds of people increase their allegiances and connections to multiple, disparate groups through the network and what kinds do not? The networks constitute an important and controversial crossing of the boundary between individuals' various group participations and commitments, and between the worlds of work and leisure. Participation in these networks is often enabled by and supported through an individual's primary employer or school, but network activities often go far beyond formal work or education responsibilities to include social discourse and entertainment uses that managers and administrators could hardly justify in strict economic terms. And these modes of communication are creating a fertile ground of controversy over fundamental notions of free speech, proprietary rights to intellectual discourse, and control of time, that have not been seen before.

One example of why these questions are raised is given in the use of networks as a participatory vehicle for peripheral employees. Senior administrators and key professionals usually have good connections and are 'in the know' in their organizations and professional communities. Employees, clients, or students who are less central by virtue of geographic location, status, job requirements, or personal attributes have fewer opportunities to make contact with others. Reducing the impediments to communication is therefore likely to affect peripheral people more than central employees, probably inadvertently. In one study Huff, Sproull, and Kiesler found that employees who used electronic mail extensively reported more commitment to their jobs and co-workers than employees who did not use the network much [14]. But this correlation was much stronger for shift workers who, because of their jobs, had fewer opportunities to see their co-workers than regular day workers did.

I and my colleagues have begun, in our study of oceanographers [10], to address whether networking has the same or different payoffs for peripheral and core scientists. Peripheral, here, does not mean unimportant, but removed from (or facing barriers to) those scientific resources necessary for doing good oceanography – remote instruments, geophysical data, global projects, disciplinary committees, important research programs, and colleagues. In oceanography, to be more rather than less peripheral is to be young, to be landlocked, or to have been trained before the development of new methods such as remote sensing. We found some evidence that, at the margin, peripheral oceanographers benefit more from network usage than core oceanographers do.

Our results also suggest strongly that no generic person model will describe network demand and success. If a more differentiated view of people is necessary, then more attention should be paid to how people actually learn and work – what kinds of access they need to what kinds of resources. Choices surrounding the development and support of networking resources need to be based on this grounding in knowledge of work, learning, and people [21].

Student and teacher roles

Using computers for instruction can unintentionally change many important aspects of life in education. For example, in one experiment, courses specifically designed to allow students to learn in an individualized manner at their own pace also caused heated competition between students. Another software program designed to reduce competition ended by increasing it.

Another unanticipated consequence of using computers for instruction is a shift in teachers' roles, most especially a shift from teachers to students in the locus of authority and control. These changes are especially likely when students use computer communications or tutoring programs that put the acts associated with learning (e.g., paying attention) under their explicit and active control. New roles are evolving for teachers from their traditional lecture and demonstration centered didactic instruction. Serving as coaches, guides, and facilitators, teachers have to set developmentally and learning-level appropriate activities in motion, foster productive discourse to advance learners' understanding, and identify and rechannel unproductive pursuits. Computers, instead of replacing teachers, demand they have new skills and roles. In addition, inquiry-oriented instruction quickly leads learners to pose difficult questions about subject matter that teachers may be ill-prepared to answer, since these questions are foundational and cross disciplines.

Teachers

Initial research on the effects of computers on skill and the content of work drew from pre-existing sociological theory. An intense debate already existed between one school that viewed workplace technologies as instruments for subordinating workers by replacing skilled craft-like jobs with narrow deskilled jobs, and an opposing school of thought that expected technologies to absorb the most routine of manual tasks, leaving jobs rich in higher-order and cognitive skills. In schools today, this debate is reflected in those teachers who have adopted computer technologies enthusiastically and in those who fear its subversion of classroom teaching.

Research on computer technologies in diverse workplaces has revealed the flaws in both these theories. First, the impact of computing on skills, although widespread, varies with specific technology and with setting. In libraries that put in networked cataloging and search systems, some librarians have become computer information professionals and some, administrative clerks. Almost identical computer systems applied to similar workforces affect work in dramatically different ways in different companies.

This research led to a thorough reworking of theories of technology and skill change. Today we realize that skill changes, although triggered by the adoption of a technology, less reflect the technology itself than they are outcomes of setting up and putting in technology, and of the structure of the workplace and groups into which the technology is deployed. Researchers such as Westin, Barley and others have identified important factors related to specific outcomes [2, 15]. These factors include: the prior history of labor relations and managerial philosophy in the organization; the size and clerical intensity of the firm; the growth rate and competitive situation of the organization; the scarcity of the skilled labor pool; the introduction of the system (e.g., top-down versus bottom-up); and the degree of dullness of the work.

Clearly, the skills of teachers might change if networks are introduced extensively into education. But the direction of these changes will be influenced by other social factors. For example, a labor scarcity of good teachers would increase their bargaining power; they could insist on open access to networks for themselves and their students, authority over curricula in networked group courses, on new approaches to assessment, and on subsidies and time off for computer training. Competitive pressures and turbulence in the industry of training or education will tend to 'select for' firms that promote teachers' intellectual development, independence, and inventiveness, all attributes required for skill advancement amidst technological change.

Conclusion

Networks alter constraints on communication and information through a confluence of communication modalities, processing power, and access to varied information sources not hitherto possible. People can communicate with one another via computer-based systems such as electronic mail and computer conferences in ways complementary to traditional face-to-face, telephonic, and written modes as well as in ways not possible with traditional face-to-face meetings or conventional telephony. In fact, the very concepts of group and collaboration must be rethought in light of network electronic groups involving hundreds of people, and computer-based collaborative work projects involving highly distributed communities of actors who seldom, if ever, meet physically. The new technologies further permit individuals, groups and organizations ready access to rich arrays of information, often in machine-readable form that permits data exchange for local or remote processing without costly conversion. Finally, these technologies operate 'on top' of communication infrastructures that are both global and always 'up', thus enabling 24 hour activity and asynchronous as well as synchronous interactions among individuals, groups, and organizations.

There are strong theoretical arguments to suggest that networks alter transaction cost structures and principal-agent relationships within and across networked organizations. Are these changes sufficient to permit shifts in educational organization? There are good, competitive reasons for these changes to appear. At the same time, we do not understand the workings of organizations fully. Many social and political factors could effect different outcomes even given the same technological changes. We need research on organization of networks as well as on the nature of social, political, consumer, education, and work networked groups within and across organizations. For instance, do the features of small collaborative groups hold when considering the diverse, distributed network 'groups' that have highly fluid membership, obscure boundaries, and very large size (e.g., greater than 200 members)? Perhaps these new social entities constitute something between what we now call groups and what we now call organizations. But it is not clear exactly what these communities are.

If networks inspire more groups, larger projects, more diverse groups, and more flexible group structures, then the educational opportunities and experiences of individuals may change. For instance, geographically or organizationally isolated employees can gain new opportunities to initiate and receive communication [7,8,24]. If management policies permit such interactions, these employees can increase both their membership in groups and their connections to groups. These interactions can increase information flow between the periphery and the center of the organization and among peripheral workers. In short, while increasing connections through network communication could increase the participation of everyone in principle, peripheral employees are likely to see a relatively greater impact than are central employees [7,10,14].

If the chain of events and consequences of networked groups looks different from a linear scaling up of individual or small group behavior in traditional educational settings, then we cannot simply speculate from traditional studies in education. Variables that seem trivial (perhaps because of low variance) in traditional groups may loom much larger in electronic groups, or variables may scale differently. It is important now to study individuals and groups on the networks, both in laboratory and in real-life settings. In that case, we may do better in understanding the mental and the social consequences of computers and networks.

References

1. Aronson, E., Blaney, N., Stephan, C., Sikes, J., and Snapp, M.: The jigsaw classroom. Beverly Hills: Sage Publications 1978

2. Barley, S. R.: Technology as an occasion for structuring: Evidence from observations of CT scanners and the social order of radiology departments. Administrative Science Quarterly, 31, pp. 78–108 (1986)

3. Clark, N. K., and Stephenson, G. M.: Group remembering. In: Psychology of Group Influence (P. Paulus ed.) pp. 357–391. Hillsdale, N.J.: Erlbaum 1989

4. Danziger, J. N., Dutton, W. H., Kling, R., and Kraemer, K. L. Computers and politics: High technology in American local governments. New York: Columbia University Press 1982

5. Diehl, M. and Stroebe, W.: Productivity loss in brainstorming groups: Toward the solution of a riddle. Journal of Personality and Social Psychology, 53, pp. 497–509 (1987)

6. Dubrovsky, V., Kiesler, S., and Sethna, B.: The equalization phenomenon: Status effects in computer-mediated and face-to-face decision making groups. Human Computer Interaction, 6, pp. 119–146 (1991)

7. Eveland, J. D., and Bikson, T. K.: Work group structures and computer support: A field experiment. Transactions on Office Information Systems, 6,4, pp. 354–379 (1988)

8. Fanning, T. and Raphael, B.: Computer teleconferencing: Experience at Hewlett-Packard. Proceedings of Conference on Computer-Supported Cooperative Work. New York: ACM, pp. 291–306 (1986)

9. Greist, J. H., Klein, M. H., and Van Cura, L. J.: A computer interview for psychiatric patient target symptoms. Archives of General Psychiatry, 29, pp. 247–253 (1973)

10. Hesse, B., Sproull, L., Kiesler, S., and Walsh, J.: Computer network support for science: The case of oceanography. Unpublished manuscript. Pittsburgh: Carnegie Mellon University 1990

11. Hill, G. W. Group vs. individual performance: Are N + 1 heads better than one? Psychological Bulletin, 91, pp. 517–539 (1982).

12. Hiltz, S. R., and Turoff, M.: The network nation: Human communication via computer. Reading, MA: Addison-Wesley 1978

13. Hinsz, V. B.: Cognitive and consensus processes in group recognition memory performance. Journal of Personality and Social Psychology, 59, pp. 705–718 (1990)

14. Huff, C., Sproull, L., and Kiesler, S.: Computer communication and organizational commitment: Tracing the relationship in a city government. Journal of Applied Social Psychology, 19, pp. 1371–1391 (1989).

15. Hybels, R. C., and Barley, S. R.: Co-optation and the legitimation of professional identities: Human resource policies in high technology firms. In: Organizational issues and high technology management. (L. R. Gomez-Mejia and M. W. Lawless eds.). pp. 199-213. Greenwich, CT: JAI Press 1990

16. Kiesler, S. and Sproull, L.S.: Response effects in the electronic survey, Public Opinion Quarterly, 50, pp. 402–413 (1986)

17. Kling, R.: Defining the boundaries of computing across complex organizations. In: Critical issues in information systems (R. Boland, R. Hirschheim eds.). pp.307–362. New York: John Wiley 1987

18. Kraemer, K.L., King, J.L., Dunkle, D. and Lane, J.P.: Managing information systems: Change and control in organizational computing. San Francisco: Jossey-Bass 1989

19. McGrath, J. E.: Groups: Interaction and performance. Englewood Cliffs, N.J.: Prentice-Hall 1984

20. National Research Council, Committee on the Effective Implementation of Advanced Manufacturing Technology, Manufacturing Studies Board, Commission on Engineering and Technical Systems. Human resource practices for implementing advanced manufacturing technology. Washington, D.C.: National Academy Press 1986

21. Sproull, L. and Kiesler, S.: Connections: New ways of working in the networked organization. Cambridge, MA.: MIT Press 1991

22. Steiner, I. D.: Group processes and productivity. New York: Academic Press 1972

23. Tziner, A., and Eden, D.: Effects of crew composition on crew performance: Does the whole equal the sum of its parts? Journal of Applied Psychology, 70, pp. 85–93 (1985)

24. Wasby, S.: Technology in appellate courts: The ninth circuit's experience with electronic mail. Judicature, 73, pp. 90-97 (1989).

25 Waterton, J. J. and Duffy, J.C.: A comparison of computer interviewing techniques and traditional methods in the collection of self-report alcohol consumption data in a field study. International Statistical Review, 52, pp. 173–182 (1984).

26 Whisler, T.: The impact of computers on organizations. New York: Praeger 1970

11
Understanding Collaborative Learning in Networked Organizations [1]

John Gundry

Digital Equipment Corporation, Newbury, United Kingdom

Abstract: This paper argues that collaborative learning is a routine occurrence in organizations that have invested in computer conferencing networks to support their business. Computer conferencing allows people to learn from each other, while they work, although the 'learning network' potential of conferencing has not received much attention. The paper looks forward to valuable exchanges between networked organizations and distance education enterprises. One result could be education designs which prepare people for working in teams.

Keywords: networking, computer conferencing, distance education, learning systems, collaborative learning, collaborative work, organizational learning, management development, teaming.

---

[1] This paper was developed during the NATO Advanced Research Workshop which was held on the schooner *Najaden* as it sailed from Copenhagen to Stockholm in the summer of 1991, and I shall occasionally refer to the *Najaden* venue. I unashamedly refer in the paper to the organization to which I belong – Digital Equipment Corporation. I do this because it represents a world class example of an environment for collaborative learning. Digital operates the largest private computer network in the world (over 30,000 nodes covering 33 countries). On this network, electronic mail, computer conferencing, videotex and a host of other information tools are available to over 100,000 people in the organization.

Introduction

This paper explores the concept of collaborative learning through computer conferencing within organizations whose principal business is not education. I propose that in organizations which have invested in computer conferencing systems, collaborative learning takes place hand-in-hand with people's use of conferencing for work.

There is, however, a paradox. While the educational world is just developing the models for collaborative learning through conferencing, in networked organizations the process occurs every day virtually without recognition or acknowledgement. This invites an interesting and potentially productive exchange of models, experiences, and research, between the educational and organizational worlds. Networked organizations provide a fascinating case study of collaborative learning, and both they and the educational world could benefit from collaboration to understanding the process more fully. The time is ripe for this. Collaborative learning in organizational life is now starting, under a number of guises, to receive explicit attention from organization development specialists and other management practitioners. Further, collaborative learning as an educational process is, as this book shows, developing as a powerful model for distance education.

Some definitions

Learning

As a non-educationalist, I am using the term 'learning' simply to refer to a process by which non-material capability is acquired; that is, acquisition of skills and knowledge.

Organizations

'Organizations' here refers to enterprises whose principal goal is the provision of goods or services, in contrast to 'the educational world' of enterprises whose principal goal is to provide environments and services for learning.

Collaborative learning

Defining collaborative learning is especially important in the organizational context, because there are other concepts that sound similar, and the definition of many of these terms is not generally agreed. The definition of collaborative learning used in this paper was generated on board the *Najaden*. It is that collaborative learning is "individual learning as a result of group process". At its heart it is a process by which people learn as a result of interactions with their peers. It is important to recognize the contrast between the collaborative learning model and the transmissive model of traditional formal education, in which interactions occur principally between the teacher and students. In the strict transmissive model, peer-to-peer interactions are not seen as relevant to learning, and may even be discouraged. The *Najaden* definition of collaborative learning is very close to that identified by Hiltz [10], who says:

> Collaborative learning is defined as a learning process that emphasizes group or cooperative efforts among faculty and students, active participation and interaction on the part of both students and instructors, and knowledge that emerges from an active dialogue among those participants sharing their ideas and information.

Group learning

The term 'group learning' is widely used in the organizational context. (It is also sometimes used in educational contexts to mean the same thing as collaborative learning [10], which adds to the confusion). In the organizational context, 'group learning' seems to describe a phenomenon whereby a set of people have learned more than the sum of all their individual learning. However, since no-one has identified the mechanism that accommodates this extra learning, it does not seem a helpful concept.

In discussions on the *Najaden,* we reserved the term 'group learning' for the processes by which individuals learn to be or act as a group: through naturally-occurring or specifically designed peer-to-peer interactions. (Following Bannon and Schmidt [6], an informal definition of a group is when the individuals in it perceive themselves as "we".) Even defined this way, however, group learning is not the same as collaborative learning. Collaborative learning emphasises learning from others, not about others.

Organizational learning and the learning organization

Another term which, in an organizational context, might seem similar to collaborative learning is 'organizational learning'. This term is used by writers on organization development such as Senge [16] to describe the process which goes on within 'the learning organization'. A 'learning organization' is one which can adapt and re-invent its structures, processes and behaviors to accommodate (at worst), anticipate, or influence (at best) external factors which will determine its survival.

It is noteworthy that while 'organizational learning' emphasises an organization's ability to develop capability for acting differently, through the adoption of new strategies, behaviors and principles, the processes which facilitate individuals learning how to do this are rarely highlighted in organization and management development texts. An implicit theme of this paper is that computer conferencing and collaborative learning processes are highly relevant to enabling a learning organization.

Collaborative Learning and Working in an Organization

Collaborative learning means people learning as a result of working and interacting with others. In business life, people work and interact with others a very great deal. Thus, I propose that organizations provide a necessary environment for collaborative learning.

Hiltz [10] identifies the basic premise of collaborative learning to be that significant learning takes place when people "actively construct" knowledge by putting new ideas into words and receiving other people's reactions to those formulations. In organizations, those active constructions take place constantly as people express, develop, explain, and apply concepts and knowledge.

By their very nature, I argue, organizations offer significant potential for collaborative learning. However, not every learning activity in an organization is collaborative learning. People in organizations go on training courses and attend other formal educational events which still use the formal transmissive educational model.

Collaborative Learning and Computer Conferencing

While working in organizations offers more potential for collaborative learning than do traditional educational processes, that potential can be greatly amplified through computer conferencing.

Linda Harasim [8] examines how online education through computer conferencing facilitates educational collaborations. She describes online education as a unique combination of five factors: many-to-many communication, place independence, time independence, a text medium, and a computer-mediated medium.

We need not be concerned here with the fact that online education through computer conferencing spans distances, is asynchronous, and takes place in computer-mediated text exchanges. What is relevant here is Harasim's account of what computer conferencing implies and offers for the educational process. She draws out the following from a substantial review of the literature:

– Computer conferencing can, with due attention, support active learning collaborations, whereby students work together.

– Computer conferencing does this because it is a many-to-many communication medium, and not a one-to-one medium (like correspondence or electronic mail), or a one-to-many medium (like videotex, or traditional distance education media such as radio, TV, and mailing lists).

– Because computer conferencing-based collaborative learning supports and encourages peer-to-peer interactions amongst students, it (a) addresses a critical learning variable, (b) increases learner satisfaction and engagement in the learning process, (c) assists learners in understanding new concepts, (d) makes learners actively reorganize their ideas and thus builds a more highly organized cognitive models, (e) can provoke conflict and thus more active and fundamental understanding of principles.

Harasim's paper elucidates the theory of the 'fit' between collaborative learning and computer conferencing, although she notes that collaboration by learning peers has not been widely considered in the distance education literature. That fit is also at the heart of a management program using computer conferencing run by the Western Behavioral Sciences Institute at the University of California San Diego. While online seminars are led by international experts, much of the program's educational value intentionally comes from the interactions between the participants themselves, who are senior executives from all over the world. Illustrating the peer-to-peer aspects of the WBSI program, here are some anonymous comments from participants [18]:

"..It offers a worldwide classroom ... and the participants offer insights that make each conference interesting." (Major General, US Army),

"..The topics we are going through and the group of people I have met enrich the way I will look at things in future." (Managing Director, Saudi Arabia),

"..for the perceptive person who expects at least half his or her learning to come from shared experience and insights among peers." (US Corporation President).

Computer Conferencing and Collaborative Learning in Digital

A knowledge network

Digital Equipment Corporation is the world's second largest computer company, with about 120,000 employees worldwide. Computer conferencing, employing the VAX Notes conferencing system, is very widely used in Digital, and in that respect, the company is a valuable case study of the potential for collaborative learning.

In October 1991, the index of publicized computer conferences on Digital's internal network showed 1876 individual conferences. Their subjects ranged as follows:

– Products (virtually every Digital product, past, present or in development has a conference devoted to it; indeed, the very first widespread VAX Notes conference in Digital was used to discuss the development of the VMS operating system);

– Work-Related Subjects (e.g. Computer-Aided Manufacturing, Gateways, Marketing, Standards, Digital's History);

– Valuing Differences (e.g. Black Issues, Christian Perspectives, Hispanic Issues, Learning Disabilities);

– Employee Interest (e.g. Amateur Radio, Boston Red Sox, Home Improvements, Twin Peaks, Vegetarian Interests, in addition to conferences about living in the districts in which Digital has major facilities).

Anyone in Digital can establish a computer conference, on their own network node (if they have one), or, with the agreement of their system manager, on the computer which hosts their account. As there is no requirement that conferences be publicized, no-one really knows the number of conferences on the network, and the list of publicized conferences is probably only the tip of the iceberg. People using these conferences span the company: from Vice Presidents to contract staff, from the sales force to circuit designers, from Boston to Australia.

No-one forces anyone to start a conference, nor to contribute to one, and so their number and vitality is a sure sign that they are serving some function for the people who use them. Those functions are various, but the work-related conferences, about research, products, services, and strategies, are used for the following:

– as a means of preparing for, following-on from, and often instead of, face-to-face meetings amongst product and business groups;

– for managing projects and collaborations dispersed over geographical and time zones;

– for brainstorming and testing ideas on new strategies from a wide variety of perspectives;

– for company-wide feedback on products, services, initiatives and policies.

But in addition to these rather directed uses of conferencing, it is commonplace for conferences to be used as a place for people to exchange information about the company and its products, services, and policies. These conferences are, then, pools of knowledge or information banks about specific subjects; and organization-wide 'help desks' and directories of who has expertise on what subject.

Conferencing in Digital has become, according to David Skyrme who has written extensively on this [17], a "knowledge network". Within Digital, people who want to know the answer to a question look into the directory of computer conferences, and then to individual conferences. If the answer isn't there, then they will post a question, and in most cases someone, somewhere in the world, will reply with an answer. Even if an answer isn't forthcoming, a browse through a conference will often identify people who are working in a relevant area, who can be contacted directly through electronic mail or telephone.

It is also interesting that it is common for a number of people to reply to a question with different answers, provoking the questioner to think more clearly about his or her query. Or browsing in a conference will alert someone to something they did not think was a question. Conferencing in Digital, therefore, not only provides people with access to a network of knowledge and knowledgeable people, but interactions with others through conferencing helps to develop the process of enquiry.

A learning network

The central thesis of this paper is that in addition to being a powerful corporate resource as a knowledge network, computer conferencing in Digital is also a collaborative learning network.

The third section of this paper identified the power of people learning from their peers through interacting with them. What computer conferencing does for Digital is to enormously widen the community of peers from whom one can learn. Rather than being limited to learning from the people with whom one works day-to-day, or can travel to meet, or from the people who have found time to put their knowledge and experiences into documents, it is possible to interact with people across the whole company.

Whom one is likely to see day-to-day is perhaps surprisingly limited by physical co-location. In a study [13] of 500 scientists and engineers in a large industrial development laboratory, it was found that people on the same corridor collaborated five times as often as people simply situated on the same floor. Collaboration dropped off sharply when people were situated on different floors, and continued to decline logarithmically as distance increased.

A similar, earlier, study confirmed that it is only very small groups who can truly co-locate [4]. It found that 25% of technical workers whose offices were less than 5 meters apart were likely to talk to each other once a week. At 10 meters or more, fewer than 10% were likely to talk once a week. When offices were 30 meters or more apart, the probability of workers talking to each other was the same as for those whose offices were miles apart. With the potential for collaborations through physical co-location being so low, the effect of 'electronic co-location' is significant, especially in anything other than a small organization.

Another aspect of conferencing which contributes to its learning potential is its constant availability at the place of work. It is not necessary to make special arrangements to 'get at' some knowledge – one doesn't even have to leave one's desk. That means that people can consult the information pool anytime they need to know something. If and when they get an answer through conferencing, it can be immediately applied in the work situation which provoked the question.

Knowledge acquired through the network is, then, often sought and applied actively in the context of real work issues. Not only is this an efficient process from the point of view of work effectiveness, but it fits exactly with a core concept of collaborative learning, again described by Hiltz [10] "... knowledge is not something to be 'delivered' ... but rather something that emerges from active dialogue among those who seek to understand and to apply concepts and techniques".

Finally, that conferencing networks offer the potential for learning outside formal educational channels was brought home to me in the case of a young man who works in our group. This young man is 21, and is a specialist in VAX system management, hypermedia, and DECwindows/Motif programming. He joined us four years ago having completed a Digital-sponsored information technology awareness course in the local town, after leaving school at 15 with almost no qualifications. Virtually everything about his specialities that he has learned since he joined Digital has come from participation in conferences. He has attended a couple of formal training courses, but he has gained most of his expertise through conferencing. When he has encountered a work-related problem that he cannot solve himself, his first reaction is to consult the network, and then to search and research for the answer or for someone who can tell him the answer.

Does Collaborative Learning Really Happen in Networked Organizations?

So far I have sought to show that the use of computer conferencing in a networked organization is a propitious environment for collaborative learning. I have also declared my strong belief that collaborative learning happens all the time in a networked organization like Digital. However, what empirical evidence can I submit that this is true?

Unfortunately, it is difficult to find examples of organizations formally recognizing or attesting to collaborative learning through conferencing. As Bannon says (in the context of how people learn to use networks) " .. note how little work has been done on the way people learn from each other, from colleagues in actual settings .." [5]. I believe that this is because learning is associated with formal educational events – such as courses, or media – such as manuals, and learning from peers goes unremarked. Put another way, people experience learning as they work, as part of their personal development, and they do not necessarily identify any particular channel of learning outside those that are well signposted.

However, if one looks at surveys of the use of conferencing for work-related activities, there is evidence that at least strongly suggests that collaborative learning takes place. In an early study, Hiltz [9], surveyed a user community of about 100 academics using the EIES conferencing system in 1977. She included (amongst a very comprehensive question set) a few questions which addressed what to me are aspects of learning. She asked how use of EIES increased the stock of ideas that might be useful to the respondent; changed their view of their work in relation to that of others; provided leads, references and other information useful to work; and increased others' familiarity in the respondent's work. On all these questions, respondents' scores were positive about EIES.

Likewise, in their questionnaire study of about 300 users of the COM computer conferencing system in Sweden, Adrianson and Hjelmquist [2] asked how conferencing contributed to non-educational work tasks. Users ranked COM highly for getting information, opinions and ideas, and spreading information – again, components of learning.

It is noteworthy, however, that in these and other studies of work-related computer conferencing, there are rarely direct questions about learning. While I take the Hiltz and Adrianson & Hjelmquist data as suggesting that learning was likely to be taking place, because of the value attached to information-sharing, none of the questionnaires explicitly asked respondents to comment on the value of conferencing for learning from others. It is only in studies of computer conferencing used for explicit educational purposes, such as Hiltz's evaluation [11] that one finds explicit assessment of the value of conferencing for collaborative learning.

In conclusion to this section, it seems that the potential of computer conferencing for collaborative learning in organizations is largely unrecognized. That may be because recognition of collaborative learning anywhere is only recent. While there are theoretical reasons to point to a tight fit between work-related conferencing and collaborative learning, it is difficult to find empirical evidence from the workplace, although I offer statements from WBSI's participants, and observations of Digital's conferencing behavior, and of one case in particular. Although researchers into conferencing have found evidence that people readily share information through conferences used for work, they have not asked those respondents directly if they felt they learned anything through conferencing. One is tempted to ask if the concept of learning at work was that outlandish.

As this is a chapter in the research section of this book, it seems appropriate to state a formal null hypothesis. My null hypothesis is that "collaborative learning does not occur when computer conferencing is used for work-related purposes and outside formal educational processes". In the remainder of this paper, I shall assume that this null hypothesis has been disproved.

Promoting Collaborative Learning through Computer Conferencing within Organizations

As my argument is that an organization's use of conferencing for work and for collaborative learning are operationally inseparable, the factors which promote collaborative learning certainly include those which promote conferencing's use for work.

The factors which determine the degree to which conferencing is used in an organization (the extent of a 'conferencing culture') are to do with:
– the nature, availability and access to conferencing technology;
– the intellectual and communicative abilities of the people in the organization;
– the familiarity of those people with the conferencing tools;
– the number, relevance, vitality, and (in some cases) the adequacy of moderation, of the conferences themselves;
– the extent to which distributing and sharing information is valued within the organization.

In this list I omit the social dynamics of conferencing within small groups (see for example [1,3,12,14]). This is because the pattern of computer conferencing at issue here is organization-wide. It occurs across hundreds, even thousands of people, the majority of whom are unknown to each other, and who would not consider themselves members of a group, and who do not a priori communicate extensively with each other.

It seems particularly important to concentrate on the type of organizational culture which values the sharing of information, because it is this shared information which populates the collaborative learning infrastructure. Again, I use Digital as an example. In passing, however, it is worth noting the hundreds of *Valuing Differences* and *Employee Interest* computer conferences, mentioned earlier, that Digital hosts on its network. In addition to their role in other respects within the company, they themselves have contributed to the development of a conferencing culture, particularly amongst employees who would otherwise not be attracted to the medium.

In terms of people's behavior, computer conferences which sustain a learning network are themselves sustained by people spending time sharing information with others. That means reading conferences, writing unsolicited information into them, writing specific replies to people's questions and discussion points and engaging in dialogue with them. If we consider people's motivations in engaging in this type of behaviour, one can identify the following utilitarian uses of conferencing:

– when contributing to conferences is in direct support of departmental goals, such as circulating material to a wide readership, or soliciting feedback on products, services and policies for which the group has responsibility;
– when contributing draws attention to their personal skills or to the work of their group.

However, there remains a great deal of conferencing activity which does not seem to fit into either of these two directly-rewarding paradigms. This is when people altruistically spend their time writing unsolicitedly about things that others could find valuable, debating with others, and responding to other people's requests for information. In Digital, such activity is informal, at the employee's own discretion, must not compromise job goals, and I have never heard of it being rewarded through the formal career advancement processes. This behavior within Digital has been described by Skyrme [17] as one of the company's principal cultural characteristics. Building on Skyrme's analysis, the values which underpin this culture appear to me as follows.

Collaboration and mutual support

Information is the company's, and not the personal possession of individuals. What is good for all of us is good for each of us.

Openness of communications

Contributors trust others to act in the company's best interests with information they gain from conferences, to cite the source of valuable information, and particularly not to use it to harm the originator.

Informality

Valuable information does not have to be exchanged at power lunches – getting it to the right place is the key mandate.

Knowledge not position authority

Information and opinions are never 'right' until tested amongst one's colleagues.

Lack of hierarchy

People do not necessarily know or care about the organizational level of those who read what they write, even when explicitly criticizing corporate actions.

Self responsibility

You and you alone are responsible for what you write into a conference. If you transgress, the moderator or your peers will certainly point it out to you.

Self-judgement

There is a lot of material in the conferences, and no-one tells anyone to use any of it. You and you alone are responsible for what you make of what you find there.

It would be wrong to get too misty-eyed about Digital's culture, and the way in which it supports open information-sharing. Of course, there are types of information which are not openly shared, and groups who do not share information. However, the culture summarized above is pervasive in many areas of the company, and is distinctive to people who encounter it for the first time.

Promoting Collaborative Learning through Computer Conferencing in Educational Contexts

A number of exercises have sought to institute collaborative learning through computer conferencing in educational contexts. Two of these are summarised below.

Hiltz [11] briefly describes the set-up of a study involving students in a writing seminar at Upsala College. Hiltz says: "All of their writing assignments were done in small groups online, and the students were asked to critique one another according to the guidelines provided by the instructor." In her evaluation, Hiltz found that those students who took advantage of this design to collaborate with the instructor and other students valued the approach, but there is a suggestion that this was only true for those students, and not for the class as a whole.

Suzanne Regan [15], at California State University Los Angeles, used the BESTNET educational network to offer a media course in which students not only worked with her to design examination questions, but their answers were visible to each other online, using the VAX Notes conferencing system. A student could choose to enter the first reply to the question, or wait to enter a later reply having read the preceding ones. They knew that Regan, as the instructor, would assign grades on the basis of the value-added of each student's answer, rather than on the basis of the common material regurgitated. Regan asked the students to join with her in marking each of the assignments, online, and obtained a general consensus amongst the students as to the allocation of grades.

Unfortunately, it is not clear what the instructor did in either of these cases to engender a collaborative learning culture amongst students. Since the effect of cultures on information-sharing is a topic of conversation in organizational life [7,19], networked organizations may have something to share with the educational world about building cultures which support collaboration. It is possible that the dimensions of collaboration and mutual support, openness and trust, lack of hierarchy, self responsibility and self-judgement are as applicable to the collaborative classroom as they are to the collaborating organization. In this respect, it is pleasing to note that the BESTNET project is embarking on a research program with Digital to understand collaborative learning cultures more fully.

The Pay-off to Organizations if Education is Collaborative

If the organizational world can help the educational world build collaborative cultures, there is every reason to believe that both parties would benefit. A recent book on distributed computer-based working in commercial organizations [7] highlights the need now being expressed by industry to form collaborating teams with widespread skills. (The book also gives an excellent overview of the organizational issues discussed in this paper.)

For example, one major aerospace company is now building work organizations which depend on the performance of multi-disciplinary teams rather than individuals. One of the barriers to team formation, however, is the individualistic view of achievement and reward held by employees. To illustrate: the company has a strategy to change its reward system so that people are paid on the basis of the performance of the team to which they belong, rather than their individual contribution. Consider your own reaction to being paid on the basis of the performance of your group or department. Consider also the parallels between team-based reward systems in the organizational context, and class-based reward systems in the educational context.

It seems that a barrier to achieving team-based work organizations is people's socialization by a competitive, individualistic educational environment. Hiltz [11] has already noted the desirability of collaborative learning as giving people experience which will ready them for teaming in later life. If collaborative learning can emerge, perhaps spearheaded through computer conferencing, as a design for educational processes, it may prepare people more readily to accept work arrangements in which teaming and collaboration is necessary.

References

1. Adrianson, L.: Psychological studies of attitudes to and use of computer-mediated communication. University of Goteborg Sweden, Goteborg Psychological Reports. 8, 17 (1987)

2. Adrianson, L., and Hjelmquist, E.: Users' experiences of COM - a computer-mediated communication system. Behaviour & Information Technology 7, pp. 79–99 (1988)

3. Adrianson, L., and Hjelmquist, E.: Group processes in face-to-face and computer-mediated communication. Behaviour and Information Technology 10, pp. 281–296 (1991)

4. Allen, T.: Managing the flow of technology. Cambridge, Mass.: MIT Press 1977

5. Bannon, L.J.: Comments from the sidelines: some thoughts on research networks and network research. Behaviour and Information Technology 10, pp. 253–256 (1991)

6. Bannon, L.J., and Schmidt, K.: CSCW: four characters in search of a context. Proc. First European Conference on Computer Supported Cooperative Work, pp. 358–372. Gatwick, London 1989

7. Grenier, R., and Metes, G.: Enterprise networking: working together apart. Bedford, Massachusetts: Digital Press 1992

8. Harasim, L.M.: Online education: an environment for collaboration and intellectual amplification. In: Online education (L. Harasim, ed.), pp. 39–64. New York: Praeger 1990

9. Hiltz, S.R.: On-line communities: a case study of the office of the future. New Jersey: Ablex 1985

10. Hiltz, S.R.: Collaborative learning in a virtual classroom. Proc. Conference on Computer-Supported Cooperative Work 1988, Portland, Oregon, pp. 282–290. New York: Association for Computing Machinery, Inc. 1988

11. Hiltz, S.R.: Evaluating the virtual classroom. In: Online education (L. Harasim, ed.), pp. 133–183. New York: Praeger 1990

12. Kiesler, S., Siegel, J., and McGuire, T.W.: Social psychological aspects of computer-mediated communication. American Psychologist 39, pp. 1123–1134 (1984)

13. Kraut, R., Egido, E., and Galegher, J.: Patterns of contact and communication in scientific research collaboration. Proc. Conference on Computer-Supported Cooperative Work 1988, Portland, Oregon, pp. 1–12. New York: Association for Computing Machinery, Inc. 1988

14. Lea, M., and Spears, R.: Computer-mediated communication, de-individuation and group decision-making. International Journal of Man-Machine Studies 34, pp. 283–301 (1991)

15. Regan, S.: Personal communication with Dr Suzanne Regan, Department of Communication Studies, California State University, Los Angeles

16. Senge, P.M.: The fifth discipline: the art and practice of the learning organization. New York: Doubleday/Currency 1990

17. Skyrme, D.J.: The evolution of a knowledge network: computer conferencing at Digital. Newbury: Digital Equipment Co. Ltd., 1989

18. Western Behavioral Sciences Institute: 1990 International Executive Forum brochure. San Diego, CA: Western Behavioral Sciences Institute, University of California 1990

19. Zuboff, S.: In the age of the smart machine. New York: Basic Books 1988

Author's notice

DECwindows, VAX, VAX Notes and VMS are trademarks of Digital Equipment Corporation. Motif is a trademark of Open Software Foundation Inc.
Views expressed in this paper are those of the author, not of Digital Equipment Corporation.

PART III

Issues in Software Design

After two thirds of a book on the 'soft' aspects of CMC, and reviews of several educational and organisational applications, it is now worth looking at the 'hard' aspects. We have determined that success (and failure) happens on all kinds of software; but in which ways has software impacted these applications? Would the IBM and Digital applications have worked on non-proprietary software? Indeed, it looks as though they would; the success factors seem to lie in the common group culture, motivations and goals of the people in these companies.

However, software design features do clearly have some influence on take-up and use of conferencing. Both Digital's product VAX Notes and IBM's three products (GROUPTALK, TOOLS and PSINET), have had relatively little outside success; at least, nothing like their internal successes. In the educational field, popular software such as Cosy and the EIES series seems to have little success in industry. Why? Certainly the needs of applications and available software serving those needs frequently mismatch. In fact, such is the rationale for tailorable software, a serious sales point for Caucus, and the central driving force behind Murray Turoff's own development efforts, which went beyond 'tailorable' to 'personally-tailorable' (PT-EIES). The inability to track readership on some distributed systems will make it difficult for them to penetrate the educational markets. Several noteworthy applications involving high level executives at the Western Behavioral Sciences Institute and the World Economic Forum required a level of ease-of-use simply unavailable on existing conferencing systems.

The papers in this Part of the book address software and system design issues in a variety of ways. Chapter 12, by Oliver Vallée, provides a useful introduction to some of the main technical and software issues, and reviews the history of CMC development. This account is complemented by the first part of Chapter 16, by Jacob Palme, which provides a detailed list of computer conferencing functions, and briefly describes how they are implemented in a number of well-known systems.

For new users of conferencing software, the design of the interface can be a key factor in determining initial uptake. The chapter by Elsebeth Sorensen reviews some of the – often unconscious – metaphors which underly interface design. She argues for a design approach based on the tool perspective, in which the user and the computer are clearly seen as being different, and in which the computer can be understood as a 'transparent' tool for group and personal communication, with features which intrude as little as possible on the communication process itself.

The next three papers provide examples of CMC software design. Chapter 14, by Gary Alexander, presents an interface for an educational CMC system specifically designed with collaborative learning in mind, with features which put a strong emphasis on people and group relationships, rather than just on the messages in the conference space. Chapter 15, by Alain Derycke, describes the design and educational use of a CMC system adapted to the French videotex standards, and then goes on to identify some of the main issues which need to be addressed in the design of the next generation of CMC systems – and, in particular, the integration of text and multi-media with synchronous and asynchronous communication modes. The third part of Chapter 16, by Jacob Palme, is a detailed case-study of the design and interface style of SuperKOM, which is a distributed conferencing system with a number of special features.

The final chapter, by Jens Ambrosius, reviews some of the hardware, software, and network architecture issues that need to be considered in implementing a conferencing environment, and identifies some of the factors relating to standards and compatability that may have hindered more widespread take-up of conferencing.

The discussions in the Software Design group on *Najaden* covered a number of important issues which need to be taken into account if CMC systems are to become more widely and effectively used for collaborative learning. These include:
– the development of better software tools for off-line working, and for the downloading and local organisation and manipulation of conference messages;
– the design of interfaces which provide participants with a sense of 'groupness' or 'telepresence' when they are using the system, and which minimise navigation problems and information overload problems (whether working online or off-line);
– an increase in the availability and functionality of distributed systems, which allow users to connect to a local machine, instead of having the whole system on one remote central server;
– the adherence to common standards which would permit transparent interchange of messages between different conferencing and e-mail systems;
– the wider development of systems which permit integration of textual conferencing with other media, at the very least to include graphics and voice annotation.

12
The Challenge of Conferencing System Development

Oliver Vallée

EuroPACE, Paris La Défense, France

Abstract: More than in most other areas of software development, writers of computer conferencing systems are faced with difficult challenges. Conferencing systems must be used if any of the benefits of computer conferencing are to materialize. Getting participation is not the job of the administrator but rather that of the software developer. This paper develops this argument, reviews the history of well-established conferencing systems, and attempts to draw some lessons along these lines.

Keywords: Computer conferencing systems, distributed systems, electronic mail, functional requirements, compatibility, social factors, network technology, operational support

Conferencing Applications: Good and Bad News

Conferencing applications are put in place to accomplish specific goals, such as reductions in travel costs, time spent in meetings, personal growth of employees, organizational development and cross communication, education and learning, and so forth. In advanced applications, computer-mediated communication (CMC) is an enabling technology permitting new social organizations, such as distance education or organizational knowledge networks, not otherwise possible. These goals are often implemented at great effort (and expense) as potential benefits are often substantial.

Unfortunately, those trying to derive these organizational benefits from CMC often find, to their dismay, that their system simply lays unused. It is difficult to get people to work together unless they enjoy themselves, and it's a mistake to take participation for granted. In certain social networks, however, participants do enjoy themselves a great deal, and place a high personal value on the relationships they build with other members. This participation brings all sorts of unexpected but well documented benefits, such as those listed above, to the organizations that have implemented these networks. From observations of various applications we can conclude that if a network is to succeed, it must exploit the personal satisfaction of its users, regardless of the organizers' objectives, which cannot be expected to drive individual participation.

To get benefits to materialize, CMC systems must motivate users to participate. This occurs not when they are forced to participate by their bosses, peers or teachers, but rather when they enjoy communicating with their online colleagues and friends, teachers and peers, students and subordinates. A CMC system must enable and encourage the creation of these valuable interpersonal relationships between its participants. The challenge of conferencing system development is not implementation of new computer architectures, network technologies, or database techniques, but rather the identification and development of the features and characteristics of software which allows the 'magic' of CMC to happen.

Successful Applications

Scientists speak of 'mentors'; businessmen speak of 'leadership'; musicians speak of 'inspiration'. Universities provide 'intellectual stimulation' in a 'learning community' which endures through an 'alumni association'. Personal and professional development requires not just traditional classroom communications between learners and teachers but on-going, long term interaction between a person and his or her peers, mentors, and colleagues. If facilities to allow this special type of communication are provided, participants will find the resulting community personally rewarding and enriching – and they will learn.

In a successful system, every participant would feel a personal loss if the online group were disbanded, even if it were reconstructed using other means of communication. This definition of success measures individual satisfaction, but does not neglect educational, economic, organizational, or productivity benefits – inevitable consequences of quality interpersonal communications. The two requirements for successful applications are not specific goals and decent software, but rather *participation* and *very special software*.

Unfortunately, development of software designed for interpersonal interaction is difficult to justify. A group will develop when the quantity of random interpersonal bonds between various members reaches a critical mass. Tools designed to enable these social processes ('chat' programs, 'profile directories') compete with 'hard' tools ('productivity tools', 'group decision support systems'). It is not difficult to guess which tools receive serious study and funding.

Historical Development of Conferencing Software

Over the years CMC design has followed technical development in computers, networks and databases, but the social technology of group asynchronous written communications is essentially unchanged from the days it was described in *The Network Nation*. The concepts of one-to-one and one-to-many communications in synchronous and asynchronous forms are as old as the first multi-user system. Electronic mail was arguably invented by Samuel Morse! Indications are that CMC, as a literary group media, will survive the coming changes in the computer field – graphics, images, video, artificial intelligence, digital sound, distributed servers, and so forth.

The history of conferencing systems can be separated into three generations of technical styles (documented below). CMC technology can be further developed not only by implementing advances made in its base of computer, network and database technology, but more importantly by using knowledge gained in recent years by the implementation of applications, whether successful or not. These applications have demonstrated the need for social features in networks such as those that allow relationship building, mutual exploration, levels of anonymity, and so forth. The isolation and development of these social features accounts for the design worthiness of the first generation of CMC systems; nearly all of them still run today, ten to twenty years after their development.

The first generation: the visionaries

Table 12.1 First generation Conferencing Products

System	Designer	Director	Organization
EMISARI EIES	Murray Turoff	Richard Wilcox Murray Turoff	Office of Emergency Preparedness New Jersey Institute of Technology
CONFER CONFER 2	Robert Parnes	Meryl Flood Robert Parnes	University of Michigan, Ann Arbor
AUGMENT		Douglas Englebart	Stanford Research Institute
DELPHI FORUM PLANET NOTEPAD	Hubert Lipinski Rich Miller	Paul Baran Jacques Jacques Vallée	RAND Corporation Institute for the Future InfoMEDIA Corporation
COM	Torgny Tholerus	Jacob Palme	University of Stockholm

The first generation of conferencing was developed in the seventies by a few leading edge visionaries who saw the computer as a communications device rather than as a computing device (see Table 12.1). Since computers were very expensive at the time, these early systems were designed as centralized information utilities on large timesharing machines, accessed by cheap terminals using modems, inexpensive phone lines, and X.25 public packet switched networks.

The second generation: portability and branching
During the 1980's, the first conferencing systems inspired a second generation of products with two important technical improvements. The first improvement was 'portability', meaning that a system can run on many different types of machines; many were designed to work on Unix, a popular operating system. A second improvement, 'branching', takes advantage of the computer's ability to manage a split of a conversation into several threads.

Table 12.2 Second Generation Conferencing Products

Name	Origin	Designer	Organization	Notable Applications
PICOSPAN	CONFER 2	Marcus Watts	NETI	The Well
CAUCUS	CONFER 2	Charles Roth	Camber Roth	MetaNET
PARTICIPATE	EIES	Harry Stevens	Participate Systems	The Source
PORTACOM	COM	Jacob Palme	Univ. of Stockholm	EuroKOM, EuroPACE
COSY		Alastair Mayer	Univ. of Guelph	BIX , UK OU

The third generation: distributed conferencing
Third-generation systems allow sophisticated distributed networks of conferences, making it possible to create networks of networks. Distributed systems use two or more host computers placed near clusters of participants. Communications are localized wherever possible, and communication centers are linked using various network technologies, ranging from simple file sharing, to the client-server architecture of Digital's VAX Notes, to the packetizing of CMC communications of a PC directly connected to Ethernets or TCP/IP.

Distributed conferencing makes possible a variety of benefits, one of which is extreme cost reductions, enabling exotic applications such as transcontinental conferencing. Distributed networks allow intra-institutional conferencing; this can be done by installing conferencing servers as gateways on large corporate networks to allow controlled access to other networks. The higher speeds of distributed conferencing makes possible more exotic features, such as seamless graphics and file transfer. Finally, local hosts often mean that the user is using a familiar system and has access to the necessary technical support; the support costs are distributed. However, distributed conferencing introduces a rather important level of complexity at the administrative level which must be isolated from the user if the application is to succeed. Lotus Notes, for example, is a product which requires significant application development effort, which may or may not result in user friendly or socially conducive interfaces.

Table 12.3 Third Generation Conferencing Products [1]

Name	Developer	Organization
EIES 2	Murray Turoff	New Jersey Institute of Technology
VAX NOTES		Digital Equipment Corporation
VM GROUPTALK	Robert Flavin	International Business Machines (Yorktown)
PSI NET	Paul Friedl	International Business Machines (Palo Alto)

Functional Requirements

With three generations of CMC software and countless applications over twenty years, one can identify parameters that are most important – the basic necessities which are most common in successful systems.

Quality

The most successful systems have exceptional design quality, are obsessively friendly, and have a professional look and feel. Successful systems must communicate the complex group communications concept with crystal clear clarity. As a social technology conferencing attracts a wide variety of users and must allow many different user approaches, from the impatient browser to the slow, structured learner. As a distributed application, often with users all over the globe, it can rely little on user support, training or documentation. Standard user friendliness concepts are highly important, such as a small, consistent vocabulary, quality context-sensitive help, and so forth.

Social factors

Software designed for a user requires 'user friendliness' but software designed for a group requires 'social funliness'. For example, live applications are far more fun than off-line uploading and downloading systems. Systems must take into account the social identity of the user using such facilities as nicknames, nationalities, organizational affiliations, biographies, and so forth, to allow for the initial processes of mutual recognition and eventual exploration; but only a few systems institutionalize such 'frivolous' details as the user's first name. In a social environment users can be quite capricious and it is important to capture the moment when he or she feels the need to write a specific message or chat with a user; the command set must be easily accessible.

Writing is an intellectual activity that must not be interrupted with the need to consult manuals, look up commands, suffer disconnections, and so forth; a proper editor is important. Poor English speakers (or rather, writers) will rarely

---

[1] Please note that the author has only included some of the more popular readily available, time-tested products. Most CMC software developers are moving towards distributed versions of their software; at the time of print, CoSy, Caucus, PortaCOM and SuperKOM are readying distributed software, but which are currently unavailable, although several have been announced for some time. These new systems are extending the definition of distributed by taking advantage of the proliferation of e-mail and internetworks as sophisticated store and forward conferencing servers. In fact, there are at least two standards, RFP-1039 and X.GPC (currently before the International Standards Organization), which are being used as conferencing/mail interchange protocols.

display their mistakes in front of a group: an online English dictionary and thesaurus will do wonders for participation.

Proper functionality

CMC is not a single media but rather a mix of medias, including not only conferencing but also mail and chat programs, which allow random and spontaneous conversations as is necessary in any social gathering. Additional media include user descriptions ('biographies' or 'résumés') and text libraries for occasional long comments or group-relevant reference information. These latter capabilities allow the establishment of identity and common reference frameworks. Also important are features that allow review and evaluation of the conference transcript, which is essentially the group's history and identity.

It is amazing how few systems have basic integration of these capabilities. At least three major groups within Digital, and one outside, have tried to integrate VAX Notes, Mail, Phone and Videotex. For example, the user's personal name in Notes is different from the one in Mail, and Phone displays no personal details, beyond the user's 'nodename' and ID code.

Compatibility

Obviously, a system must be accessible by users and compatible with their equipment. Cheap hardware such as the Radio Shack Model 100 or 200, long loved by CMC users, is rarely a solution. Even when accessing a system that does not require special full screen emulation, such as EIES2, or a keypad, such as VAX Notes, or ANSI graphics, such as PSI-NET or any bulletin board, it suffers, like many laptops, from a small, grey screen, unsuitable for many older people, such as senior executives, who find it difficult to read, and who don't like to read messages as they scroll a few lines at a time. An industry oxymoron is the "multi-standard" modem. Huge networks of IBM and DEC terminals in thousands of companies are still unable to access remote hosts for logistical and accounting reasons. At the very least a CMC system requires a good X.25 configuration, with a direct dial capability, and ANSI compatibility. Soon we'll see audiotext integration and Fax output – it will be possible to call the host and have waiting comments and messages faxed to you, even if you've left the laptop at home.

Network technology

Applications with highly dispersed users are the most troublesome – and the most personally interesting. Special considerations for cost control are imperative. Downloading is one undesirable solution, as is participation off-hours (not for serious applications). Distributed conferencing, either at the 'client server' level or of the store-and-forward kind, is highly cost effective at the transcontinental level, and is efficient when acting as intra-organizational gateways.

Operational support

The lack of operational support in conferencing systems has allowed the author to earn a very good living over the past ten years. Installation itself requires a good knowledge of the social environment and should not be done by the average 'techie'. Maintenance (daily backups, monthly billing, statistics, occasional archival, security checking) requires special skills not found at the user level. Management of membership is extremely time consuming; a small educational application with fifty classes of fifty participants will require the maintenance of 2500 memberships every quarter or semester. Accounts, groups, and conferences must be created, backed-up, managed, archived, and deleted. Finally, automated user support is generally ignored, but leads to direct cost savings when properly designed.

Looking to the Future

Kiosk pricing is a recent innovation that has not yet caught the imagination of the major networks. Invented by France Telecom, and available in many countries through the Infonet consortium, kiosk pricing removes the burden of pricing, billing, and collecting from the host provider to the network company because the user actually pays the network, who pays the host for the user's time. This leads to an unusual situation where the network companies actually care about users and host providers much more than those who simply bill the host. It should be noted that billing is a major ordeal for most host providers, and collecting even more so.

Fax and audiotext are short term remedies which will continue to be important to travellers, those with hardware or software failures, and for those few members in a group that might not have access to compatible equipment. Audiotext allows a user to dial in with a normal touch tone phone and request that his or her messages and comments be faxed to the home, office or hotel.

Meeting the Challenge

The challenge of CMC development is in the development of those social factors which enable the formation of personal relationships which participants find rewarding. When this challenge is met, conferencing applications generally succeed by the more tangible and traditional measures.

Many organizations are attempting to operate social networks on CMC systems. Many successful projects can be found, and also many failed projects based on good ideas and poor implementation. In Europe, projects such as EuroPACE, EuroKOM, the UK Open University, the World Economic Forum's WELCOM project, the DELTA projects, the applications at Neurope Lab, X-ON, and in Stockholm, and the tremendous volume of traffic on the corporate and academic networks, indicate the level of interest in interpersonal group communications. If the challenge is met, CMC will attain even higher levels of success and broaden its horizons to new applications.

13
Metaphors and the Design of the Human Interface

Elsebeth Korsgaard Sorensen

UNI•C (The Danish Computing Centre for Research and Education), Aarhus, Denmark

Abstract: As it stands, computers and computer systems are relatively new phenomena in our daily life, and we do not have any norm or tradition for a particular use of language, when we speak about these technologies. Therefore, we must use concepts and terms from domains with which we are already acquainted, and which – in some areas – are similar to these new phenomena; in other words, we must use metaphors as a means both to perceive and understand these new technologies, and to communicate around them.

Keywords: conferencing systems, metaphors, design perspectives, human communication, interface, language as action, cognition, metaphorical structuring, symbolic tool, work organization.

Introduction

Computers and computer systems occupy increasingly more space in the daily life of the average individual. As a result of this situation, demands and expectations in relation to the skill of the average individual arise in terms of being able to understand and apply computer systems in a goal-directed and relevant manner. The interface of a computer system should promote and support the user's understanding of the system. The task of 'communicating' the possibilities of a system to the user is not only of great importance, but also a precondition for the relevance and possibilities for application of the system. This 'communication' takes place from the screen to the user – in other words, it is built into the design of the interface of the system. Thus, the basic requirement of the design of an interface is pragmatically and functionally oriented, in as far as the interface as clearly and unambiguously as possible should be able to 'communicate' the various possibilities and limitations of the system to a typical user without technical expertise.

The type of communication which should take place from the system to the user is usually information concerning 'where' in the system the user is taking action (the current state of the system), which actions may possibly be carried out, and which items the user may choose as objects for these actions.

From the point of view of the user, all actions in a computer system have to take place in terms of manipulation of symbols, as this is the only level at which it is possible to apply computer technology. In general, the application of this technology is predetermined in a very fundamental way, requiring a certain level of abstraction on the side of the user, from carrying out actions in a concrete manner to carrying them out symbolically.

One of the strongest, most dynamic, and transcending communicative mechanisms of our natural language is the use of metaphors. In interface design for computer systems, metaphors are also used to create and shape the communication from the screen to the user. The use of metaphors is usually manifested at two levels: the designer's latent perception of what it means to use a computer system to carry out certain work tasks; and the direct use of metaphors in the design of the communication from the interface.

This paper deals with the general use of latent metaphors in the design of computer interfaces, and discusses one specific choice in relation to conferencing systems. As a background for discussing the role of metaphors in interface design, the next section contains a presentation of some theoretical views on the role of metaphor in linguistic communication. The following section contains an account of various latent perspectives – based on metaphors about the computer or computer system – behind design of interfaces in general and conferencing systems in particular. The final section presents a theoretical basis for the most appropriate choice of perspective for computer conferencing systems.

The Role of Metaphor

As a background for understanding the effect in general of the use of metaphor in the design of interfaces for computer systems, this section covers certain linguistic theories concerning the role of metaphors in linguistic communication. The theoretical views presented here are chosen on the basis of a particular view of language and linguistic communication. A closer look is taken at the ways in which production and interpretation of metaphors take place [5], as well as at a certain understanding, relevant in this context, of the role of metaphors and the way they function [4].

The fundamental view of language which lies behind the following account of the communicative importance of metaphors has moved away from a traditional, rational, view of language (understanding language merely as a means of description without any social role) towards an understanding which is existentially and phenomenologically more fundamental, namely language as a dynamic, social and interactive phenomenon: language as action, (represented by for example the philosopher, Martin Heidegger).

A widely accepted model of linguistic communication (based on a view of language as representation) portrays communication as transfer of information – a process in which a certain fixed piece of information such as a message, thought or feeling, is transferred from a speaker to a listener. The message is perceived as being independent of prior encoding and later decoding processes:

> Meanings are objects.
> Linguistic expressions are objects.
> Linguistic expressions have meanings (in them).
> In communication, a speaker sends a fixed meaning to a hearer via the linguistic expression associated with that meaning.
>
> On this account it is possible to objectively say what you mean, and communication failures are matters of subjective errors: since the meanings are objectively right there in the words, either you didn't use the right words to say what you meant or you were misunderstood.
> [4, pp. 2–6]

Such an understanding of language and linguistic communication is often accompanied by a view of the function of metaphors as being mostly poetic, decorative or rhetorical [1]. However, this view of the role of metaphor is not acceptable if one views humans as fundamentally linguistic creatures, and the use of language as a dynamic, social and interactive process involving the total communicative context.

Contrary to the views held by a number of theorists, the legitimacy of metaphors is not only rooted in poetry, decoration, or rhetoric. Metaphors and metaphorical concepts are not exclusively a phenomenon of language – they are also a part of the human cognitive system. Lakoff and Johnson claim that human ways of thinking are to a great extent metaphorical, as the human cognitive system is structured and defined metaphorically, and that metaphors structure how we perceive, how we think, and what we do. Metaphors permeate not only our entire language, but also our thoughts and actions; metaphors move structures of consciousness.

Our conceptual system is not something about which we are very conscious. As, however, communication among people is based on the same, shared conceptual system with which we think and act, language may be perceived as an expression of this system. The concepts which guide our thoughts are not only of intellectual relevance. They also decide how we perceive, how we move around in the world, and how we relate to other people. In other words, our conceptual systems play a large role in how we define our daily reality. Lakoff and Johnson, at a more concrete level, describe the essential meaning of metaphors as follows:

> The essence of metaphor is understanding and experiencing one kind of thing in terms of another.   [4, p. 5]

The circumstances which allow us to understand (or focus on) one particular aspect of a phenomenon in terms of something else are at the same time hiding other aspects of the concept of concern:

> In allowing us to focus on one aspect of a concept (...), a metaphorical concept can keep us from focusing on other aspects of the concept that are inconsistent with that metaphor. [4, p. 10]

As a consequence, metaphorical structuring is only partial, in the sense that it emphasizes some aspects of a phenomenon and not others.

More concretely, one may ask how it is possible for a person to invent the idea to say something specific, when, in fact, he means something else; similarly, one may wonder how another person who hears this specific message is able to find out or guess the intended right message. How can the receiver possibly know that what is actually said deviates from the real intended message?

A fundamental precondition for any communication at all seems to be some shared logical rules or principles, conscious or unconscious, among the interlocutors, with respect to the understanding or interpretation of the metaphorical meaning.

First, the listener must possess some kind of strategy for deciding whether he should seek any metaphorical meaning at all in the message: a shared strategy between speaker and listener, on the basis of which the listener is able to decide that the message should not be taken literally. The most common principle is that the message would appear erroneous if taken literally.

> Where the utterance is defective if taken literally, look for an utterance meaning that differs from sentence meaning. [5, p. 105]

Secondly, if the listener has 'decided' that the message in question should be perceived metaphorically, he must have some principle or other for 'extracting' possible 'true' interpretations. Thus, in other words, there must be some shared principles between speaker and listener which associate the metaphor used with the possible interpretations. One of the principles defining how the various possible alternative meanings are extracted may be described in the following words:

> When you hear "S is P", to find possible values of R look for ways in which S might be like P, and to fill in the respect in which S might be like P, look for salient, well known, and distinctive features of P things. [5, p. 106]

Finally, as the third requirement, the listener must possess some principles for restricting the variety of possible interpretations, and find the one which is most probable. Speaker and listener must have some shared principles for performing this restriction, on the basis of their shared background knowledge. One of the principles for this restriction is described as follows:

> *Go back to the S term and see which of the many candidates for the values of R are likely or even possible properties of S. [5, p. 106]

As it stands, computers and computer systems are relatively new phenomena in our daily life, and we do not have any norm or tradition for a particular use of language when we speak about these technologies. Therefore, we must use concepts and terms from domains with which we are already acquainted, and which – in some areas – are similar to these new phenomena. In other words, we must use metaphors as a means both to perceive and understand these new technologies, and to communicate around them.

For many people the computer has become a tool in their daily work. There is nothing particularly radical in applying a new tool. The radically new with respect to computers and computer systems is that they are symbolic tools, which represent the surrounding world in terms of symbols on the screen, and that the actions which the user may take have to be carried out by manipulating symbols. It is not possible for the user to see what is happening in the machine, and it is not necessary in order to use the tool. But it is necessary to understand the 'symbolic work' and to be able to speak about it.

In order to meet this requirement, metaphors are used in the design of computer systems at two levels, one of which, in particular, is expanded on in the next section.

Latent Metaphors and Perspectives in Interface Design

This section deals with the designer's perspective when designing the interface for computer systems in general, and conferencing systems in particular. In order to perceive and understand the computer technology and to be able to communicate around it, metaphors are used in the interface design at two levels [6]. The first level is the (conscious or unconscious) implied perception of the designer of what it is like to apply a computer system in carrying out certain work tasks. This latent perception will always mark the way in which the communication or interaction with the interface is shaped, not only in the choice of metaphors in the concrete design of the interface, but also in the construction of the interactive process of communication between the user and the screen. The other level is the designer's use of metaphors in the direct design of the screens of the interface. In this context it is what is called here the 'latent perception' of the role of the computer which is in focus.

When designing an interface for a computer system, the designer – before starting to design – always brings along an implied idea of what it means and what it should be like to carry out certain tasks using the computer system in question. Regardless of whether this idea or perception is conscious or unconscious, it will always have a fundamental impact on some of the analyses and decisions made in the design process. In other words, this underlying perception will always to some extent influence the way in which the communication from the interface is constructed. Moreover, the latent metaphor also has a tendency to influence the language which develops in order to discuss and understand the potential and capacity of the new technology.

Bearing this in mind, it seems obvious that it is desirable for a designer to be conscious about his perspective on the work process, as this is likely to create an interface which communicatively is more clear, homogeneous and coherent.

There are four distinct perspectives on the work process which predominate in interface design, each based on different metaphorical concepts of humans and computers and computer systems [2]. The first two of these (the system perspective and the dialogue partner perspective) imply a view of humans and computers or computer systems as belonging to the same category. The other two (the tool perspective and the media perspective) are alike in that they deny that humans and machines are similar, and in that they use technical concepts from other areas to understand the role of the computer.

The system perspective

The first, the system perspective, is a perspective which was very common in the early days of computers and computer systems, where – contrary to now – the designers themselves were also the users. In the system perspective humans are perceived as machines, and consequently the human way of functioning is perceived as being equal to that of machines. The work processes of the user are interpreted and modelled in the interface design according to the communicative processes characteristic of programming languages. This is mirrored, for example, in the command language of the interface (e.g. GET, BUFFER), as well as in the way these commands have to be issued by the user.

Within the world of conferencing software, VAX Notes represents an example of a system with a latent system perspective behind the design of the interface [6]. This view is reflected both in command language and structure, and in the dialogue process between the user and the system. The work processes of the user are understood as and modelled after those taking place in programming languages.

The system perspective is very useful in the technical design of computer systems; but it does not lead to a good interface design. Firstly, most command names and terms are likely to be alienating, especially to inexperienced users without any technical background, and this may cause too many breakdowns in the user's understanding of the system and the work tasks which he may carry out.

Secondly, it is not possible for the user to rely on his pre-existing linguistic knowledge and experience as a help towards remembering the various commands. In other words, the user needs to learn a 'new language'.

The system metaphor is also reflected in the language which develops and is used to speak about the system, in as far as it appears very technical: GET THE BUFFER, INVALID PARAMETER DELIMITER, etc.

Finally, the interaction with such a system is usually command based, which means that the user's interaction with the system is supported by memory exclusively, rather than by the principle of recognition (as is the case with menu-based systems).

The dialogue partner perspective

The other perspective within which humans and machines are perceived as being entities of the same kind is the dialogue partner perspective. Within this perspective it is the computer which is viewed as playing the same role as humans. In other words, humans are used as a metaphor to understand the electronic technology. The resulting interface design is constructed in such a way that the interaction between the user and the screen imitates the interaction that takes place among humans. This perspective lies behind a large proportion of the initiatives within the area of artificial intelligence. In the interface this perspective expresses itself more concretely, for instance, in linguistic phrases which are formed in a way that suggests cognitive processes in the computer Typically, the feedback reactions from the system are constructed in a way that simulates human linguistic utterances (e.g. I DON'T UNDERSTAND).

The interface design of a conferencing system such as Caucus mirrors the dialogue partner perspective behind the design of the interface [6]. Among other things, this expresses itself in the communication between the user and the system, which is constructed, linguistically, as a dialogue between two humans.

This perspective on the role of the computer is also mirrored in the way people communicate about the computer system: "... and then it asks for my number", "... and then I get an answer", "... it answers in a way which I'm not used to", "... then it comes and wants my number", etc.

Like the system perspective, the dialogue partner perspective is not ideal with respect to interface design of computer systems, as it creates an undesirable understanding amongst the users, of the system as a mystical organism possessing competences relating to the user's work processes. Such a system does not stimulate and support the confidence of the user with respect to the carrying out of his work tasks.

The tool perspective

The tool perspective implies a view of the computer system as a tool with the same characteristics as other tools. The symbolic world of the interface of the computer system is aimed at mirroring and 'resembling' the real world and work situation of the user. The idea behind this type of design is that the interface of the system should stimulate the user to forget that he is working in a symbolic world, so that he is allowed to concentrate on the goal of his actions. The interface should create the illusion that the user works on 'real' objects and performs 'real' actions on these objects. Systems whose interfaces are designed on the basis of this principle are usually menu-based and have an interface which more directly uses spatial metaphors in order, symbolically, to create a resemblance to the physical reality of the user. For instance, words and concepts are used which indicate how objects physically are organized in a room or different types of rooms.

CoSy and EIES2 are examples of conferencing systems designed from the tool perspective [6]. Characteristically, these conferencing systems also make use of room metaphors (a writer's desktop) in the more concrete design of the interface. This reflects an attempt to create an illusion of a 'natural' work environment and organisation with the intention of supporting the user's orientation in the system as well as the organisation of his work.

An attractive property of the tool perspective is that it seems to comprise a wider view of the work processes and work organization of the user, as it stimulates him to maintain his concentration on the goal of his actions, as opposed to concentrating on the tool he is using in the process of reaching this goal. On the basis of this view it is possible to design the interface in such a way that the user is able to make use of his pre-existing assumptions and knowledge about work processes and organization. Moreover, as the form of interaction in interfaces designed with an underlying tool perspective is usually menu-based, it is possible for the user, with respect to commands, to rely not only on memory but also on the principle of recognition.

The understanding of the role of the system as a tool is reflected linguistically through the use of space-metaphorical concepts and terms: "... could you go into the conference and summarise our view", "... I go out and into mail", "...I can go in and get hold of the information", "... it must be lying in another conference", "... I don't really know where I am", etc.

The media perspective

As with the tool perspective, this last perspective does not assume that humans and computers are adequate metaphors for each other. In this perspective the computer system is understood as a medium through which people communicate. Any linguistic message from the screen is seen as information which may or should be subject to interpretation by the user. Familiar media metaphors are used to make the role of the computer system comprehensible (e.g. papers, books, etc.). In the media perspective the user should not at all be stimulated to forget about the symbolic nature of the computer system. On the contrary, he should be supported in keeping a critical distance from any text or message which appears on the screen.

The use of the media perspective in interface design is claimed to emphasize to the user the idea and feeling of collaboration. However, it could be argued that a latent media perspective, with its focus on transfer of information and on the ways in which this can be facilitated, generally affects the logic and accessibility of the interface, which consequently appears conceptually much more complex and difficult to use.

Several conferencing systems seem to have a latent media metaphor behind the interface design. PortaCOM, SuperKOM and Parti all represent examples of products where the interface design is based on a media perspective [6]. The underlying focus in the design seems to have been directed towards the creation and transfer of information, and the different ways in which these processes can be eased. Although, in for example PortaCOM, an attempt has been made – in the more concrete design of the interface – to convey to the user the idea of familiar physical activities (e.g. the concept of mail), the media metaphor and perspective is reflected in the general choice of commands. In Parti, there are no signs of a similar attempt to create an illusory world, in which the user can carry out his different work tasks, manipulating 'objects' through 'actions', corresponding to his 'real' world. This is reflected in the main grouping of actions that the user can perform (read information, produce information, change information, overview information, control access to information, etc.). Generally, the media perspective in these systems discloses itself in the command language, syntactically as well as semantically.

Also the language which is used to speak about and understand systems designed on the basis of the media perspective mirrors the metaphor: "... all the remarks he (the designer) is writing probably mean something", etc.

The acknowledgment of the effect and strength of metaphors in linguistic communication in general, and in these latent metaphorical concepts in particular, points to the fact, that in order to achieve a coherent and adequate design it is of great importance for the designer to be clear and conscious about his latent perspective on the role of the computer before starting to design. Being theoretically aware may even allow him to choose and make use of his concept in a goal-directed manner. There is no doubt that the latent metaphors and concepts of the role of the computer have a great impact on the way in which the interaction between the user and the screen is shaped. In particular, this is reflected in the linguistic choices and the linguistic organization of the menus and commands, as well as in the character and in the linguistic form of the feedback.

Conferencing Systems and the Tool Perspective

This section deals with the choice of the tool metaphor as an adequate latent metaphor behind the design of interfaces for conferencing systems.

The ultimate goal of conferencing systems is to facilitate and ease communication and collaboration among people separated in time and space, in an adequate manner. The special conditions operating in a communication which takes place independently of time and space, and the resultant total communicative dependence on the written message, create a need for an interface which is able to promote and support this goal in the best possible way.

At first sight, the media perspective behind an interface design for conferencing systems seems a good choice, especially as the system actually functions as a medium for human interaction. However, considering more carefully the need of the individual user and his specific communicative situation, this view does not seem adequate. For the individual user, the communicative reality with which he is dealing presents itself at two levels: the designed, formalized communication between the user and the screen, and as the very dynamic interaction among people [7].

Between these two levels of communication there exists a relationship of dependence, as the communication between the user and the system (screen) predetermines the dynamic communication between people. In order for any human communication to be made possible, it is essential that the interaction between the user and the system takes place without breakdowns in the user's understanding of the system and its communicative possibilities. These requirements are closely associated with the tool perspective. This is because of the transparent way in which an interface designed on this background functions, the ultimate goal being that it should appear as a good, familiar and well functioning tool – one which does not distract by demanding the user's attention, and that ideally should be devoted to the goal of his action, namely dynamic interaction among people. At this point, in order to provide a more elaborate theoretical argument for my view of the role of breakdowns, I turn to some existential-phenomenological thoughts of Martin Heidegger [3].

Martin Heidegger does not only keep a critical distance from the linguistic views implicit in the rational tradition. He also denies its perception of cognition as being a result of a process of distant reflection – a process which is fundamentally based on a dualistic view of an objective world of physical reality and a subjective mental world of the individual's thoughts and feelings. Instead of accepting this ontologically dualistic view and understanding of the world, Heidegger is occupied by trying to understand – as a basis for further inferences – what it really means to exist. He argues that 'being-in-the-world' in a state of 'throwness' is more fundamental than subject/object dualism, and he rejects both the simple objective stance (the objective physical world is the primary reality) and the simple subjective stance (my thoughts and feelings are the primary reality). Heidegger views humans as 'being-in-the-world' in a kind of 'throwness', and claims that human beings have primary access to the world through pragmatic involved action, as opposed to distant detached reflection. Some of Heidegger's points resulting from these views are:

– It is not possible to make explicit (turn into objects) all our beliefs and assumptions, as there are no neutral viewpoints from which we can see or

observe our beliefs as things or objects, since we ourselves are always placed within the framework they provide.
- Practical involved action and understanding is more fundamental than detached theoretical reflection and understanding, as we have primary access to the world through unreflected practical involvement; detached contemplation may be fruitful, but it remains an exercise in cognition as praxis.
- It is a basic characteristic of humans that we are always in the process of doing something and, in doing something, we use things which surround us; we understand the things we use in terms of what we use them for.
- We do not primarily relate to things through mental representations of them. For example, when using a tool in a purposeful activity, the ability to act comes from the familiarity with the activity, rather than with the knowledge of the tool (e.g. a hammer). The things we use for a particular purpose are primarily existing for us, and the things we cannot use in what we are doing are exist for us secondarily. When we use a thing, it exists for us only in terms of its function. In the view of Heidegger, "what really is, is not defined by an objective omniscient observer (...) but rather by the space of potential for human concern and action" [8], as it seems meaningless to speak of the existence of objects and properties in the absence of purposeful activity with the implied possibility of breaking down.

As long as a thing fulfils its purpose it remains 'ready-at-hand' or unreflected (transparent) to the person who is using it; if it does not fulfil its purpose any more in the use situation, a breakdown happens in the person's understanding of it; the thing becomes 'present-at-hand' or reflected to the person. In other words, understanding is to be able to use a thing (a tool) unreflectively (without breakdowns):

> The hammer presents itself as a hammer only when there is some kind of breaking down or unreadiness-to-hand. Its 'hammerness' emerges if it breaks or slips from grasp or mars the wood, or if there is a nail to be driven and the hammer cannot be found. (...) As observers, we may talk about the hammer and reflect on is properties, but for the person engaged in the thrownness of unhampered hammering, it does not exist as an entity.   [8, p. 35]

Moving back to computer conferencing and the choice of latent metaphor behind the interface design, Heidegger's theory and his view on breakdown support the choice of the tool perspective. The interface of conferencing systems, developed as a means to enable communication among dispersed groups and people, should be designed in a way that allows the user to keep his focus on the purpose of his action, rather than on the means which brings him there (this view does not agree with a media perspective, as the idea behind this is to stimulate reflection).

In conclusion, we can summarize the advantages of using a tool metaphor for understanding and comprehending the role of a conferencing system as follows:
- It comprises the whole work situation and organization of the user.
- Due to well chosen metaphors with spatial orientation and accompanying well chosen words organized in semantic fields, the user is provided with a possibility for working in a familiar reality (although symbolic in nature), and he is able to use his pre-existing assumptions and knowledge.
- Due to the generally menu-based interface, the user is provided with the possibility of applying the principles of both memory and recognition in his interaction with the system.

– As, among other things, the philosophy behind the tool perspective is that the interface should support the user in forgetting the symbolic nature of the system, this perspective produces an interface design which does not aim to attract attention. In other words, it is designed not to cause breakdowns in the user's understanding and as a consequence forcing him to reflect and concentrate his attention on the system (the tool) itself. The user is supported in keeping his attention directed towards the goal of his actions: the dynamic linguistic interaction with other people.

A tool perspective behind the design of interfaces for conferencing systems may be envisaged as having more widely reaching implications for the interactive potential of conferencing systems. An interface which is designed for 'involved action' and which does not 'ask for attention' is likely to make available to the interlocutors the optimal possibility for creating a new 'interactive reality', as it offers an opportunity for using the written word in an ontologically different manner [7]: a movement towards using the written word in a much more interactive way than it is traditionally being used. Instead of supporting the adoption of the conditions of traditional written interaction (using the written word in a detached and reflected manner), a tool perspective behind the interface design of conferencing systems works towards an incorporation of the dynamic, social and interactive aspects of human communication.

References

1. Albech, U.: Dansk stilistik. Copenhagen: Gyldendal 1973

2. Bøgh, P. A.: Semiotics and informatics: Computers as media. In: Information, technology, and information use. (Ingwersen et al. eds). London: Taylor Graham 1986

3. Ehn, P.: Work-oriented design of computer artifacts. Stockholm: Arbetslivscentrum 1988

4. Lakoff, G., and Johnson, M.: Metaphors we live by. Chicago: University of Chicago Press 1980

5. Searle, J. R.: Expressions and meaning: Studies in the theory of speech acts. Cambridge: Cambridge University Press 1979

6. Sorensen, E.K.: A comparative evaluation of CMC systems. Aarhus: Jutland Open University 1990

7. Sorensen, E.K.: Dialogues in networks. Aarhus: Jutland Open University 1991

8. Winograd, T. and Flores, F.: Understanding computers and cognition: A new foundation for design. Norwood, N.J.: Ablex 1986

14
Designing Human Interfaces for Collaborative Learning

Gary Alexander

Centre for Electronic Education, Faculty of Technology, The Open University, United Kingdom

Abstract: Collaborative learning, as opposed to individual learning, is known to provide an effective and efficient means of learning. Using computer-mediated communication (CMC), it can be incorporated into distance learning. This chapter describes the collaborative learning approach to be adopted in a forthcoming experimental course. It then describes the design of the interface for a CMC system to support it. Following a discussion of interface styles, it presents draft designs for four 'views' of the conference system: a personal view, a conference system overview, a conference overview, and a message view. The design attempts to convey the illusion of the presence of the members of the collaborative group ('telepresence'), and provides convenient tools for collaboration.

Keywords: collaborative learning, computer conferencing, distance learning, human interface, graphical interface, telepresence.

A personal note

This chapter comes at an interesting time for me. I have been developing prototypes for advanced human interfaces for (CMC) systems for a number of years. My participation in the discussions on board the *Najaden*, where this book was formed, helped me to advance my understanding of those interfaces significantly. Upon returning from the *Najaden* Workshop, I checked my local CMC system, and found that a new project I had proposed had been funded. It is an educational experiment in the form of a pilot course on Renewable Energy, in which the educational methodology is to be collaborative learning using CMC.

As a result, I have decided to use this chapter as an opportunity to describe a first draft of the interface for the CMC system we hope to implement for this new project. It will include most of the material I had otherwise intended for this chapter, and will build on many of the ideas which were discussed on the *Najaden*. It should provide an application of the theoretical ideas discussed in several of the other chapters of this book. Of course, the designs I will present are in no way definitive: many other choices could have been made regarding almost all of the details. Nonetheless, I hope this case study will be informative and will tie together some of the ideas expressed elsewhere in the book.

Collaborative learning at a distance

My interest in CMC stems from a belief that collaborative learning has significant advantages over individual learning. I work for a distance learning university, which for 20 years has developed mass media techniques for individual distance learning. With the technology of CMC now available, collaborative learning at a distance has become possible.

By collaborative learning, I mean a structured learning experience designed so that the learner interacts with a group of peers. I see three principal strengths to a learning strategy which takes collaboration as its starting point. Firstly, the learners have the benefit of other perspectives on the material they are learning. The group inherently brings with it a wider range of experience than does any individual member. This enables learners to obtain help from their group, and to tackle larger projects than they could individually. Secondly, the learning experience can be structured so that students will find themselves presenting and explaining parts of the material to other students. Discussion with peers can be more relaxed and free than with a teacher. By communicating what they have learned to others, the material will become more integrated into their general understanding. (...as in the old adage, the best way to learn something is to teach it!). Thirdly, working with a group is highly motivating to people. The group provides a pace for its members. People want to be seen to be doing their best. The support and sense of identity provided by the group allays fears and builds confidence.

Collaborative learning cannot be guaranteed to occur successfully simply by giving students a CMC system and telling them to get on with it. It is far preferable to devise activities in which collaboration is an essential part. All of the following group activities will take place through the medium of CMC.

Our proposed experimental course will consist of a set of collaborative projects. The students will form themselves into 'collaborative learning groups' for each project, which will have as its output a group report. Each student will contribute one or more sections to the group report, and some will take on other tasks as well, such as group coordination, editing, or research. The initial activities in the course will be for the students to introduce themselves to each other, noting each others' skills and abilities. They will be asked to form groups such that people with appropriate interests and abilities are available to take on each of the range of tasks required. Associated with each student group will be one or more tutors. Although the principal responsibility for the project will rest with the group, the tutors will be available for advice and assistance with group coordination, and as guides to the course materials.

The course materials will not provide a pre-digested route through the intended content of the course. Rather, they will consist of a set of texts, reference materials, computer models and audio-visual materials giving a wide coverage of the subject matter. The materials will be supplied in the form of print, video tapes, and a CD-ROM containing the computer-based materials. Students will be expected to use the course materials to research the areas of their contribution to the group report. They will have access to the other students and tutors through the CMC system for help with this research. They will then be asked to submit drafts of their contribution to the group and will receive comments on it from other students. Their final drafts will reflect these comments. All students will be expected to comment on the drafts of one or more other students, and will generally be expected to be familiar with the entire content of the group report.

The educational approach thus requires students to take a very active role in their own learning: searching for the material they will need from a set of resources, presenting material to their peers, and critically evaluating the work of their peers, all within a supportive framework.

The student's performance will be assessed on a three-part basis: the standard of the overall group report, the standard of their contribution to the group report, and a score given by the other group members assessing their assistance to the group. The purpose of this strategy is to create conditions in which collaboration is clearly in everyone's interests, so that group synergy is maximised.

Features to Enhance Collaborative Learning

There are a number of design features of a CMC system which can assist and support collaborative learning. Some of these are basic to any CMC system:
– The system must be used! This means that using it must be desirable to the learner. The equipment needed must be readily available. The cost must be low enough not to be a barrier. Learning to use the system, and operating it once learned, must be easy and enjoyable (as noted by Oliver Vallée in Chapter 12).
– The process of making connection should be automated and the cost of connection should be minimised.

Some of these features are to create and maintain a sense of group identity. This is the 'telepresence' which was much discussed on board the *Najaden*:
– The system will provide information about the other members of a student's group; aside from the usual background information and lists of interests, it will be used to create joint expectations about the contributions of each to the group project.
– As will be described in more detail below, we plan to design the human interface so that it emphasises people, not messages; images of faces will be used to give a sense of personality and the system will normally show who has been

present since you were last connected; contributions of each individual will be easily followed.

Some features will support the specific collaborative activities the students will undertake:

– The most important tools needed are for joint authoring, and students must be able to easily circulate draft documents and other materials to each other and to comment on them; since a conference system is generally structured in terms of contributions with a series of comments on them, the prime requirement here is to integrate the conference system with the student's more general document generating tools.

– Some materials the students will handle will not be in the form of conference messages, including graphics, computer models, external reference materials; there is thus a need to permit transparent transfer of files between students, that is, to exchange materials without the need to go into some separate program, set up file transfer protocols, etc.

– Easy extraction of material for re-use is essential; a CMC system is one tool among several the students will use, and the information received through it must be searched, digested, re-used and linked to other information.

Online versus Off-line Working

Some early strategic decisions have to be made in the overall design. The first of these is the assumption that students will normally be working off-line. We will provide them with a 'front end' program which automatically connects to the host computer at intervals they set, then sends and receives all waiting messages and files. Once disconnected, the system then will repackage the information received, setting up its own database and linking structures, integrated into the other course materials and tools we will be providing.

The principal reason for doing this is to keep connection costs low. If students work online, the connection time is determined by the time they take to read, think, and answer. High speed modems are of no benefit. For serious collaborative effort, they might be spending several hours a week online, with resulting costs which would be unacceptable. If they work off-line, then efficient connection algorithms and compression techniques can use the modems to their best effect, keeping connection times to a minimum.

A further advantage of working off-line is that the student can compose replies to any messages at leisure, free from the pressure of connection costs building up. The disadvantages of working off-line are more limited access to the facilities of the conference system. Searching and browsing will be most convenient for what has already been downloaded, and will require extra time and effort otherwise.

The choice of interface styles

The second major strategic decision is the basic style of the human interface. Computer interface design has gone through considerable development over the past ten years, but most CMC systems are still using interfaces of the style which was common at the beginning of that period. The reason for this has been a desire to allow access by a wide range of equipment, but nonetheless, many proponents of CMC systems strongly defend their interfaces as modern and friendly.

The earliest mode of interactive computing used teletype machines as terminals. The computer offered the user a short string of characters as a prompt and the user typed in a reply. This style of interface is called a 'command line interface' (CLI). A teletype machine prints one line at a time. It cannot erase what it has already typed or go back to retype earlier lines. On the other hand, the roll of paper provides a permanent record, and the user can always look back along it to see what occurred earlier.

When cathode ray tube (CRT) based terminals replaced teletypes, the software that went with it was initially unchanged, producing what is called a 'glass teletype' style of interface. Unlike a paper teletype, material which has scrolled off the top of the screen often cannot be retrieved. This is the style of interface which still dominates CMC systems.

A command line interface (CLI) requires a knowledge of the specific set of commands and syntax required at any point. Generally, the prompt supplied changes with the context (i.e. between reading and writing messages, or between entering the system and within a specific conference) and the set of commands, and sometimes the syntax changes too. This provides a great learning load on the novice user. The result is that most users learn only the most basic commands and never get to use the more sophisticated features of the system. However, careful thought as to the choice of commands and default behaviours can make a system relatively easy to use. For example, in CoSy, repeatedly hitting <return> at every prompt will take users through all their new conference messages.

In the hands of an expert user, the command line interface has the great advantage over later interface styles that rich syntaxes are possible. This enables users to give complex commands in a few words. (Of course, experts who use several CMC systems curse the fact that each has a unique syntax and vocabulary. Not only are the commands for identical actions totally different, but the names of data items are different: 'mail' in CoSy is a 'message' in Caucus, etc.)

The next development in interface styles was to present the user with a 'menu': a list of numbered commands, to which the reply was the number of the command desired. The user no longer had to memorise the commands. However, this approach is slow and cumbersome, because to invoke the richness of the command syntax of the CLI, several layers of menus and submenus are required. Nonetheless, some CMC systems which claim to have 'user friendly' interfaces today, do so because they have taken this step! The basic presentation metaphor is still the glass teletype.

The next generation of interfaces used the ability of the CRT to paint anywhere on the screen to create new styles of interface objects and new ways of interacting. The so-called 'WIMP' (window/icon/mouse/pointer) interface put information in windows (which could scroll back), and used icons to represent some objects. Interaction is generally achieved by pointing with a mouse or other device. The three principle ways in which commands are presented are in pop-up menus (and menu bars), palettes and dialogue boxes. A pop-up menu bar allows a large set of commands to be presented and organised logically while taking up a very small part of the screen. Palettes and dialogue boxes overlap the main data temporarily, so make for efficient use of the screen area. All these devices allow the user to select commands by pointing so no memorising is needed. However, I must say that simply implementing a WIMP-style user interface is no guarantee that a system will be easy to use.

The full WIMP style interface requires graphic-oriented hardware. It is thus not possible to use such an interface on a 'terminal', where the interface is generated on the central machine. As explained by Jens Ambrosius in Chapter 17, the use of personal computers as terminals is now becoming more and more common. It is thus possible for the interface to be generated on the PC instead of by the central computer.

The current generation of personal computers are all capable of handling graphic-oriented interfaces, but there is still a large installed base of machines which cannot handle them. Nonetheless, character-based interfaces sharing many of the characteristics of a WIMP interface can be used on them, and in fact are used in some of the newer CMC systems (e.g. SuperKOM: see Chapter 16).

In the glass teletype style of interface there is generally virtually no consideration of the aesthetics of the presentation. In WIMP style interfaces, there may be some consideration for the overall screen layout and presentation, but information is still usually presented in a completely abstract way. The latest generation of interfaces, often associated with multi-media presentation, relies much more heavily on graphic design to set contexts and create expectations in the user. In this way, interfaces can be created which are much more intuitively understandable. It is the approach we intend to pursue.

We plan to use a graphic-style user interface, running on a personal computer (an Apple Macintosh initially), which acts as a 'front end' to a conventional conference system. Because of the special features added by the front end, the conferences will not be fully accessible to people using the conference system without it.

An Interface Design for Collaborative Learning

In this section I will present a 'first sketch', an outline of the design we are preparing for our experimental course which will be using collaborative learning by CMC. Much of this design is new, although it is an outgrowth of earlier work, and much of the underlying functionality (and additional details) will be taken from earlier work.

As described by Elsebeth Sorenson earlier in this book, the choice of metaphor is crucial for the designer, and it is best if it is explicit. The metaphor we are using is that of a tool for collaborative work groups, but a tool designed in such a way as to reinforce the concept of 'telepresence' (creating the illusion of the presence, and even the closeness, of other people who are, nevertheless, distant in space and in time).

The current state of our design, as will be described below, does little more than embody the current state of our attempt to convey the metaphor of a tool for collaborative work groups which emphasises the notion of telepresence. There are many other important features of interface design which will not be covered. Worth mentioning are the need to group controls understandably, to ensure that the most used commands are readily accessible and require minimal effort to give. At a different level, it is vital that people can navigate through the maze of messages easily. This can be facilitated by a combination of graphic presentation to display the structure, and flexible controls to allow access to it.

With a graphic style user interface, the basic issue the designer must face is the overall architecture of the system as presented to the user. How is the overall functionality to be separated into different views of the system? The user needs to be able to view the structure of the conference system as a whole.

We currently envisage four principal views: an overview of the conference system ('The Electronic University'); an overview of each conference; a message view (which will include comments on messages, and with variants for replies); and a personal view, giving information about each of the participants.

I will start with the personal view, as that sets up the basis for the group metaphor. A draft of it is shown in Figure 14.1. In the left hand corner are a personalized face icon and a personalized monogram. These are used elsewhere in the interface to provide instant recognition. In addition, whenever the face icon or monogram appear elsewhere, they can be used to bring up the display of the personal view, thus providing an easy reminder of who has sent any message.

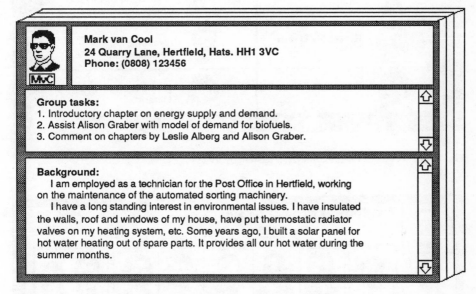

Figure 14.1 A design for the 'personal view'

One of the first tasks in the course will be for participants to create their own personal view, including a face icon and monogram. The face icon will be created by each user by customising a face from a library of faces. It needn't be realistic, and could even be symbolic if desired. The monogram will be created by choosing a font for the initials and drawing a border. Face icons such as these, built on a 32 by 32 grid, can be represented as 256 hexadecimal characters and so can easily be transmitted to all users.

Notice that prominent in the personal view is the list of tasks that individual has agreed to contribute to the group. That will be completed during the process of forming the collaborative groups. Its purpose is to ensure that all members of the group are agreed as to what is expected from them.

The other three views show successively more detailed descriptions of the CMC system. The most general is the conference system overview, for which a draft design is shown in Figure 14.2. It shows a list of the conferences (and mailbox), with a number indicating the number of new items received in that conference. Each conference also includes a face icon of the person who is moderating that conference, to emphasize the personal links. The list will be scrollable, so that more than 8 conferences can be accommodated.

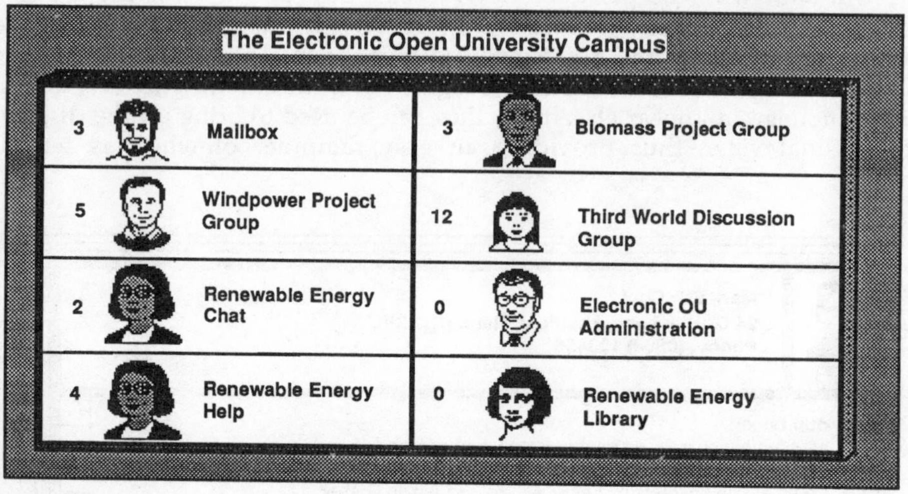

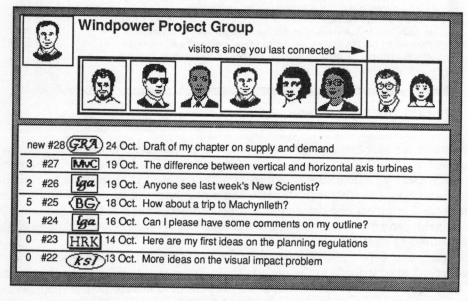

Figure 14.2 A design for the conference system overview

Figure 14.3 A design for a conference overview

At the next level of detail is the overview of a conference, which is shown in Figure 14.3. This shows the activity of the collaborative learning group itself, so it is here that the metaphor must be brought out most strongly. Along the top is a row of face icons showing who has been active in the group since the user last connected. The box around a face icon will be used to indicate that that person has made a contribution (i.e. the others, people who have connected and have read messages but have not contributed are not left out.) Again this will be a scrolling list so that a larger group can be accommodated. The lower part of the view shows the list of current main messages, with the latest on top. To the left is the number of new comments which have been received since the user last connected (or 'new' if the main message itself is new.) The authors are identified by their monograms (although face icons, or simply names may finally be used.) Again, this will scroll to allow older items to be viewed.

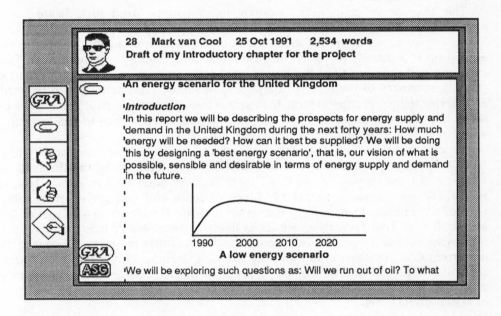

Figure 14.4 Draft design for a message view

The final view, and the one which is most important as a collaborative learning tool, is the message view. A draft of our design is shown in Figure 14.4. It is intended to facilitate the creation of joint documents. The metaphor presented is that of a document with a margin to which comments and other materials can be attached. By using this metaphor for messages, the CMC system will be integrated with other tools for creating documents and linking them to notes, references and other materials. However, the metaphor is sufficiently general to be used for casual discussion and other forms of interchange normally associated with CMC.

The message view presents a scrollable document, designed to permit comments to be associated with a specific paragraph. The presence of a comment will be indicated by the personal monogram of the sender (the principle use of the monogram). The monogram acts as a button: the comment will appear in a pop-up window, as though it was clipped to the document. Comments which apply to the message as a whole can also attached. They will appear in order of creation at the end of the document, extending its scrollable contents. This metaphor thus provides users with a rich, flexible structure which can be used either as the basis for building a joint document, or as a well-defined strand of a discussion.

The palette of icons on the left of the message offers the user a choice of ways of commenting on the main message. The monogram is used to attach marginal comments. The paper clip is meant to be used for private notes, again which pop-up to be read. Creating them will be the same as creating comments with the monogram, but they will not be transmitted to the host computer. A second use of the paper clip icon will be to link the message to other documents, models, educational materials, etc.

The 'thumbs-up' and 'thumbs-down' icons will be used to indicate basic agreement or disagreement, and will form the basis of a simple polling system. For example, someone might ask a question of the whole group, ("Are we all agreed on this plan?") to which members will reply using the thumb icon. The front end will combine all of the thumb icons for a given paragraph and present a running summary of the results in a pop-up window. We intend this to be used as a device to help groups to steer themselves towards consensus. It is intended to serve a similar function in CMC to those occasions in a face-to-face meeting where people nod agreement at some proposal.

An editor will be included with the front end which has the functionality of a fairly basic word processor. It will be available for general use by the students, in addition to forming part of the CMC front end. As illustrated in Figure 14.4, it will allow for a certain degree of choice of fonts and text styles, plus some embedded graphics. These will be converted into ASCII code using a sub-set of the Microsoft Rich Text Format, which looks likely to become a *de facto* standard, for transmission to and from the host computer. We feel that the text-only constraint of current CMC systems is too limiting for joint documents. On the other hand, the editor's features will be limited to keep the burden of learning to use it to a minimum. The added expressiveness this editor provides will also be welcome in casual discussions.

Conclusion

In this chapter I have presented the reasons why we are trying to introduce collaborative learning as the educational strategy for an experimental distance learning course, and have described the preliminary designs for the human interface of a communication system to support it. The starting point was the type of activities we will use as the basis of a collaborative learning experience (principally joint authoring of documents), and the CMC strategy is intended to support that. Our designs have attempted to bring the people and the group relationships to the foreground, rather than the messages. We have also tried to use metaphors and provide tools which facilitate joint activities and promote agreement. All of the devices and metaphors we have used build on well established principles of face-to-face group work. If they work as we imagine them to, we will have developed a distance learning environment using CMC with the excitement, fun and effectiveness which truly answers Oliver Vallée's challenge.

15
Toward a Hypermedium for Collaborative Learning ?

Alain Derycke [1]
CUEEP Institute, TRIGONE Laboratory,
Université des Sciences et Technologies de Lille, France

Abstract: The use of Computer Mediated Conferences (CMC) has gained popularity in various fields of human activity. Some pioneers have reported experiments in the field of education either to support remote learners in Open Learning institutions, or to teach at distance. We have designed the first generation of a CMC system tailored for education, based on the French videotex network. We have also tested this, and a summary of the first results is reported here. The human communication process, even if it is mediated by a computer, is very complex and requires the contribution of disciplines such as psychology, linguistics, and social sciences. The design of a new generation of CMC system adapted to educational goals is an ambitious task, which calls for very flexible work-benches to allow for multiple and various experiments. It also needs to solve a number of fundamental issues, of which seven are highlighted, and to explore new foundations and paradigms for such a design.

Keywords : computer supported collaborative learning, groupware, hypermedia, hypermedium, multimedia, teleconferencing, conversation, videotex, conference server, communication modes, human factors, group problem solving.

---

[1] I would like to acknowledge the invaluable contributions of my colleagues Danièle Clément, Christian Ladesou, and Claude Viéville in the preparation of this paper.

Introduction

The CUEEP, an Institute of the University of Lille, is involved in further education and in research and development in educational engineering. It has a wealth of experience in the use of computer assisted learning (CAL) and in the design of multimedia packages for open learning. In the last two years there has been a major shift towards the design of a global architecture for an open learning system based on advances in new communication technologies.

This is being done through the setting up of networks either at the level of the classroom and learning resource centres (local area networks), or at a regional level. Previous experience, especially with LANs [6], has convinced us of the need to find a balance between the necessary individualization of learning (self-paced, plurality of cognitive styles) and the need to promote socialization and cooperation amongst learners, especially for those who are distance learners. We have called this concept 'cooperative autonomy' [6].

The second generation of open learning systems, or Open Universities, is characterized by two things: the first is the 'mediatization' of the curriculum in various forms (paper, TV, audio...) and the second is the asynchronous delivery of the contents of courses. In spite of its success, this second generation model has severe drawbacks, especially in respect of the interactivity of the learners with the media, and their isolation. Of course, the use of courseware can reduce the first drawback, and teletutoring by telephone or periodic meetings can decrease the impact of the second one.

But we think that a broader vision which takes into account not only the advances in new communication technologies, but also new theories of education, is necessary to set up a third generation Open University.

For this purpose, it is important to conduct both theoretical and experimental research. In this paper we will emphasize one aspect of our work devoted to the use of multimedia computer conferencing systems in distance education. From our first experiment with the computer conferencing system we have designed, we can highlight seven of the major issues that must be addressed by the next generation of conferencing systems dedicated to education.

Computer Conferencing in Distance Education: the CoCoNut Project

The computer conferencing system

Conferencing systems have gained in popularity during the the last few years. These are asynchronous or 'connection-less' communications systems: the actors (e.g. learners, tutors, teachers) do not interact with the network at the same time. The messages, usually textual, are stored on a conference server. These are different from electronic mail because they are more group-oriented. The earliest use of such systems was in the field of cooperation between scientists or managers to help them discuss topics and problems in which they were interested. Nowadays, a widespread public uses computer conferencing (in the form of bulletin board systems, or BBS) to exchange information in various domains of interest, from computer programming to astrology.

Hiltz [13] has shown the importance of computer conferencing systems in education and she has stated that "it was recognized by those who followed this path (introducing CMC), that communication was an important part of the educational process; communication not just between teacher and student, but involving peer-group reinforcement among students as well". In spite of this premonitory view, CMC has only recently received interest from the educational world. This is due on the one hand to the cost of hardware and the availability of computer networks, and on the other hand to the difficulty of finding a place for these tools in the educational process, even in distance teaching.

Some pioneers have conducted experiments. Haile, for example, [11] discovered that conferencing was qualitatively different from an electronic mail system and can provide an educational environment which fosters group-oriented communication and greater interactivity.

The design of a conferencing system supported by a videotex network

For two years we have had launched an ambitious multi-year, multi-disciplinary research project call CoCoNut, for Cooperation and Communication Network Utilities for teleTutoring. The project is related to the study of various communication tools for the setting up of a third generation Open University.

Beside theoretical research work, a number of prototypes are being designed and tested. There are two important sub-projects :
– the first one deals with small group multimedia real-time interaction, which is a form of computer assisted audio conferencing or electronic blackboard [5];
– the second project (presented here) deals with asynchronous communication with a larger audience.

We chose to design a computer conferencing system from scratch for three reasons. Firstly, even if good systems existed, like CoSy or Parti, they were not available to us when we started our project, and our first evaluations showed us that these systems were relatively complex for the novice user. Secondly, we wanted to take advantage of the success of the French videotex network. There are more than 400,000 *Minitel* terminals in the homes of our Region. So, for part of our experiments, it is not necessary to provide terminals to the learners. Other advantages accrue from the videotex network such as equal access and cost throughout the country, and a relatively well known user-interface (e.g. the keyboard and special function keys of the *Minitel* terminal). And thirdly, we wanted the system to act as an experimental platform, so it was important to have access to the software source code and resources, and to be able customize and make incremental changes to the system.

Figure 15.1 gives a general overview of the architecture of our system. The videotex server is based on a set of Unix minicomputers linked by an Ethernet LAN. The CMC system is implemented in C language and is built on top of a videotex software kernel. This is viewed as another service which is accessible in the same way as other videotex services (information systems, traditional electronic mail, text retrieval systems etc). The conferencing system is coupled with a database and some procedures to up-load and down-load data other than text. The conferencing system is accessible either from a *Minitel* terminal or from a PC microcomputer. In the latter case, the PC emulates the *Minitel*, but it also offers other possibilities such as exchange of data, computer programs, and graphics.

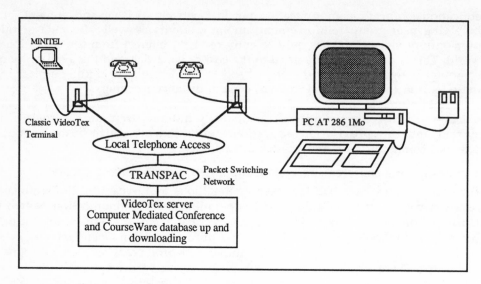

Figure 15.1 General architecture of the CMC network system

The user interface was kept simple, with only a few commands and a syntax very similar to the guidelines of the French videotex system. All the documentation needed by casual users is summarised in a six page booklet. Of course, there are other functions which are available for the experienced users (teacher, tutor, some learners) or for the system administrator, but they are not available to the other users.

For the presentation of the structure of the various conferences or sub-conferences we have used the metaphor of the electronic campus: conferences take place in different rooms where it is possible to discuss specialized topics with other people. We have also provided some rooms for informal conversation, for example the 'café'.

A structured conference for case study activities

A case study example

The case study is a good example of the use of computer mediated conferences for education, as it illustrates many of our key concepts in open learning. Here, it is not the result which is important but it is the process, the construction of the solution. We do not expect each learner to build his own solution, but we want them to collaborate, and exchange ideas to construct a solution. In arriving at this solution, the role of the teacher is to collect all the data from the simulated situation and to set the objectives. Thereafter, he divides the group into several subgroups and has to organize their work. The simulated situation must have a critical level of complexity in order to force the learners to cooperate. Sometimes, the learners would like to ask questions from experts in a particular field. Specialists can easily participate in this case study because there are few or no constraints on their time-table. The teacher can also play the expert role. After a given time, the teacher, who has observed all the subgroups, asks the participants to work out a unique solution amongst the different possible ones. The solutions are compared, discussed and analysed by all participants. The learners have also to argue their positions and to criticize the other solutions. While in subgroups the messages were less formal, less structured, but here the teacher requires discipline in the process. This requirement is due to the number of participants, which can be more than twenty.

There are clearly two levels of exchange during the conference: within the subgroups, when proposals are made and discussed; and during the plenary discussion, when each member can propose modifications, extensions, and adaptations to this first proposal. From time to time, the teacher has to summarize the state of the work so that participants do not become confused. Each member is able to switch easily at any time from the subgroup to the plenary situation.

An analysis of the activity

We have derived a group communication model of the case study activity based on four categories: roles, functions which can be applied to messages, types of messages, and rules [20]. These are summarised below.

Roles: In a case study these are:
– Participant: this user can browse and write messages.
– Organizer: normally the teacher, who organizes the conference, and asks each subgroup to propose its solution.
– Expert : a person who is able to answer a question asked by a participant.

The *functions* which can be applied to a message are well identified:
– Send a message within or to a subgroup.
– Send a message to the group.
– Ask for a vote.
– Note a proposal.
– Modify a previous message.
– Cancel a previous message.

The *types of messages* used in the group situation are :
– Continuation: when the text is too long, a user can use it to link two messages.
– Cancellation: when a member wants to cancel an earlier message.
– Comment: when a member wants to comment on a message.
– Proposition: used by a participant to propose the solution of his subgroup; it can also be used by the organizer to propose a compromise between several solutions.
– Modification: used by a participant or by the organizer or one of the experts to modify the content of a proposition.
– Extension: used by a participant, by the organizer or the experts to introduce an extension to the proposition.

The following messages can be used by all members within a subgroup:
– Conversation: the most current message in a subgroup.
– Question: used to ask a question of another member of the conference.
– Response: to answer a question.

The following messages are used to vote:
– Motion: contains the text which must be voted.
– Bulletin: transports the answer of a particular participant.
– Result: to disclose the result of the vote.

The *rules* coordinate the conference. They specify what to do when a message is read by a user or when a fixed time has elapsed. From these conditions, rules determine the function to execute, and the member who can or must do it. All the types and rules are described in a notice given to all the members of a conference.

Experimentation of the Conferencing System in Open Learning

We have conducted several experiments with our system in the framework of the development of Open Learning in our Institute, to give more choice as to the time, the rhythm, and the place of learning. Distance teaching/learning is only one mode of education we are developing amongst others.

But before we can draw conclusions from our experiments it is necessary to give some background to our analysis, as communication between humans is very complex and can carry of lot of different interpretations or points of view.

Some human factors for the analysis of the experiments

There are different levels of analysis of the process of communication via a computer conference. In reality, these levels are very intricate and correspond to different human factors with regard to the specialism or background of the observer.

We can roughly separate different types of human factors into four groups :

– *Ethical, political or social factors*: is this use of CMC compatible with the development of democracy? More generally, how does the use of new communication technology fit in with the political project of a new generation of Open University, of open learning? Other problems occur with respect to privacy, legality, etc.

– *Social psychological factors* which deal with the organization of groups, the interaction between their members, the place and value of etiquette, the evolution of meta-communication, codes and conventions etc. From our pedagogical point of view, emphasis was put on the social construction of knowledge and the necessity of cooperation and emulation [8].

– *Cognitive psychological factors* deal with the ability of the users to interact with the CMC system to accomplish different tasks in relation to the general goal. This is also, in the pedagogical field, the development of transverse skills with regard to access to information and the development of a plurality of learning styles.

– *Sociolinguistic or conversational factors* which are related to discourse analysis, turn-taking, and speech act theory [1, 17].

All these human factors have already been examined in other analyses of CMC experimentation – see for example [3]. Our project and observations are transverse to these factors, because we want to have a global view which puts emphasis on the total education process. It is important to note that these human factors are important not only for providing us with information on the experiments, but also to modify the existing CMC system, or to provide a basis for the design of a new system.

A first analysis of our experiments

Conditions of experimentation

Four different groups of learners at undergraduate level have tested our system. In this first stage all access was through a *Minitel* videotex terminal. Nobody reported difficulty in access to the terminal. For two of these experimental groups

CMC plays only a secondary role, with most of the educational process still remaining traditional: multimedia package delivery, distance tutoring by telephone, periodic meetings in learning resource centres where the learners can meet others following the same curriculum. Informal assignments are given via CMC. In presenting the potential of CMC, emphasis was placed on conviviality and free use.

The two other experimental groups are of more interest for us, because we have chosen to give a more important, central place to conferencing in the learning process. Learners received a formal assignment which obliged them to use the system. Their interaction with the system was part of the process of assessment. Two types of activities were chosen :

– *A group problem solving activity*: it is recognized that this kind of pedagogical activity is a promising potential of CMC in education [2]. The activity was organized around a collective mathematical game (Math-Hangman). The moderator of this conference has a lot of experience in the management of a traditional classroom with this collective game. It must be noted that in this game all propositions made by a learner must be submitted to the group and that a proposition is applied to the problem only if it receives a majority agreement.

– *A case study activity*: this activity takes place in an economics course of the company included in a broader curriculum for the training of office automation system managers. The case study is used as a synthesis of the course. The assignment is a study of the investment in office automation in small or medium sized companies. The moderator gives the first questions and the general direction. The activity implies that the group designs a collective set of questions for an investigation in the companies. He chooses the panels of company representatives. Each learner has one or two companies to interview and he reports the results of the investigation via the conferencing system. The results are collectively discussed (validity, generalization, etc) and a collective report is written. This approach is close to that of project work pedagogy envisaged as a special form of distance education [7].

The data we have available to analyse the experiments include:
– the report of the tutor/moderator: observation during the briefing and de-briefing sessions in traditional classroom meetings, assessment results, etc;
– the history of all the messages exchanged during the CMC sessions (one, two, or three months);
– non-directive interviews with some learners.

A synthesis of our first results
The first analysis is related to the usage of our CMC system. We have not encountered real difficulties. In fact practically all the learners (aged from 19 to 30 years) had already used the videotex system, both the terminal and the access procedures. They reported no difficulty in learning to use the CMC system. Fortunately the complaints were directed to the general videotex system: lack of a professional keyboard on the terminal, small screen with only 40 columns, slowness of response, etc. But these drawbacks are well known to learners, and thanks to the French videotex success everyone accepts them.

At the social psychological level, all our investigations confirm the results of previous experiments [3]. The lack of meta-communication, even if new textual conventions can be found, seems to present difficulties at the first time of use.

But after a first step this difficulty seems less important and most of the textual conventions disappear.

The major problem which appeared from our experiment is due to the multiple threads of discourse resulting from the asynchronous writing of messages in the CMC system. In this first version of our system there is only a time stamped on the messages when they are created, and a sequence number which indicates the chronological order in the CMC server. Because it is difficult to have a contextual view of a particular message and because tools to give a graphical historical view of the conference with different links between messages do not exist, learners are sometimes lost. Some messages ask: "... could someone tell me what we are talking about?". Currently, the only solution to this problem is for the moderator to periodically summarise a sequence of messages.

For us the asynchronous nature of communication is probably the most important characteristic which we will take into account in the design of new CMC systems. This has been recognized by major specialists in the CMC man-machine interface fields [4,15].

At the linguistic or conversational level it appears that roughly 50 percent of CMC messages are not really related to a conversation process [4]. As a matter of fact, it is difficult to attach these messages to a particular turn taking aspect of the conversation. However there are some sequences of messages which really can be analysed as conversation: in general it implies only two participants and the time between the different messages tends to be shorter than average. In fact, there is a shift towards a more real-time interaction. It can also be noted that, in such cases, the involvement of the participants seems to be higher.

At the pedagogical level, two important characteristics have been observed, especially in the second two groups. The first one is relative to meta-cognitive information given by some learners. They reveal difficulties in organizing their learning and in criticising the pedagogical values and methods used in the teaching of the course (especially about papers or reference books). But at this stage, it is difficult to use this information for tutoring.

The second one is the difficulty in organizing cooperation between learners. The main goal is buried in the 'noise': messages about the organization, cooperation and co-ordination of points of view which are mixed up with other ones relating to social activities. The operation of sub-conferences is not a good solution in this case, and we find there is a lack of structuring tools which would enforce structure and cooperation. The free form of the textual messages is not well adapted to these goals.

With the first generation of CMC the only way to overcome these difficulties is to create a precise and well-accepted protocol between the users (this can be explained during a meeting at the beginning of the conference) and to give an important role to the moderator (tutor).

There is a tension between free (unconstrained) access to the system, which would encourage participation, and the need for structuring (and thus constraining) the activities. One solution might be to design new communication tools by tailoring the CMC system for this type of application. This is similar to the approach of microcomputer systems: between the general programming language which gives the programmer the freedom to implement anything, and the specialized applications, there is a place for generic tools like spreadsheets.

Seven Issues for the Next Generation of Educational CMC Systems

The theoretical issue

It is important to have a strong background in theory to give a solid foundation to the design of new CMC systems. These theoretical approaches are related to the different levels described earlier. At the philosophical or political level it seems that new approaches like contextualism [21] could give a methodological framework to reformulate group meetings and collaborative work. The evolution of general theories of education must also be taken into account. We are especially interested by the post-modernist analysis of pedagogy [10], because it reflects our assumption that a balance between individualization and socialization (i.e. acceptance of the difference) is a democratic requirement.

At the linguistic or conversational level it appears that speech act theory and its extensions could be a basis for the design of collaborative systems which favour participation and co-ordination [22].

The multimedia issue

One of the most important deficiencies of our CMC system is its textual orientation, with two severe drawbacks: none of the verbal cues found in traditional teaching, and the related psychological problems; and it is difficult to use this kind of CMC in the field of sciences, for example, because of the lack of pictures, complex drawings and the possibility of exploiting them. This can be partially overcome by use of tools to down-load and up-load data other than textual messages. This is only possible with a microcomputer connected as a terminal. But a major problem still remains with the integration of the different media, especially voice.

Voice annotation is still at a research phase. In the real time mode of interaction it is easier to use voices, texts and pictures simultaneously [5]. The emergence of new powerful networks like ISDN will surely facilitate the task at the transport level.

The navigation issue

This is an issue related to the problem of multiple threads of discourse, and the disorientation of some users. It is a problem well known to Hypertext/Hypermedia (HT/M) specialists (for a good introduction see [14]). There is a need for special tools to help user navigation. In the HT/M field these tools are called browsers. The most important requirement for a new kind of CMC system would be the availability of a historical browser which could give not only a chronological view of the stored messages, but also the context of the writer of a particular message. This problem is close to one encountered in the field of collaborative writing of texts and the management of different versions of the same text. Research in the HT/M domains will probably give the first elements of solutions [12]. Another problem with consulting messages is the problem of information overload. It is important to design access filters which select messages, not only by date and name of sender, but also by the categories (types) of messages. It is also possible to use some active messages, i.e. messages with a relatively autonomous behaviour, which can collect, for example votes and acknowledgments.

The group structuring issue

For the design of new CMC systems dedicated to, or tailored for, education it is important to make it easy for the moderator (tutor, but also for the learners themselves), to organize and structure groups in relation to the pedagogical goals and the social and psychological characteristics of the target audience [3]. The COSMOS project, oriented towards office automation use of CMC, proposed a special system language for this purpose. Although it is a good solution for professional users who personalize their own environment, it seems difficult to apply in the field of education, which is characterized by occasional users. Perhaps visual programming will be a solution.

The textual conversation issue

At first sight, the possibility of conducting a dialogue through textual messages can appear strange. Linguists and speech act theorists have shown that a message text is an utterance of a conversation, so that CMC can be analysed in the light of conversation theories. However, the different asynchronies introduced by the storage of messages and asynchronous access introduce some important differences to a conventional spoken conversation. One solution is probably to design a system interface based on the 'conversations for action' paradigm [22,4].

In the education field the challenge is to design a system which favours interactive participation, without hierarchical and incentive management of the sort found in the corporate environment.

The specialization issue

If we want to support the learning process efficiently with a CMC system it is important to provide more tools to support the activity of the learner in relation to the pedagogical goal. It is not possible to have an integrated tool which is tailored to all kinds of activities, including debate, discussion, case studies, brainstorming, etc. We do not think that artificial intelligence and expert systems approaches can provide solutions to these high level human activities. The tools must only be considered as systems to reveal and facilitate the processes of human intelligence. Some developments have occured in this respect with tools to support discussion, for example the Euclide systems [18], or to support brainstorming decisions, like the Colab project [19].

The integration issue: towards hypermedium

From the overview of the first six issues it appears that a CMC system tailored to education could be very complex to design. There is a danger of setting up a system which is composed like a puzzle of various tools. The challenge is to design a new system with a homogeneous interface where the communication act is central. The use of hypermedia and courseware must be integrated in this communication environment. A lot of research work must be carried out to determine the best approach for the human-computer interface to such a system. It is important that this integrated environment is underlain by only one or two powerful metaphors, such as the desktop metaphor in the world of office automation.

Another challenge is to integrate the two fundamental modes of communication: asynchronous and synchronous. This is not an easy task because in asynchronous communication the elements of the conversation could be viewed as an exchange of documents (text, audio annotation, etc). However, in synchronous communication the document is only an object of the conversation, which is organized around it. The audio channel is then the most important one. It is the same if the use of video conferencing is planned.

The integration problem occurs at two levels. Firstly, at the network level the different streams of communication (text, audio, image, moving video) must be synchronised and controlled (for example: detection of the speaker). In some cases the transport of all the media can be integrated on the same packet network, depending on the available bandwith. Secondly, at the interface level, the system must enable the user to shift gracefully from asynchrous to synchronous modes, or even to use the two modes simultaneously (for example two people discussing in real-time a document they are writing collaboratively in the asynchronous system). [2]

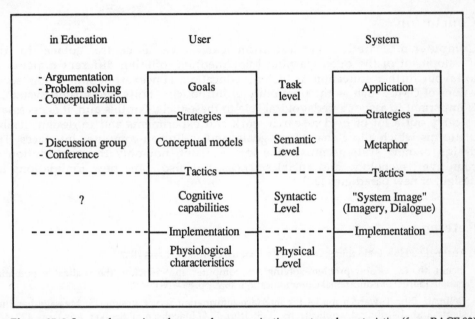

Figure 15. 2 Layered mapping of user and communication system characteristics (from RACE 92)

The integration could be based on the concept of HyperMedium described by Gaines, which is close to our aims for the design of a third generation Open University:

> The hypermedium concept is significant in capturing the computer-supported, open-ended access to a diversity of media that offers many possibilities for creative thinking, problem solving and networking by individuals and dispersed groups. [9]

To achieve the integration goal, it is important to have a clear view of the interaction between users and the communication system. For this purpose, a layered approach can be used to clarify this complex task. The layered model

---

[2] The integration of different media channels and different modes of communication for collaborative learning is the core of the CO-LEARN project, accepted in Phase II of the DELTA Programme of the Commission of the European Communities.

proposed by the EEC RACE Programme [16] is very useful as a starting point of analysis and requirements for designing a new communication system (see Figure 15.2). The users have goals, purposes or intentions concerning a particular task employing conceptual models (i.e., ways of thinking about how to reach their goals and purposes and how to satisfy their intentions) which reflect their cognitive abilities and physiological characteristics. Each of these layers can be mapped into related features in a communication system. Metaphors, for example, have to be designed to match the conceptual models held by the target users. The model also implies that a mismatch at any level may prejudice the success of the communication system. The challenge is to design applications which give an active mediation to support pedagogical goals. At the semantic level the system must present only a few metaphors which have a common 'feel' and which are in accordance with the learning activity.

Conclusion

Computer-mediated communication can have a central place in the development of the open learning hypermedium, offering different dimensions to favour further education or lifelong education. However, in spite of the social values of CMC, such as the possibility of introducing noise into a rigid system, it is important to assign a pedagogical role to these tools. For this aim, it is necessary to carry out a lot of field research work and experiments and to design flexible platforms which allow changes in goals, and in human-computer interfaces. The design of new systems must take into account, not only the contribution of cognitive psychology and social sciences, but also some new foundations for design, or new paradigms [22].

References

1. Austin, J.L.: How to do things with words. Oxford: Clarendon Press 1962

2. Beckwith, D.: Group problem-solving via computer conferencing: the realizable potential. Canadian Journal of Educational Communication, 16,2, pp. 89–106 (1987)

3. Bellman, B.L.: Toward a model for interface information server design. In: Message handling systems and distributed applications (E.Steffernd, O.J.Jacobsen, P.Schiker eds.) pp 427–445. Amsterdam: North-Holland 1989

4. Bowers, J. and Churcher, J.: Local and global structuring of computer mediated communication: developing linguistic perspectives on CSCW in Cosmos. Proceedings of the CSCW'88 ACM Conference, pp. 125–139. Portland, Oregon 1988

5. Derycke, A. Viéville, C., and Vilers, P.: Cooperation and communication in Open Learning: the CoCoNut Project. Proceedings of the WCCE'90 IFIP Conference, Sidney. In: Computers in Education (A.McDougall and C.Dowling eds.), pp. 957–962. Amsterdam: North-Holland 1990

6. Derycke, A., Loosfelt, P., and Viéville, C.: Towards pedagogy in networks. Proceedings of the ICCAL Conference, University of Calgary, May 1989, pp 93-98

7. Dirckinck-Holmfeld, L.: Project pedagogy and computer mediated communication in distance learning. Proceedings of the WCCE'90 IFIP Conference, Sidney. In: Computers in Education (A. McDougall and C. Dowling, eds.), pp. 963-970. Amsterdam: North-Holland 1990

8. Doise, W. and Mugny, G.: The social development of the intellect. London: Pergamon Press 1984

9. Gaines, B. and Vickers, J.N.: Hypermedia design. Proceedings of the RIAO 88 Conference on User-oriented content-base text and image handling, pp. 14–23. Massachusetts: MIT, March 1988,

10. Giroux, H. Border pedagogy in the age of post-modernism. Journal of Education, 170, 3, pp 162–181 (1988)

11. Haile, P.J. and Richards, A.J.: Supporting the distance learner with computer teleconferencing. 15th Annual Conference of the Northeastern Educational Research Association, New York, October 1984

12. Halasz, F.G.: Reflections on Notecards : seven issues for the next generation of hypermedia systems. Communication of the ACM. 31, 7, pp. 836–852 (1988)

13. Hiltz, S.R. and Turoff, M.: The network nation: human communication via computer. Reading, MA: Addison-Wesley 1978

14. Nielsen, J. Hypertext and hypermedia. San Diego, CA.: Academic Press 1990

15. Norman, D.A. and Draper S.W.: User centered system design. Hillsdale, N.J.: Lawrence Erlbaum Associates 1986

16. RACE: Operation 92 – Advanced communications technologies in Europe. Brussels: Commission of the European Communities 1990

17. Searle, J.R.: Speech acts. Cambridge: Cambridge University Press 1969

18. Smolenski, P., Fox, B., King, R., and Lewis, C.: Computer-aided reasoned discourse, or how to argue with a computer. In: Cognitive sciences and its applications for human-computer interaction (R. Guindon.ed.). Hillsdale, N.J.: Lawrence Erlbaum Associates 1988

19. Stefik, M. et al.: Beyond the chalkboard : computer support for collaboration and problem solving in meetings. Communication of the ACM, 30, 1, pp. 32-47 (1987)

20. Viéville, C., Clément, D., Demerval, R., Derycke, A., and. Ladesou, C.: To promote cooperative education in open learning by a dedicated computer mediated conference and groupware. Proceedings of the 12th Educational Computing of Ontario and 8th ICTE, pp. 609–611. Toronto 1991

21. Whiteside, J. and Wixon, D.: Contextualism as a world view for the reformation of meetings Proceeding of the CSCW '88 ACM Conference, pp 369-376. Portland 1988,

22. Winograd, T., and Flores, F.: Understanding computers and cognition. Norwood, N.J.: Ablex 1986

16
Computer Conferencing Functions and Standards

Jacob Palme

Department of Computer and Systems Sciences,
University of Stockholm Royal Institute of Technology, Sweden

Abstract: This paper makes a comprehensive inventory of functionalities often available in computer conferencing systems. Each function is described, and the terminology used to refer to this function in well-known systems is included. The paper further discusses why standardization of computer conferencing is of value, and which different interfaces can be covered by such a standard. A short introduction to current models for standards in this area is included. Finally, the design and user interface of one particular conference system, SuperKOM, is shown.

Keywords: computer conferencing, bulletin board systems, ISO, CCITT, terminology, KOM, SuperKOM, EIES, groupware, computer-supported cooperative work, group communication, message handling, electronic mail, standardization.

Introduction

This chapter consists of several parts. The first part describes the main functions in computer conferencing systems, both functions which almost all systems have, and functions only available in a few systems, but of value for distance education. For each function, the chapter describes how the function is implemented in some well-known conference systems and which terms are used to describe it. The chapter can be used as basis for a wish-list when procuring conference system software.

The second part discusses how standards for computer conferencing can be developed and describes the status of work in this area within ISO and CCITT.

The third part discusses the design of one particular conferencing system, SuperKOM, whilst the fourth and final part presents the main principles of computer conferencing as seen from the user interface of one particular system, the SuperKOM system.

Computer Conferencing Functions and Terminology

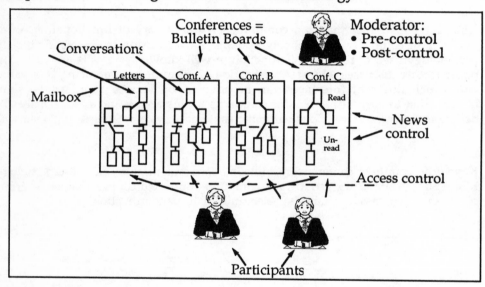

Figure 16.1 Terminology of computer conferencing

Figure 16.1 gives a pictorial introduction to the main terminology used in computer conferencing. The list which follows presents, in sequence, the functions displayed by conferencing systems, and indicates the terms used to name them in a variety of different existing systems. [1]

---

[1] The various terms used in different systems are given with the system name in parentheses. By (ISO) is meant the proposed terminology in the latest version of the ISO/CCITT working paper, to become a forthcoming standard for computer conferencing. The standard is not ready, so the term may change [7]. By (KOM family) is meant all the systems in the KOM family of conference systems: COM, PortaCOM [13] and SuperKOM [11, 12]. By (EIES) is meant both EIES1 and EIES2 [15,17].

Items

Inter-personal message

• Function: Items of text sent to individually named recipients.
• Terms: Message (EIES, Caucus), Mail message (CoSy), Inter-personal message (X.400), Letter (KOM family).

Contribution

• Function: Items of text sent to groups of recipients. In advanced systems, items can contain drawings and voice. Such items are called multi-media items.
• Terms: Contribution (ISO), Article (Usenet News), Comment (EIES), Entry (KOM family), Message (CoSy), Item (Caucus).

Notification

• Function: Various kinds of notifications to a user when things of importance to that user happens, such as the re-sending of his/her contributions, their removal by the moderator, the addition of the user to a new conference etc.
• Term: Notification.
• Implementation: The type of notifications available vary between systems. Some systems present notification as news items, other only store them so that the user can request them when they are needed.

Conference types

Conference

• Function: A set of participants and a set of contributions which they all can read and usually also write.
• Terms: Bulletin Board, Group activity (ISO), Conference (EIES, SuperKOM, CoSy, Caucus), Meeting (PortaCOM), Newsgroup (Usenet News).

Open conference

• Function: A conference which any participant can make himself a member of.
• Terms: Open (ISO, KOM family, CoSy, Caucus), Public (EIES).

Closed conference

• Function: A conference to which only the owner or moderator can add members.
• Terms: Closed (ISO, KOM family, CoSy), Private (EIES, Caucus).

Restricted conference

• Function: A conference to which some, but not all, participants can make themselves a member.
• Terms: Restricted (PortaCOM), Open for (SuperKOM).
• Implementation: The group of people who are allowed to add themselves as members to a restricted conference are often defined as the set of members in another conference.

Protected conference

• Function: A conference on which no information, not even its name, is available to non-members.
• Terms: Protected (KOM family), Hidden (EIES), Confidential (CoSy), Unlisted (CoSy, Caucus).

Write-protected conference
• Function: A conference to which only some of the members can add entries.
• Terms: Write-protected (KOM family), Read-only (CoSy, Caucus).
• Implementation: Note that the right which is controlled is not the permission to write, but the permission to add contributions. The person who has these rights (usually the moderator of the conference) can thus add not only his own, but also entries written by other participants.

In Caucus, every conference can have full and read-only members, so a write-protected conference in Caucus would simply be an ordinary conference which has some read-only members. In KOM, there is for every write-protected conference a superconference. If a member who is not allowed to write into the conference tries to add an entry, the entry is instead sent to the superconference. In SuperKOM (version 2.3) write-protection only applies to original contributions, not to replies on them. A member can however set his membership so that he only sees the original contributions.

Subconference
• Function: Conferences within conferences.
• Terms: Subconference (ISO, SuperKOM), Topic (CoSy).
• Implementations: In CoSy, everyone who becomes a member of a conference automatically becomes a member of all topics within that conference. In SuperKOM, the subconference is announced in its superconference, and for open subconferences, members of the superconference can add themselves as members if they so wish. In SuperKOM, sub- and subsub-conferences can be nested to any depth.

Operations on conferences

Suspension
• Function: The temporary cancelling of all rights to add entries to a conference or a conversation, usually controlled by the moderator.
• Terms: Suspension (ISO), Closed/open (EIES), Frozen(Caucus). Suspension in Caucus applies to conversations, not to conferences.

Announcement
• Function: Aids for the creator of new conferences to announce their existence and for participants to be informed when new conferences are created.
• Terms: Announcement.
• Implementations: In SuperKOM, announcements of new conferences are handled in a similar manner to other contributions, and can be sent to any conference. Usually, such announcement messages are sent to special announcement conferences. By becoming a member of an announcement conference, a user will be told of new conferences announced in it, just as viewing ordinary new contributions in a conference, but in a special format suitable for choosing whether or not to join the new conference. In many other systems, there is a special facility for telling users of new conferences, for example when they log into the system.

Conference directory
• Function: Aids for finding which conferences exist.
• Terms: Directory (SuperKOM, EIES), show command (CoSy), List conferences (Caucus).

• Implementations: There are usually commands to list all conferences. The listing can in some systems be restricted to certain types of conferences (e.g. only open conferences), to only direct or indirect subconferences to a certain superconference (SuperKOM) or to only conferences which have been active (received new contributions) recently (COM, PortaCOM). There is also often a facility to search the directory of conferences based on words in the name of the conferences and/or additional keywords on them.

User directory
• Function: To find and read information about other users.
• Terms: Directory (SuperKOM, ISO, EIES), Presentation (KOM family), Profile (Caucus).

Item directory
• Function: Aids for finding contributions and other text items.
• Terms: Directory (SuperKOM), index (EIES, ISO, Caucus).
• Implementation: The item directory is a way of assigning keywords to contributions and other text items and for finding them from their keywords, subjects and/or text contents via text retrieval commands. Such directories can be closed within a certain group, or localized to only a certain conference or group of conferences.

Create conference operation
• Function: The creation of a new conference.
• Terms: Create conference (KOM family), Mod new (CoSy), Start (Caucus).
• Implementation: In some systems, all participants can create new conferences, in some systems only certain privileged participants. In some systems, the owner of an installation of the system can choose whether all or only some participants can create new conferences. In a system with subconferences, the rights to create new conferences can vary with the level of the conference in the hierarchy.

Membership application
• Function: To apply for membership in a conference.
• Terms: Become member of (KOM family), subscribe (Grace), join (CoSy).
• Implementation: For some conferences, called open or public, some or all participants can make themselves members of the conference. Some systems have a special facility for applying for membership to a closed conference, these applications are then either granted or rejected by the owner or moderator of the conference.

Withdraw
• Function: To withdraw from a conference.
• Terms: Withdraw (KOM family), Resign (Caucus, CoSy).
• Implementation: In some systems, all members can always withdraw from conferences. In other systems, withdrawal is controlled by the moderator. In some systems, a member who has withdrawn is allowed at a later time to make himself a member of the conference again.

Conference archive
• Function: The facility to retrieve already seen contributions – one of the major differences between conference systems and distribution lists. Usually, new members of a conference can read contributions written before they joined.
• Terms: Conference archive, Review seen (KOM family), View all accepted (EIES 2).

Membership lists

• Function: The capability to find who are the members of a conference, and sometimes also how much they have left unread in the conference.

• Implementation: This facility is available in most conference systems. It is useful because a person who writes in a conference wants to know who will read or have read his contributions.

Special procedures

Moderator

• Function: A role with special privileges for a certain conference. Typical such privileges are to remove any entry from the conference, to add and remove members, to suspend and close the conference. In pre-moderated conferences, the moderator must approve each contribution before it is accepted and made available to the conference members. In post-moderated conferences, the moderator does not approve items in advance, but can remove items after they have been sent out. The advantage with pre-moderation is that unnecessary duplication and non-pertinent items can be avoided in groups with very heavy load. The disadvantage with pre-moderation is that it slows down the group interaction very much. Typical delays between a contribution and replies to it are six hours in post-moderated conferences compared to one week in pre-moderated conferences.

• Terms: Owner, Moderator (ISO, CoSy, EIES), Organizer (SuperKOM, Caucus).

• Implementation: The moderator role is in some systems split into several roles, such as an owner (who controls membership), an editor (who can remove contributions) etc.

Roles

• Function: When special rules apply to a conference, these rules will organize the members into groups with different capabilities.

• Terms: Roles.

Office procedures

• Function: Special rules applied to certain conferences. A set of rules, written in some kind of programming language, controls the actions in certain conferences.

• Terms: Office procedures. The conference, which has special rules, may sometimes not resemble any ordinary conference at all, and the term domain is then preferred to the term conference.

Commitment

• Function: Handling of information about tasks, priorities, promised delivery dates, who has promised to do what.

• Terms: Commitment.

Deferred operation

• Function: The storage of operations to be performed at a later time.

• Term: Deferred delivery (X.400), deferred operation.

• Implementation: There should be a possibility for users to find their deferred but not yet executed operations, and to modify or delete them.

Joint editing

• Function: Support for the joint editing of a text by a geographically distributed set of users.

• Term: Distributed authoring, joint editing.
• Implementation: Systems with such support are able to hold a master copy of the document, to stop two users from modifying the same part of the document simultaneously, and to have discussions hanging on pieces of the draft document.

Voting

• Function: Support for sending out vote queries and counting the replies.
• Term: Voting, balloting, polling.
• Implementation: Various algorithms for counting and presenting the result of the vote are used.

Data base

• Function: Data base facilities built into the conference system.
• Implementation: Contributions can be found by database queries. Sometimes information can be created by automatic combining of information in other contributions.

Contributions

Anonymous/Pseudonymous contributions

• Function: The possibility to write contributions where the author's name is withheld from the readers of the contribution.
• Terms: Anonymous, pseudonymous contributions. In the latter case, a pseudonym chosen by the user replaces the normal author name. EIES and Caucus have such a facility for writing pseudonymous contributions.
• Implementations: In most systems, it may be possible using privileged commands to find out the real author of an anonymous or pseudonymous contribution. In some systems, it is possible to write personal replies to the author of anonymous or pseudonymous contribution without knowing the name of the person behind the pseudonym.

Submit contribution

• Function: Submitting contributions to a conference.
• Implementation: This right is usually open to all members of the conference. It can be restricted to only the moderator. In those cases, other members can sometimes submit contributions, but they are not added to the conference until they have been approved by the moderator. Some systems also allow non-members to send contributions to all or some conferences.

Multi-recipient submission

• Function: Submitting the same contribution to more than one conference, and possibly also as personal mail.
• Implementation: In the KOM family, any participant can send a contribution to several conferences and/or personal recipients. Group replies are normally sent to the same set of conferences and personal recipients who received the replied-to entry. In EIES 2, a contribution always belongs primarily to one conference. But a contribution or a set of contributions in one conference can be submitted as attachments to contributions in other conferences.

Group reply

• Function: The ability to send a reply to all recipients of the replied-to item.
• Terms: Comment (KOM family, CoSy), Add response (Caucus) Reply all, Group reply.

• Implementation: There is often a way to let some special recipients see a particular item without forcing them to see all replies to it.

Obsoletes

• Function: The ability to change already submitted contributions.
• Terms: Obsoletes (X.400), change entry (SuperKOM), update (CoSy), change item and change response (Caucus).
• Implementation: In SuperKOM, recipients of an obsoleted contribution will be shown that this contribution obsoletes a previous contribution, and can with a special command see the text before the change.

Delete contribution

• Function: The ability to remove or delete contributions.
• Terms: Remove, delete, erase, withdraw.
• Implementation: In some systems (KOM, PortaCOM), removed items will not be visible even to those who have already received them. In other systems (SuperKOM) it is not possible to remove items from the mailboxes of the recipients, but they can be marked as deleted, which means that they are not shown as new.

Body types

• Function: The ability to send contributions containing other data than ordinary text. Examples are word processed documents, spreadsheets, executable object programs, graphics etc. A special case is where a contribution contains a program in a top-level language, which is executed when the recipient reads it. This facility is called activity in EIES 2 and delayed command in COM.
• Terms: Attachment (EIES 2), Body part types (X.400).
• Implementation: In EIES 2, such data can be put into attachments to ordinary contributions. In X.400, each message can consist of several body parts, each of a particular type. Usually, there are safeguards to protect the recipient from being mistreated by such executable entries.

Expiration times

• Function: Expiration times of various kinds on contributions.
• Terms: Expiration time, validity time.
• Implementation: There are two kinds of expiration time. One is the time before which a contribution may not be deleted, the other is a time after which a contribution should not any more be available. PortaCOM has such a facility. In SuperKOM, entries can be marked as archived to protect against purging.

Security

• Function: Use of special cryptographic security facilities to stop misuses like reading of items by non-authorized users, falsifying items, ensuring that the author of an entry is the one given etc.
• Terms: Encryption, electronic signature etc.
• Implementation: The various facilities are described in great detail in the X.400 messaging standard (not in the 1984 version of it).

Reading

News control

• Function: The facility to find only unseen contributions.

• Terms: News control, conference marker, view full text (EIES 2), read next unseen/entry/comment/letter (KOM family), Carriage Return key only (KOM family, CoSy), Show new (Caucus).

• Implementation: There are two two main methods. One is via a conference marker, which for each conference marks how far in the list of contributions the user has read. This method (used in EIES 1, CoSy, PortaCOM) has the restriction that it will only work if users read contributions in sequential order. The other method is by information for each participant of which contributions that participant has read or not read. This method is used in SuperKOM, EIES 2 and Lotus Notes. A special problem is how to handle the case where a user is a member of more than one conference, and an entry was sent to each conference. Those systems which allow participants to submit the same entry to more than one conference usually have a facility so that such double members will not be shown the same entry as new more than once.

Filters

• Function: The storage of a series of conditions, which are applied to new contributions to find those that satisfy certain criteria.

• Term: Filter.

• Implementation: Filters can operate on the incoming contributions for a particular participant, or on the whole stream of publicly available contributions. Selected contributions can be sorted into folders in the workspace of the user, or submitted to special conferences for receipt of filtered contributions.

Management

Purging

• Function: Purging of old contributions.

• Terms: Garbage collection, cleaning, purging.

• Implementation: Most conference systems have some facility to automatically remove old contributions to save disk space. A good purging system should not delete a contribution before the deletion of group replies on it.

Distributed operation

Distributed service agents

• Function: Distributed functionality I: Several conference system installations can be connected and run conferences in parallel.

• Terms: Distributed operation, parallel conferences. This functionality is available in EIES 2, SuperKOM, Caucus and Lotus Notes.

• Implementation: The implementations vary in the ease with which this is handled. In older systems, like PortaCOM, concerted action by moderators of both systems is needed to set up parallel conferences. In newer systems like EIES 2 and SuperKOM, conferences will automatically be copied in parallel to all hosts where there is at least one member of the conference.

Distributed user agents

• Function: Distributed functionality II: Support programs for conferencing in personal computers and workstations.

• Terms: User agent, PC version.

• Implementation: In some implementations, the PC version mainly handles the user interface, but retrieves data when the user asks for it from the central systems. This method (used for example in the MacCOM and EasyCOM front-end programs for PortaCOM) often give long response times and delays unless the connection to the main system is very fast. Other implementations keep a complete one-user conferencing database on the PC/workstation, so that a user need only connect to the network to upload and download news. The user can then use the conferencing system off-line, and even read conference by conference and write new entries off-line. Systems in this category are SuperKOM and Lotus Notes. The SuperKOM user interface can either be used locally in the PC or in a Unix server on the network, while Lotus Notes always runs the user process in the PC of the user. The advantage with a full database in the PC/workstation is very fast response times for most commands and that one saves the cost of keeping a telephone line open during the whole session. The disadvantage is that it becomes more difficult for a user who wants to access the system sometimes from a PC at work, sometimes from a PC at home, sometimes from a third PC on travel.

Inter-personal mail standard support

• Function: The ability to co-work with electronic mail.

• Implementation: In most systems, this only means that you can send e-mail messages from conference systems. In some systems (PortaCOM and SuperKOM) it is also possible to receive incoming e-mail directly into conferences, and to make external e-mail mailboxes into members of conferences.

Standardized connection to other conference systems

• Function: Capability to co-work with other conference system installations, so that parallel conferences can be run even though the sites use different conferencing software. Note that this is more than only the capability to interwork with other systems for the sending and receipt of personal electronic mail.

• Implementation: This requires a standard for the interchange of information between the systems. No full such standard exists. However, some systems (PortaCOM, SuperKOM and Caucus) can communicate using the Internet/Usenet messaging standards.

Geographical/organizational restriction

• Function: A contribution can be sent to a conference, but be distributed only to a subset of its members, e.g. only to members within a certain country or a certain organization.

• Terms: Geographical/Organizational restrictions on distribution.

• Implementation: This facility is available in Usenet News. The existence of this facility is controversial, since some people say that it would be confusing and unwise to have such subsets of recipients. There are however obvious advantages, such as posting a notice that you want to sell a car only to recipients within your own geographical area.

Conversational support

Conversation scanning

• Function: The capability to scan conversations in various ways. This function allows a user to find, from one contribution, the other contributions which are related to it by being replies to each other.
• Terms: Conversation, thread, tree.
• Implementation: This capability is available in some conference systems, for example those in the KOM family and Caucus. In Caucus, a conversation is handled in many ways similarly to conferences in other systems, users can thus see lists of conversations, find a conversation from its title etc.

Membership in conversational branches

• Function: The capability to move conversational branches from one conference to another, and to add and remove recipients from conversational branches. Users can also themselves withdraw from reading further entries in conversations of less interest to them.
• Implementation: This capability is available in SuperKOM. The Participate conferencing system has some of this capability.

Special support for distance education

Exams

• Function: Support for giving exams to students on distance education courses.
• Implementation: An exam facility typically will deliver the exam with a limited time for the student to answer each question, and where the student cannot take the same exam with the same questions more than once. In this way, cheating can be controlled.

Teacher questions

• Function: Teacher asking questions to students in distance education courses
• Implementation: A typical implementation of this is where the teacher posts a question, the replies from the students are collected, and the students are not shown the replies from other students until they have answered themselves, or until the teacher makes the replies available.

Referring to passages within contributions

• Function: The ability to write replies directed at certain words, phrases or paragraphs of a previous contribution. This has many uses, one of them is in distance education, where it makes it easier for the teacher to correct and comment on papers written by the students.

Computer Conferencing Standards

With increasing use of electronic mail and computer conferencing, people will more and more often be required to participate in conferences in different installations with different software. And most people are not willing to go to the trouble of connecting to several different conference systems. This is especially true if they also have to learn different user interfaces to different shades of functions. This problem can be solved by standards.

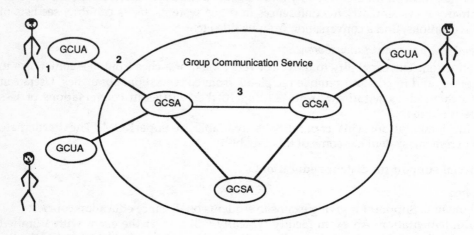

Figure 16.2 Group Communication Architectural Model

In order to understand the alternative options for writing standards, the model shown in Figure 16.2 can be used. In this model, each user is connected to a User Agent or Group Communication User Agent (GCUA) which handles the interaction with that user, and maybe also a personal database of messages for that user [1]. Each GCUA is connected to a multi-user server, called GCSA (Group Communication Service Agent) in Figure 16.2. The GCSA can communicate with other GCSA's.

The digit 1 in the figure represents the interface between the user and the conference system, as shown on the user screen. Many modern conferencing systems have a software component which runs locally in the personal computer or workstation of the user. The digit 2 in the figure represents the communication between such a software component and a server. This means that for some conference systems, no such interface 2 exists. The digit 3 in the figure represents the communication between two conference systems, of the same or different type. A standard for computer conferencing could standardize any of these three interfaces, numbered 1, 2 and 3 in the figure.

Standardizing the interface 1 would thus mean that the words and commands used in the actual user interface are standardized. The disadvantage with such standards is that they hinder future development of new and better user interfaces. Because of this, standards organizations usually avoid standardizing this interface.

Standardizing the interface 2 would mean that the user can buy one piece of UA software, with one type of user interaction. This UA software could then connect to several different conference systems, but the user would still have the same user interface. The disadvantage with standardizing 2 is that all conference systems do not use such personal computer software, and that different systems divide the task between the GCUA and the GCSA in different ways.

Standardizing the interface 3 would mean to provide a standardized way of different conference systems to communicate with each other. All existing standards mainly standardize this interface.

The following standards exist today:
– The Internet mail standards [3], [14]. These are mainly standards for inter-personal mail. They are widely used, but have very limited functionality.
– The ISO/CCITT X.400/MOTIS standards [2]. These have much more functionality than the Internet mail standards, especially in the areas of notifications, body types and distribution lists.
– The Usenet News standards [5]. This is a rather limited standard for the exchange of information between GCSA' s.

ISO and CCITT are working on the development of new standards. These may be ready in a first version in about 1995. ISO/CCITT standards are based on the Open Systems Interconnection model [6]. This model provides basic facilities for the interconnection of systems. The Remote Operations Service (ROS, [9]) uses OSI to make it easy to develop new protocols. A special language, Abstract Syntax Notation 1 (ASN.1, [8]) is used to define the format of the data structures exchanged between systems in a computer-type-independent way.

The forthcoming ISO/CCITT standards are going to define an architecture, i.e. a description of the different types of nodes (like GCUA' s and GCSA' s) which can connect. They will then define a common information model, a view of the database organization in group communication systems. They will define the user functionality in what is called an Abstract Service Description. They will then define the operations in the protocols to be defined, like the protocol between a GCUA and a GCSA (2 in the figure) and the protocol between a GCSA and another GCSA (3 in Figure 16.2). The forthcoming ISO/CCITT standard will contain a basic general group communication model, and define applications based on this general model. Example of such applications are basic computer conferencing, voting, joint editing, distance education, office procedures etc.

Design of the SuperKOM System

Part of the history of computer conferencing is shown in Figure 16.3., which also shows how SuperKOM was designed with knowledge of many existing conference systems like EIES [17], KOM [11], Parti(cipate)[10] and Usenet News [5]. The very first conference systems in the world were Emisari (designed by Murray Turoff) and Forum-Planet (designed by Jaques Vallée) [16]. The idea originally came from the Delphi method used in futurology. Around 1980, a number of different conference systems were designed. Typical of these systems was the centralized view, assuming that all users connect to one central host. The newest systems (Usenet News, EIES 2 [17], SuperKOM) differ from these systems in their distributed [14] nature, where users are connected to many different hosts, working together via computer networks.

Our design goals were to incorporate in a simple and general-purpose structure the main concepts of several older systems. In addition to the features described earlier in this chapter, we also wanted to support the ideas and functions listed below. Information on how we have tried to meet the design goals described below can be found in [11].

Allow the sending of messages to more than one conference

One and the same message can be submitted or re-submitted to more than one conference. Users should still not be shown the same message more than once, even if they are members of both conferences.

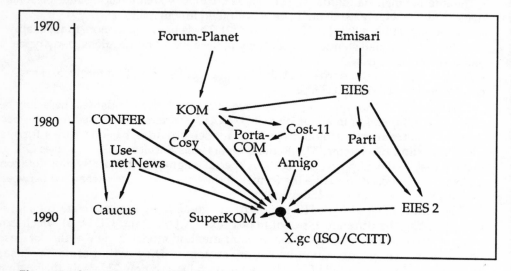

Figure 16.3 SuperKOM dependence on previous systems

Integrate personal mail with group communication

Each person has a personal mailbox, which looks very much like a conference with only one member. Thus, a message can be sent or re-sent to any number of personal mailboxes and/or conferences, and a user would still not be shown the same message as new more than once.

Natural default recipients for replies

Comments (replies) to messages are by default sent to all recipients of the commented message. The originator of the comment should of course be able to change this default set of recipients. For example, if a message was sent to conference A, conference B and as personal mail to a users C and D, then the default set of recipients for a comment on that message would also be conferences A and B and users C and D. It should also of course be easy to write a reply which is only sent to the author of the commented entry.

Easy forwarding of conversations to additional recipients

Suppose that in this way, a series of messages are exchanged between the same users. And suppose that one of them decides that some outsider or group of outsiders should take part in this discussion. It should then be simple to send this discussion to additional recipients, which may be users or conferences. In SuperKOM, we chose to give the person forwarding a message to additional recipients, two options on how the forwarding should work. With one of the options, only one single message and nothing more is forwarded. This option is in SuperKOM called *single copy*. The other option is to forward the whole conversation, or a whole branch of the conversation, to additional recipients. This option is called *for information*. With the second option, also forthcoming, not yet written messages in the forwarded conversation or branch will automatically be forwarded to the additional recipients.

Our experience with SuperKOM has shown that this is a very valuable facility. There often occurs cases, where you want to send whole conversations or branches in them to additional recipients, and to be able to do this with just one single command is very useful.

Users should be able to join and withdraw from conversations

There should be strong support for conversations. In principle, anything that can be done to a conference, should also be allowed for any conversation or any branch of a conversation. Users should thus be able to browse conversations, read news one conversation at a time and be able to become members of (be shown) messages from any branch of any conversation, and to withdraw from (not be shown) the messages from any branch of any conversation. This should, just like for conferences, apply also to not yet written, forthcoming messages in the conversation.

Hierarchical conference database

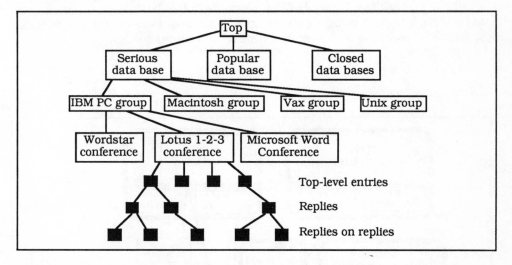

Figure 16.4 The hierarchical conference database

Another design goal for SuperKOM was that the database of the existing conferences should itself be structured, so that conferences can be organized into groups, departments and other hierarchies of conferences to suit different needs (see Figure 16.4). One subordinate node in the structure can be superior to more than one superior node. Our experience is that this is a valuable feature, but that one should not overdo it, creating an unnecessarily complex branching structure in practical usage of the system.

Built-in general purpose directory and information retrieval system

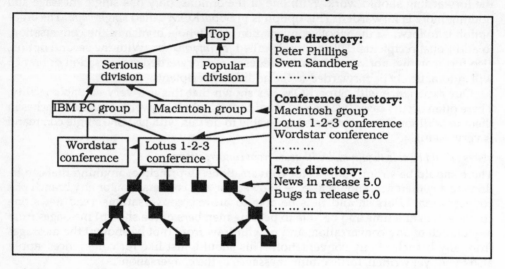

Figure 16.5 The central directory

It should be possible (see Figure 16.5) for any node in the database (user, conference, conversation, branch, message) to be assigned a name or keywords in the directory system, so that users can find them by information-retrieval queries.

A distributed system

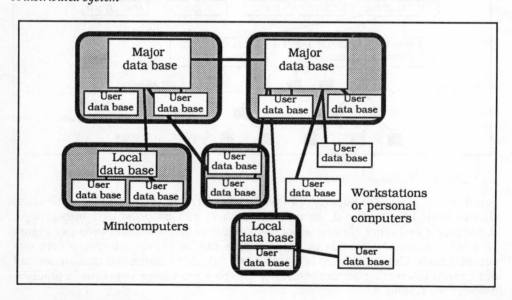

Figure 16.6 The distributed database

Finally, SuperKOM was to be distributed (see Figure 16.6). By this we meant that the database could be distributed on many hosts, each containing only the activities of interest to the users at that host. All features of the conference system should be available also in the distributed environment. For example, if a moderator moves a message from one conference to another more suitable conference, the effect of this action should be applied automatically to all hosts where this message occurs. In principle, the distribution of the database should be transparent to the users.

X.400 and and Internet mail compatibility

SuperKOM should allow connections to other mail systems, using the X.400, Unix Mail, Internet and Usenet News messaging protocols. Users in such other message systems are in SuperKOM called *external* users.

It should not only be possible to send mail to external users. It should also be possible to include their names as members of conferences in SuperKOM. If their message system only has electronic mail, and not conferencing facilities, the SuperKOM conference will then appear to them as a distribution list. It should also be possible to nest SuperKOM conferences with distribution lists. The conference would still look as a conference to SuperKOM users, and as a distribution list to external users outside SuperKOM.

It should be possible, from other mail systems, to send messages to SuperKOM, both to individual SuperKOM users and to conferences.

All the facilities described above for handling multi-recipient and multi-group messages, forwarding of conversations etc. should of course also be available for recipients in other messaging systems connected via X.400 or other mail protocols. The only limitation would be that external users can only use the commands available in their message system. Thus, external users cannot themselves give commands for example to withdraw from conversations.

A general-purpose and easily extensible internal database structure

The database should be structured in a simple and general-purpose way, so that it easily can be extended with new facilities, like for example support for voting, joint editing and other more advanced group communication tasks.

The User Interface to SuperKOM

A brief description of the ways in which the main features of computer conferencing are presented in the SuperKOM interface is given below

Showing the news

The first thing which a user sees with when entering a conference system is usually a list of all conferences with new contributions in them, with information on how many new items there are in each of them (see Figure 16.7).

Reading conference by conference

The user will then read the news in one conference at a time (see Figure 16.8). Within a conference, the user will read the news one conversation at a time. The user can decide the order in which the conferences are read. Once a user has stored in the database the order in which the user wants to read conferences, it is very easy for the user to read news at later times in the same order – the user need only push the RETURN key to read news.

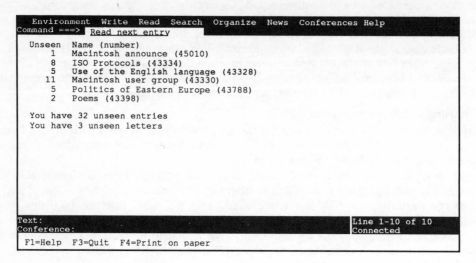

Figure 16.7 Showing the news

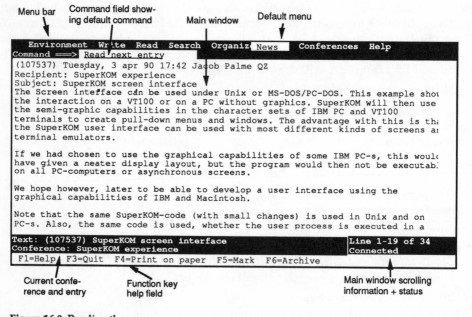

Figure 16.8 Reading the news

Writing replies

Users can give commands either by using the keyboard, or by pulling down a pull-down menu, as is shown in Figure 16.9.

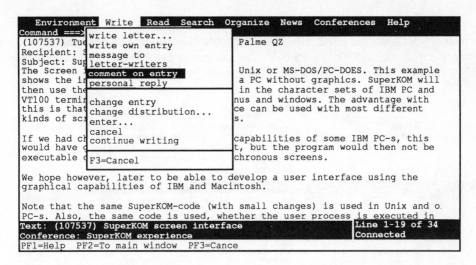

```
 Environment  Write  Read  Search  Organize  News  Conferences  Help
Command ===> write letter...
(107537) Tue write own entry          Palme QZ
Recipient: S message to
Subject: Su  letter-writers
The Screen   comment on entry          Unix or MS-DOS/PC-DOES. This example
shows the i                            a PC without graphics. SuperKOM will
then use the personal reply           in the character sets of IBM PC and
VT100 termin                          nus and windows. The advantage with
this is that change entry             ce can be used with most different
kinds of scr change distribution...   s.
             enter...
If we had ch cancel                   capabilities of some IBM PC-s, this
would have  continue writing          t, but the program would then not be
executable  F3=Cancel                 chronous screens.

We hope however, later to be able to develop a user interface using the
graphical capabilities of IBM and Macintosh.

Note that the same SuperKOM-code (with small changes) is used in Unix and o.
PC-s. Also, the same code is used, whether the user process is executed in
Text: (107537) SuperKOM screen interface          Line 1-19 of 34
Conference: SuperKOM experience                   Connected
PF1=Help  PF2=To main window  PF3=Cance
```

Figure 16.9 Pulling down the write menu

When a user writes replies, the screen is split in two windows, an upper part showing the contribution which the user replies to, and a lower part where the reply is being written (see Figure 16.10). The user can easily jump between these two windows and scroll them during the writing of the reply. The user can also, if desired, read other earlier contributions in the upper window while writing his reply in the lower window.

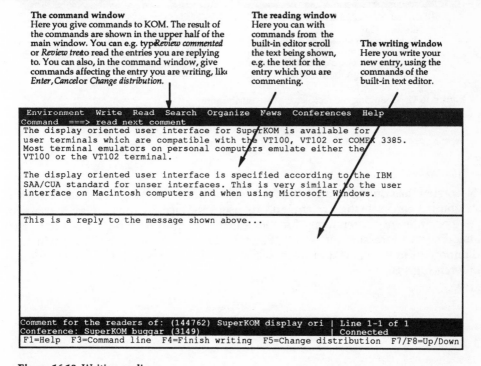

The command window
Here you give commands to KOM. The result of the commands are shown in the upper half of the main window. You can e.g. type *Review commented* or *Review tree* to read the entries you are replying to. You can also, in the command window, give commands affecting the entry you are writing, like *Enter, Cancel* or *Change distribution*.

The reading window
Here you can with commands from the built-in editor scroll the text being shown, e.g. the text for the entry which you are commenting.

The writing window
Here you write your new entry, using the commands of the built-in text editor.

```
 Environment  Write  Read  Search  Organize  News  Conferences  Help
Command  ===> read next comment
The display oriented user interface for SuperKOM is available for
user terminals which are compatible with the VT100, VT102 or COMEX 3385.
Most terminal emulators on personal computers emulate either the
VT100 or the VT102 terminal.

The display oriented user interface is specified according to the IBM
SAA/CUA standard for unser interfaces. This is very similar to the user
interface on Macintosh computers and when using Microsoft Windows.

This is a reply to the message shown above...




Comment for the readers of: (144762) SuperKOM display ori | Line 1-1 of 1
Conference: SuperKOM buggar (3149)                        | Connected
F1=Help  F3=Command line  F4=Finish writing  F5=Change distribution  F7/F8=Up/Down
```

Figure 16.10. Writing replies

Recipients of replies

Replies to conference contributions are normally sent to all who read the replied-to entry, but the user can change this if s/he desires to send the reply to for example only a subset of the recipients of the replied-to entry (see Figure 16.11).

The entry
Number and subject of the entry whose distribution is being changed

Link area
Here you choose what kind of link you want to add or remove from the entry. You move to the chosen link type with the arrow keys, and can then add or remove the X in front of the chosen alternative with the space bar.

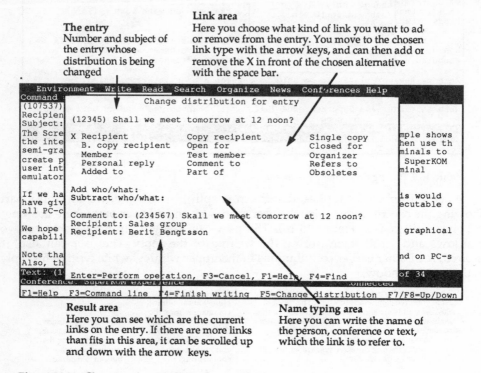

Result area
Here you can see which are the current links on the entry. If there are more links than fits in this area, it can be scrolled up and down with the arrow keys.

Name typing area
Here you can write the name of the person, conference or text, which the link is to refer to.

Figure 16.11 Changing the recipients of a contribution

Conclusion

This review has demonstrated the factors which need to be taken into account in designing a conferencing system, and its user interface, in such a way that a wide range of different conferencing functionalities and needs can be catered for, at the same time as addressing the issues of standardisation in software design, which are so important in the context of inter-working and communication between different conferencing systems.

References

1. Benford, S. and Palme, J.: Developing standards for OSI group communication. (Not yet accepted for publication)

2. CCITT: Message Handling Systems: System Model – Service Elements, Recommendation X.400, 1988 (Also published as ISO International Standard 10021).

3. Crocker, D.H.: Standard for the format of Arpa Internet text messages. SRI, California: Network Information Center RFC822 1982

4. Hiltz, S.R. and Turoff, M.: Structuring computer-mediated communication systems to avoid information overload. Communications of the ACM, pp. 680–689 (July 1985)

5. Horton M.R., Adams R., Standard for the interchange of USENET messages. SRI, California: Network Information Center RFC 1036 1987

6. International Standards Organisation: Basic Reference Model for Open Systems Interconnection, ISO 7498 (1984)

7. International Standards Organization: Group communication functionality. ISO/IEC JTC 1/SC 18/WG 4 document N1144 (January 1990)

8. International Organisation for Standardisation - Information Processing Systems – Open Systems Interconnection – Specification of Abstract Syntax Notation One (ASN.1), ISO 8824 1986

9. International Standards Organisation: Information Processing Systems – Text communication – Remote operations (ROS), ISO 9072 (1988)

10. Keehan, Michael T.: The Participate computer conferencing system. AFIPS Office Automation Conference, Los Angeles, February 1984

11. Palme, J. and Tholerus, T.: SuperKOM – Design considerations for a distributed, highly structured computer conferencing system. (To be published in Computer Communications in 1992)

12. Palme, J.: SuperKOM – a distributed computer conference system. Proceedings of the IFIP Symposium on Message Handling Systems and Application Layer Communication Protocols, Zürich. Amsterdam: North-Holland 1990

13. Palme, J.: Data Base Structure in PortaCOM. Byte Magazine, December 1985

14. Postel, J.B.: Simple Mail Transfer Protocol. Network Information Center RFC821, SRI, California 1982

15. Turoff, M.: Computer-mediated communication requirements for group support. Journal of Organizational Computing, 1, 1, pp. 85–113 (1991)

16. Vallée, J.: The Forum project – network conferencing and its future applications. Computer Networks, 1, pp. 39-52 (1976)

17. Whitescarver, J. et al.: A network environment for computer supported cooperative work. Proc. of the ACM SIGCOMM '87 Workshop: Frontiers in Computer Communications Technology, pp. 230-244. ACM Press 1988

17
Hardware and Software Architecture in Computer Conferencing Systems

Jens Ambrosius

Sant+Bendix, Arhus, Denmark [1]

Abstract: The use of Computer Conferencing Systems (CCS) has so far been very limited. Why is this the present situation? Is the problem due to lack of user friendliness or functionality, or is it because they do not fit in with other systems? This paper discusses the different possible answers.

Keywords: central environment, distributed environment, hybrid architecture, standards, different operating systems, layered software approach, user interface, systems and program development.

---

[1] At the time of writing this paper, the author was working at the Danish Technological Institute, Arhus.

Introduction

Many people would argue that there is no real issue in talking about hardware and software architecture in connection with the use of Computer Conferencing Systems (CCS). Others would claim that interesting aspects might be discussed, but that the real issue is the user interface and functionality of a CCS. In this chapter, the drawbacks of both arguments mentioned above will be explained, and some different approaches will be shown to be of significance to the use of conferencing systems.

The chapter describes the different existing hardware and software platforms used in conferencing applications. There is no 'golden truth' or right answers with regard to choosing architecture for a CCS. The task, the role, the equipment available, and the users' background will always define the demands when choosing the right system.

The first part of the chapter will discuss hardware architecture, and the second part will deal with software architecture. In the summary some guidelines are presented for choosing an appropriate system.

Hardware

Central environments

In many large organizations, the architecture of the data processing system is based on mainframe computers, and this will probably be the situation many years from now. This indicates that a CCS intended for this kind of environment should be based on the same kind of architecture as the environment in order to be able to reach all users. Also, the problem with isolated environments in these organizations should be taken into account.

If the workstations in this environment are based on PC's, there are various possibilities for the design of the system. The quick and on-going improvement of performance and high resolution graphics increases the possibilities of making user interfaces for the inexperienced user. One could call it the Mac or Windows approach. The database can be executed on the mainframe while the user interface is taken care of by the PC. This approach also allows different user interfaces, as long as the interface with the database is equal to the interface on the different PC's.

In traditional mainframe environments, terminals were quite frequent as workstations. During the last few years the situation has changed, however, so that now PC's are very often used as 'terminals' to mainframes. This recent development doesn't, however, change the fact that millions of text-based terminals are used. So, if a CCS is based on a mainframe (or several mainframes), the limits of terminals have to be taken into consideration. This is particularly problematic in connection with user interface design, since only text and very simple graphics are possible in the world of terminals. This situation contains two possibilities: either to limit the system to be text-oriented, so that all the users will have the same interface; or to have a system that is able to handle two interfaces – one for the simple terminals and one for the more sophisticated PC's, able to offer advanced graphics. The latter possibility can be difficult to use in real-life situations, since the users have to consider the type of other users' workstations when submitting mail or conference comments to the system. In terms of user friendliness and 'telepresence', for example, this approach could prove to be fatal for the use of the CCS.

In every CCS, the communication links are vital. This applies for both the possible communication links between the database systems and for the links between the system and the users. If the CCS is based on databases on different mainframes, the communication links between these have to be fast and dependable. No matter whether the software is distributed in one or the other way, the communication between the systems is of great importance. If the line 'goes down', so that one or more messages do not reach a conference, the confusion that this can cause in a discussion can be fatal.

Communication lines between the user and the system are not that sensitive in terms of dependability. One can always try again if the telephone lines are busy, for example. On the other hand, the nature of the links is important: it is not possible to depend on X.25 links, if there are participants in countries or areas where these are not commonly used or available. It is not possible to depend on telephone links and modems running at 2400 Bits/sec. in areas with very poor line quality – line noise and bad telephone connections can easily disrupt the screen presentation of text.

The capacity of the communication links has a great impact on the way that the user will experience the system. There are lots of examples of very good conferencing systems, where the limited telephone line capacity has spoiled the users' desire to use the system. There should be consistency between the capacity on the communication lines and the capacity in the system. It is the old story of the weakest link in a chain. Also, the need for file transfer of reports, spreadsheets, graphics, etc. will suffer greatly with low capacity lines.

The security aspect of the communication links can be divided into two different areas. The first is line availability. It is well known that a system based on telephone links is more fragile in terms of 'hackers', since everybody has access to this network. A system based on a packet switched network is safer in this sense, because fewer people have access. The second area is security with regard to the validity of the data being transferred on the communication lines. The different types of networks offer different types of error correction. As a guideline, ISO (International Standards Organization) based standards will give the highest level of error correction.

Distributed environments

Distributed environments have mainly been achieved by using minicomputers or PC networks. However, the discussion about mainframe, mini- and micro computers has become somewhat difficult recently: on the one hand, the so-called minicomputers have worked their way up into the mainframe world, microcomputers have worked their way up into the minicomputer world. As a result, the definition of minicomputers can be said to be a multi-user, multi-tasking computer with a proprietary architecture and either a proprietary or Unix operating system.

By the end of the 1980's, the minicomputer solutions were often used, mainly because at the time, there was a trend towards departmental solutions. The proprietary operating systems have been loosing market share, whereas computers based on the Unix operating system have gained ground during the last couple of years. Furthermore, some systems have been specially developed for distributed environments. Examples include EIES2 and SuperKOM, which

present different solutions as to how the database architecture is defined. With a distributed architecture in mind, the questions to be considered are:
– Is the database placed on one computer?
– If the database is placed on more computer, how is it organized: similar databases on each computer, or each computer with a part of the database, or one main database and user databases on adjacent machines?

The nature of the communication links between the computers also needs to be considered, as is well known to people who have actually worked in distributed environments. A breakdown of communication lines can have a fatal effect on how these systems function on a daily basis. Seen in this light, an architecture with similar databases on each computer is preferable, but this will require that each system has a large memory overhead in order to be able to handle the situation. On the other hand, a distributed database architecture can optimize the use of the system, but this will require very stable and adequate communication lines. And these are not always available!

The very fast growth of PC networks has also influenced computer conferencing, and the first new systems have seen the light of day. The best known, currently, are Caucus and LotusNotes. The first one is a dedicated conferencing system, whereas the last one is a groupware development system, also very well suited to be used for conferencing. It is evident that whatever one's opinion of PC networks, they have now become so widely used that this architecture must also be taken into consideration when talking about conferencing systems. On the one hand, PC networks pose a problem with regard to database design, but on the other hand, it will be a challenge, because the very user-friendly interface will make a simulation of the user's normal work routines possible. As this is a very important argument when discussing conferencing systems, this possibility should be explored and tested. However, it is quite as evident that the possibility of 'data anarchy' in connection with these architectures is much larger. A good deal of education and data discipline will therefore be necessary.

As regards operating systems it is clear that over the next few years, a variety of different systems (DOS, Apple OS, OS/2, Unix for PC's) will be required to co-exist. As a result, the design of computer conferencing systems must be based on this variety of operating systems and must support all of them – at least this will be the case for the CCS placed with the user (UserAgent). For as long as a VT100 user interface was sufficient, the problem was never that big. But now, as demands for a graphical user interface are increasing, everybody will have to make a stand with regard to the different systems. Generally, the problem becomes evident when people from several different sectors or institutions must work together via a computer conferencing system. In the publishing and design sectors, for example, APPLE is very often used, whereas many other industry sectors typically prefer either DOS, OS/2 or Unix.

Security in a PC network depends highly upon the network administrator. From a security point of view, the optimal PC network is based on diskless PC workstations. However, this is sheer utopia as things stand today. It is, therefore important to draw the attention to access rights, passwords, file locks, etc. in order to make sure that unauthorized access to the computer conferencing system is impossible. One factor that can really put an end to all use of computer conferencing systems is the feeling of lack of the necessary integrity and discretion.

As is the case with other architectures, the security of communication links is a very important issue in PC network architecture. In this connection, it is important to note that there are not so many different possibilities for communication between PC networks as is the case for other architectures. For example, it is not possible at this moment to connect more Lotus Notes networks with other communications links than those of the public telephone network. As several of these systems are based on identical databases on all the network servers, communication can soon prove to be a bottleneck when using the systems. These factors should be considered, ensuring that the communication between the distributed databases takes place on high-rate data network such as X.25, ISDN or leased lines.

Also in the world of PC networks, accessibility of the communication links can prove to be a problem. No matter how well-functioning a computer conferencing system we have, it can turn into a total failure if the communication links necessary are not available. This applies for both the user-to-system interface and the system-to-system interface.

The sensitivity with regard to security that applies to all distributed systems also applies to distributed PC networks. Computer conferencing systems will in certain situations be very sensitive to interference from outsiders. However, in situations where data is neither secret nor 'fragile', the sense of integrity will be very important. The security of the communication between PC networks used for a computer conferencing application, therefore, must have a high priority.

The capacity of the communication links between the particular networks is of great importance in connection with the use of systems based on graphics. Capacity is not quite so important for systems based entirely on text. If communication takes place on 1200 Bit/sec. telephone lines, graphics cannot be transferred. Not even the use of compression techniques will make this possible, because the graphic will still be 'heavyweight' files requiring high-rate communication lines.

Hybrid Architectures

If a system is based on a hybrid architecture (mainframe, minicomputer or PC), it is important to make sure that documents need not be converted from one format to another. People will not use a system that requires its users to consider which format a particular document has been generated in. This means that certain architectures have a potential built-in risk that users, in advance, will reject a computer conferencing system.

Standards

Specific standards in connection with computer conferencing systems were discussed in the previous chapter of this book. Here we deal with the still increasing number of general standards relevant to both hardware and software. It is important to distinguish the international standards, e.g. ISO (International Standards Organization), from the so-called *de facto* standards. ISO standards are internationally accepted standards, not generated by specific vendors, which means that they are 'open'. *De facto* standards – such as VT100 terminal emulation (Digital) and 3270 emulation (IBM) – are standards set by vendors, and they are often widely used.

The physical, electrical, and functional means used to connect the different units in a computer are called the computer's bus system. The bus is often realized by means of a printed card with several connectors in which units like the CPU, RAM, disc, communication cards, etc. can be connected. Most vendors of computers, except vendors of PC's, use their own bus systems. Vendors can thus not use units produced by other vendors in their own computers. However, several vendors now produce cards that can be used in different computers. The so-called 'Plug Compatible' computers produced by some vendors are, among other things, bus compatible with IBM computers. Three main systems are found in the PC world: Apple, ISA (EISA) and MCA. None of these are compatible with each other. This can be an important factor to consider before purchasing and using, for example, multimedia cards for computer conferencing systems. If graphics or picture/video are to be used in the conference, the same format must be used, otherwise these media cannot be used effectively.

The interface – the point at which users access a computer system – is described in several layers, starting with the physical interface, i.e. plugs, voltage levels, impedance, etc. Then the logical interface is described, i.e. the interaction between equipment and communication (one-way/two-ways/simultaneous etc.). For interfaces as well, different standards exist, i.e. standards set by vendors, *de facto* standards, and international standards. It is important to find out whether the user equipment to be connected to computers running computer conferencing systems can use an interface that supports the function offered by the system.

Software Systems and Architecture

Proprietary operating systems

Proprietary operating systems have always been – and still are – the most widely used ones. These operating systems are developed by vendors, and most often they are developed to be used on specific computers or series of computers, and are closely connected to the computer's hardware architecture. This is a great advantage which has often optimized the total capacity and functionality of the systems. Furthermore, these systems are often used for specific purposes, like technical data processing, office automation, online processing, etc. In some cases this can prove to be an advantage (e.g. if the systems are only to be used for the above applications); in others this can be a disadvantage. There is a huge difference between a technical application processing calculations and an application handling information exchange. The first application requires a large capacity in the CPU, whereas the last requires much of the input/output capability of the system as well as of the distributed nature of the total system. Over the last few years, the Unix operating system has gained ground in all types of data processing applications, and has become a more or less international standard. Partially compatible versions are still found, but IEEE, among others, has defined a standard, Posix (Portable Operating System for computer environment: IEEE Unix.). The future will clearly bring a higher degree of conformity into the Unix market, so that the original plan of a common unified operating system will be realized. This way the users can choose freely the type of hardware for their systems.

With regard to computer conferencing systems, more are being developed for Unix environments. On the one hand, this means safeguarding future developments, but on the other hand, it restricts a large-scale distribution at present, since the proprietary systems are used much more widely used than Unix.

The layered approach

A few years back, software was structured as isolated applications in which each module took care of everything from the user interface to communication with external units. This has been changed during the past years. At present, a so-called layered architecture is used, particularly in communication systems. This architecture divides the software up into a number of layers, each of these layers with a well-defined function. This allows integration with other programs using the same type of layered approach. For example, if a five-layer model is used, two peer-layers in two different programs will be able to communicate with each other without having to worry about the function of the upper or lower layers. The interface between two layers is described in detail, so that several programmers independently can take part in the same software development, because they know which data they get from the upper layers and which from the lower layers, as well as how to send data to the upper and lower layers.

ISO (International Standard Organization) has standardized a layered architecture for CCS, the so-called Reference Model. This model specifies seven layers. Coexistence with other applications has been a great problem for conferencing systems. As mentioned before, they have been isolated from other applications. Following the introduction of the ISO Reference Model and the standardization with regard to how data must be represented in databases (ASN #1 – Abstract Syntax Notation #1), the possibility for conferencing systems to coexist with other applications has been created. For example, the system can draw upon data directly from the company's Account Application and thus automate the information flow.

The user interface

A lot of debate still surrounds the issue of user interface design, and there is clearly no agreement on what counts as being best in this field. From the perspective of the software engineer and his or her attitude towards the user, the best description has been provided by Ben Schneiderman:

> Successful designers go beyond the vague notion of 'User Friendliness' and probe deeper than a checklist of subjective guidelines. They must have a thorough understanding of the diverse community of users and the tasks that must be accomplished. Moreover, they must have a deep commitment to serving the users. [1]

The user interface is not an unambiguous objective item, but a parameter determined by the specific situation, dictated by different factors, such as:
- the designer's explicit or implicit assumptions and metaphors
- the equipment available
- the user's skills
- the capacity of the communication links.

A text-oriented interface is in many cases a necessity, because the available equipment can only support this type of interface. In these cases, the designer has a limited number of possibilities at his/her disposal. It is important that the user interface selected is well-known to the user and that it is used in other applications. It is also important, for example, that the same terminology as well as function keys are used in order for the computer conferencing system user to feel comfortable when using the the application.

If a graphical user interface is possible, the CCS designer has more possibilities, since one can choose between text and graphics. Some differences in the graphical interface have to be discussed, however. The most widely used graphical systems are APPLE and Windows (3.0), and they are dissimilar in many respects. So, if a CCS is to be used under both systems a common denominator has to be found in order for all users to have common access to the conferencing system.

As metaphors used in the interface are discussed elsewhere in this book (see Chapter 13), we will only mention here that it is important for the designer to know the user's conceptual framework in order to be able to use metaphors familiar to the user in the interface.

Multi-media

There has been little progress so far in integrating other media than text into computer conferencing systems. There have been some attempts to integrate graphics of a proprietary nature in different systems, but other media such as pictures, video and voice have not been possible yet. Some tests have been performed with e.g. distance education workstations, but there has been no integration between the systems: the workstations have been made of isolated technology islands. It is interesting that in a time where multi-media is such a 'hot' issue in connection with education, nobody seems to be concerned about the real integration of these media with computer conferencing systems.[2] One of the reasons is the lack of standards in this field. Other reasons are the price of multi-media equipment, and the limited capacity of existing communication lines. With the decrease in equipment costs and the evolution of ISDN communication links, these barriers should be crossed in the very near future. Maybe the new possibilities for using different media in conferencing systems will be the event that brings computer conferencing more widely into the commercial marketplace.

Systems and program development

Developments in programming languages and tools have been explosive during the last five years. The languages have become more sophisticated with regard to built-in facilities (procedures, function calls, etc.), and the surrounding tools have provided the programmers with the possibility of structuring software development in a better way. CASE (Computer Aided Software Engineering) tools are the most prevalent here.

Traditional programming tools like C, Pascal, RPG, etc. were/are first and foremost used in connection with the programming of functions and in

---

[2] Although a number of current European DELTA projects (e.g. CO-LEARN) are working on the integration of multi-media tools with text-based conferencing. (ed.)

connection with information processing. They are used less in connection with information exchange. For computer conferencing systems this has resulted in the use of programming languages that by their nature are not particularly well-suited. This does not mean, however, that computer conferencing systems cannot be developed by means of traditional programming languages, but the process is difficult and the systems are difficult to maintain and expand.

Object Oriented Programming (OOP) Languages (e.g. SmallTalk, C++, etc.) have resulted in the possibility of applied programming using tools based directly on the exchange of information. Furthermore, the advantage of OOP languages is that the individual routines (Classes) can be used for other purposes as well by changing qualifications in the existing routines.

Fourth generation tools have created a new possibility for structuring databases in connection with computer conferencing systems. If the fourth generation tool has an Active Data Dictionary, the data structures will only have to be changed once in the program, after which the program automatically updates the changes in the remaining part of the application.

In order to obtain reliable systems which are easy to maintain, it is essential to use standard components like databases (e.g. SQL), user interfaces, networking programs etc. Too often in the past, different developers of computer conferencing systems have invented their own components. The lack of stability and difficulty in maintaining these systems, have perhaps been amongst the most significant reasons for the so far limited success of computer conferencing systems.

Summary

Like other applications, computer conferencing systems are subject to the conditions set by the environment and by the users. Before choosing a computer conferencing system, the conditions under which the application is to be used must be defined. The following questions need to be addressed:
– what kind of equipment is available?
– what are the user's characteristics, in terms of education, experience, and motivation?
– what is the organisation's capacity for operational and help facilities?
– what are the communication links?
– what is the actual purpose of using the computer conferencing system?
If these questions are answered, there might be a good chance that the appropriate conferencing system is chosen.

References

[1] Schneiderman, B.: Designing the User Interface: Strategies for Effective Human-Computer Interaction. Reading, MA: Addison-Wesley 1986

Index

Printing: Druckhaus Beltz, Hemsbach
Binding: Buchbinderei Schäffer, Grünstadt

NATO ASI Series F

Including Special Programmes on Sensory Systems for Robotic Control (ROB) and on Advanced Educational Technology (AET)

NATO ASI Series F

Including Special Programmes on Sensory Systems for Robotic Control (ROB) and on Advanced Educational Technology (AET)

NATO ASI Series F

NATO ASI Series F

Including Special Programmes on Sensory Systems for Robotic Control (ROB) and on Advanced Educational Technology (AET)